For Dennis,
who made this book
possible in so many
ways — & gave it a
happy ending.

Love Life,
with Parrots

Love—
Cappy

Cappy Love Hanson

Love Life, with Parrots

Copyright © 2014 Cappy Love Hanson

Printed in the United States of America.

Credits
Cover created by Joleene Naylor.
Cover image courtesy of dreamstime.com.

ISBN: 1505275423
ISBN-13: 978-1505275421

This book is dedicated to all the loves of my life—

those with hair on their chests and those with wings.

ACKNOWLEDGMENTS

No expression of gratitude can adequately repay the gift of time to write this book. To my husband Dennis Michael Gordon I owe the chance to live my dream.

I gained the courage to write this book because of a conversation with New Mexico writer and photographer Beverly Claire Jones. When I sidestepped the commitment by asking, "What if I don't finish it?" she replied, "What if you do?" That single response swept aside my resistance.

My grateful thanks for feedback and suggestions go to Jay Treiber, who read an early draft of the book; and to members of the Cochise Writers' Group and High Desert Writers' Association: Mary Alexander, Katherine Baccaro, Annette Cafazza, Kelli Calhoun, Leslie Clark, Tina Durham, Mimi Ferraro, Tatiana Koslova, Ross Lampert, Ted Mouras, Joseph Quinn, Lars Samson, Carol Sanger, Stephen Smith, Debrah Strait, Susan Struck, Kathy Swackhamer, and Susan Trombley.

Lastly, I have to acknowledge Peaches, Maggie, Willie, and Sunny, not only for brightening my life and for being the subjects of this book, but for their help in typing the manuscript. Each contributed unique spellings and unusual punctuation which, regrettably, had to be deleted.

PEACHES

If having problems meant that a person was still among the living, then I was fully alive as I stepped out of the warmth and light at Noah's Pet Arcade in Albuquerque and into the chill of a New Mexico winter night.

I had a double grip on the risk of heartbreak. In one hand, I held Perry's, where a band of pale skin circled his wedding-ring finger. In the other, I carried a mesh and cardboard box containing a peach-fronted conure. Peaches, as I'd tentatively named him, was a mostly green, hand-sized South American parrot in questionable health. Conure males and females looked alike, so I had a fifty-fifty chance of getting the gender question right.

Perry and I had interviewed perhaps a hundred parrots during our day-long search for a companion bird for me, in pet shops from the volcanic West Mesa to the upthrust Sandia Mountains. When the time came to either choose a bird or start our drive north empty handed, this was the parrot I had insisted we come back for.

Peaches had compelled me in a way both mystical and spooky. We'd first seen him early in the afternoon, when he was slumping toward a doze—or so I thought, until beams of white light shot out of his eyes and traveled a foot and a half before dissipating.

My mouth had opened, but no words had come out. Perry had stepped away to play with a puppy and hadn't seen what happened.

What *had* happened? A year earlier, Feathers—my gray-cheeked parrot companion of seven years—had died. I was determined not to let grief trick me into believing that I had found his spirit in another body, although Feathers himself had taught me to expect a sign. In a cage containing twenty who looked just like him, he'd stood apart and gazed straight into my eyes: *Ah, you've come for me at last.*

Peaches' eye-beam trick was different. He seemed unaware of me. I couldn't shake the idea that the life force was leaving him, an impression intensified by his dull plumage. Yet when Perry and I returned at sunset, Peaches was leaning forward on his perch, wings held out to make himself look more intimidating as he screeched at a larger mitred conure in a nearby cage. He expanded and contracted his pupils so that his eyes appeared to flash. The bare skin around them, circled with tiny orange feathers, added to the neon effect. So did the orange band above his beak.

Perry and I nestled our cargo into the extra-cab section of my sky-blue Datsun pickup Macha. No longer feisty, Peaches stood at the back of the box, head turned away, shivering and breathing in frightened gasps. My impulse was to warm him against my body and stroke his ruffled feathers, but he would only have struggled and bitten in terror.

As I climbed into the passenger seat and buckled up, a memory of Feathers ghosted through my mind: how he had squawked a greeting every evening when I came home from my dental receptionist job, groomed my hair, and dug into his food. He had put on a show of normalcy until it was too late to cure the infection he had concealed. Was Peaches hiding a similar secret?

Peaches rode silently in the dash lights' dim illumination and the musical undercurrent beamed out by a local oldies station. So did I. I couldn't get out of my mind the promise I had just broken. When Feathers had died, I'd vowed never to bring home another creature taken from the dwindling wilderness. Now I was.

This was late 1989, almost two years before the Wild Bird Conservation Act would outlaw the wild parrot trade in the United States. While news and nature shows provided heartbreaking images of how the birds were brought here, pet shops continued to stock their cages with low-cost wild parrots, as though the supply was endless.

Not one of the birds Perry and I had seen was domestically bred. I could have gone home without a parrot—it seemed a righteous if painful choice—but when the manager at Noah's made a show of looking at his wristwatch, I'd glanced up past Perry's close-cut reddish beard to his lively green eyes, seeking—what?—approval, support, direction?

Perry shrugged and raised his eyebrows, acknowledging the

simple truth: *Your call.*

I couldn't leave Peaches. Behind my decision lay the certainty that he would get no medical help if he stayed there. It would be cheaper for the shop to let him die, toss him out with the trash, and order another parrot.

Was paying to rescue a possibly sick bird a smart choice? No more than paying with the coin of love to rescue a man at the end of an unfulfilling marriage, when he was just beginning to deal with a raft of emotional baggage.

* * *

I had plenty of emotional baggage of my own, which made itself obvious an hour later, as Perry swung Macha onto St. Francis Drive in Santa Fe. I longed for a lifetime of going home together. In an hour, however, he would drop me off at my apartment and drive his truck to the house he had once shared with his wife and children. He needed quiet time alone—something I understood from my own divorce nine years earlier—but our partings left me with an ache in my throat.

I salved my sadness with gratitude. It was Perry's Christmas generosity, along with that of my parents in Southern California, that enabled me to have another parrot. With the scientific precision that made him a good engineer, Perry had figured out the most efficient route to all the pet shops and had done all the driving.

Peaches was still huddling at the back of the box when we pulled up to my apartment building on a volcanic mesa in the Atomic City of Los Alamos. As Perry started his pickup, I unloaded my living cargo under the frozen sparkle of stars and hurried up the heated stairwell, bringing Peaches home.

CONNECTING

In three days, the only thing that changed was that Peaches now stood on a wooden dowel perch in the cage that had once housed Feathers. He turned toward the white brick wall as I crossed the room, showing me his iridescent back. His long tail flicked dismissively against the cage bars.

I paused; so did he, crouching motionless. He looked more like a painter's brush stroke in light and dark greens than a living creature. My closeness with animals had always redeemed me in a life where human affections could be uncertain. But would Peaches and I ever bond? This was life with an alien—a four-ounce foreigner whose latter-day-dinosaur intelligence told him to fear and avoid me.

The way Peaches hunched reminded me of a cartoon vulture. This was life and death to him, though, so I couldn't laugh. Besides, worry knotted my stomach. I'd made an appointment for the following day to have Dr. Kathleen Ramsay look at the black, tarry substance that streaked Peaches' droppings.

That wasn't my only concern. Peaches' initial reactions seemed normal enough. To transfer him to his cage on top of my two-drawer filing cabinet, I'd caught him in a towel. His eyes had widened, and his heart pistoned. He stabbed his sharp black beak through the fabric like a sewing machine needle, bloodying my thumb and forefinger.

By now, though, he should have shown some interest in his surroundings. He should've stopped reacting to the apartment as The House from Hell and to me as Ms. Clear and Present Danger. Didn't the forty-three-year-old woman he caught glimpses of—long hair and a size extra-large, casual wardrobe—look more like an earth mother than a predator?

Not to Peaches. Turning his back was not the sign of trust I'd tried to convince myself it was. He was avoiding eye contact with yet another human captor as he confronted unpredictable dangers without his wild flock to alert and protect him. By freezing, he hoped to make himself invisible until Ms. Clear and Present went away.

Peaches was the ultimate outlander in my 1940's efficiency apartment, seven thousand feet up on the piñon- and juniper-studded Pajarito Plateau, a continent away from the deciduous South American forest where he'd hatched. I'd hoped that my crocheted afghans, hand-ruffled curtains, and art posters would appeal to his color vision, that my tropical houseplants would help him feel at home. But he knew he was in a strange land and was snubbing all strangers.

I sat down at my desk to keep from looming over him. Predictable as his mistrust was, it stung. Nothing challenged my self-image like an animal who didn't recognize me for the friend I intended to be. His resistance struck a note of recognition, though. I could dig in my heels, too. I appreciated that large stubbornness in such a small package.

These thoughts propelled me out of the chair, and I paced around the twelve-by-fifteen-foot portion of the apartment that served as living room, dining room, bedroom, and office. Then I sat down again and cocked my head. "Hi, Peaches parrot. Beautiful green Peaches parrot." Cocked the other way. "How ya doin', Peaches? It's all right."

His silence and posture said it all: *Yeah, right, lady. Everything's just dandy.*

Peaches had no reason to trust me or any other human. I could piece together a rough scenario of his capture, probably in Brazil. If he was taken as a baby, his captors either hacked into his nest cavity several feet up in a termite mound or chopped down his tree. Perhaps half his brothers and sisters died.

If Peaches had already fledged, he would have been caught in a net or on a glue-smeared branch. He might have struggled for hours or days, vulnerable to predators, starvation, and dehydration.

Peaches and the other survivors were thrust into dirty cages, transferred overland and by boat, and flown to the United States in a cold cargo hold. Their food was the cheapest available and probably not fresh. Their water was contaminated with parasites, bacteria, viruses, and the birds' droppings. Fewer than half the captured birds survived to enter their thirty-day quarantine in Chicago.

Quarantine, intended to keep disease from spreading to the outside, did nothing for the birds themselves. Parrots from all over the world, in various states of health, were crammed together. Their immune systems were stressed, and many were unable to fight off illness. An Asian parrot might have no natural resistance to an African disease. Workers had hundreds of birds and other animals to process every month and could give the parrots only minimal attention.

No wonder Peaches turned away and watched me covertly. The prey-animal placement of his eyes on the sides of his head helped, giving him nearly 360-degree vision. Aside from keeping his back to me, he never let me see him move.

I got up and paced again. This time, I caught sight of the pet bird magazine I'd left lying open on the dining table. The headline suggested a solution for one of my concerns. I sat down and read about mimicking a bird's vocalizations—parroting the parrot—to speed up bonding. Even though my psittacine diction was imperfect, my syntax suspect, and my vocabulary meager, I thought it might work.

The catch? Peaches was filling his Minimum Daily Screech Requirement and then some, but he wasn't making the softer sounds I hoped to woo him with. Could a misspoken squeak or squawk alienate him further?

I was forced to count on Peaches' ability to listen past the lingo and read my good intentions from my tone, my body language, and the fact that I fed him. At least I put food in his dish. He still wouldn't take so much as a sunflower seed or apple chunk from my fingers, though he was eager enough to bite me.

I sat down near him, cleared my throat, and tried my limited vocabulary—kisses, whistles, squeaks, ticks, and chucks. Peaches stood stone still, head down, wings folded across his back like a shield.

I sighed and turned away. Then I had a flash of inspiration: If copying his vocalizations didn't work, what about mirroring his body language?

Swiveling the chair so my back was to him, I sat still, arms crossed, eyes focused on the framed cover of a *Writer's Digest* issue where I'd had a poem published. I remained as silent and motionless as Peaches while the red numbers on the digital clock crept through five minutes, six, seven.

Peaches' tail feathers brushed the cage bars. Disadvantaged by a predator's forward-facing eyes, I chanced a slow glimpse over my shoulder. Peaches was standing on his top perch, not only facing me but leaning forward, staring right at me. His wide-eyed expression seemed to say, *You can't do that. That's* my *tactic.*

My held breath collapsed as I thanked the Green Parrot Goddess, a deity I imagined looked out for little guys like Peaches. Here was a wild-caught bird, with no reason to acknowledge another in a long line of humans, condescending to communicate.

Or maybe he wasn't condescending. Peaches was a social being, and I was the only flock substitute around. He wasn't seeing anything special in me. He was displaying his adaptability and his will to live.

Still, I couldn't keep from laughing with delight. Peaches blinked and turned his head away but watched with one eye as I chatted in English and my best Parrotese. He even offered a grudging response: a couple of low, gravelly whistles.

Even small conures were a lot more intelligent than the derogative *birdbrain* suggested. The trick was to be smarter than the parrot. If that required failing at a well-thought-out approach and stumbling onto one that worked, so be it.

I couldn't kid myself, though; there would be more bitten fingers. The cost of Peaches' capture could not be justified. Perhaps he could still live a happy and satisfying life, if he hadn't picked up some terrible disease in Brazil or Chicago.

The thought of what Dr. Ramsay might have to say the next day made my jaw tighten.

VET VISIT

The following morning, Peaches backed away as I secured his cage door and the smaller openings for changing his food and water. It was more than idle curiosity that made him cock his head and study my fingers. He attempted to nip me, then tugged at the ties and tried to untwist them. When he couldn't get them loose, he complained in a creaky voice.

Then he looked straight into my eyes. This was as encouraging as the kisses and whistles he offered for conversation. I did my best to imitate them.

Next, I taped the waste tray at the bottom of his cage so it couldn't slide out. I pictured Peaches wriggling through the opening and getting loose during the drive. I pictured myself on hands and knees, twisting to reach a frightened, biting parrot among the seat springs. I pictured myself visiting the chiropractor.

Peaches quieted when I covered him with a towel to keep the north wind from chilling him. I carried him down the inside stairs and along the walk to Macha. As soon as I removed the towel and belted the cage into the passenger seat, Peaches reached between the bars and bit the seatbelt.

I kept the towel on the seat so I could cover his cage if the passing scenery alarmed him. Just the opposite: He straightened and looked around, clinging to the bars to get a better view of the forested Jemez Mountains rising behind Los Alamos and the mesas that spread out from them like fingers, all shining with a layer of snow.

As we left town, he gazed up the steep tuff wall rising on one side of the Main Hill Road, then down at the pine-carpeted canyon on the other. Every time the road turned, he made nervous little *raw-w-wks*.

"Backseat driver," I said. "All right, passenger seat."

Raw-w-wk, ahk ahk.

"Oh, now that you've decided to talk, you have to have the last word?"

Raawwk!

On our forty-minute drive to Española, Peaches leaned forward to register each landmark—the water tanks at Totavi, Black Mesa's volcanic mass, the bridge over the depleted and frozen Rio Grande.

He was so alert that I wondered if this trip was necessary.

Perry had wondered, too. He'd stayed over the night before and, in the spirit of saving me a few dollars, had said, "Peaches passed quarantine. Doesn't that mean he's healthy? He doesn't look sick."

I reminded him of how Feathers had tricked us into believing he was healthy. Wild birds might drive away a sick one because it would attract predators. The flock was a bird's source of safety, so no individual wanted to expose a weakness. Whatever trust and affection Feathers had felt for me, they hadn't overcome his survival instinct.

* * *

While Peaches and I waited to see Dr. Ramsay, we had the company of several people with dogs and/or cats. The other pets showed too keen an interest in Peaches for his comfort or mine, straining at leashes and pet carriers to get a closer look—or taste.

I was about to retrieve the towel from the truck and cover Peaches when a man let his German shepherd-cross dog surge to the end of his lead. The dog thrust his soft nose against the cage bars. Peaches lunged and bit it, sending the dog yelping back to his owner.

"Serves him right," the man said.

I glared and thought, *The bird should have bitten you.*

To ease the tension, a woman with a gray tabby cat and a black mongrel puppy—the kind we called Chimayó retrievers because black Labrador crosses were so common in that community—asked how I had become interested in birds.

I gave her the standup-comedienne answer I'd developed when I had Feathers: "I have a bird instead of kids. Parrots go from babyhood to young adulthood in a year. They don't scream to have their diapers changed in the middle of the night. The terrible twos are over in a month. They don't need braces, and you don't have to work overtime to pay their college tuition."

Actually, my fascination with birds had begun with Great-Aunt Ardie, our family's amateur ornithologist. My younger brother Vance and I liked to tease her, "Did you see any yellow-bellied sapsuckers today?"

Ardie's passion primed me, though I didn't realize it until I was in my twenties. My husband Thor (yes, *Thor*) and I were planning a canoe trip with some Southern California friends, and one mentioned the birds we might see.

Studying a Peterson's field guide, I realized there was more to avian life than the finches, sparrows, mockingbirds, starlings, and crows we saw in our Anaheim yard. On the trip, I made my first entry in the bird log I've kept ever since: *great blue heron, Colorado River between Blythe, CA, and Yuma, AZ.*

That winter, the local newspaper announced a weekday Audubon Society tour of the Back Bay, a saltwater estuary less than an hour away in Newport Beach. I wasn't working and decided to go.

My eyes widened as I approached. Thousands of ducks and shorebirds blanketed the low-tide mudflats. Flocks of sandpipers flew up and wheeled as if connected by strings.

Experienced birders almost fell over one another to help novices recognize the birds and learn their habits. The mysterious avian names sang in my head: willet, godwit, bufflehead, gadwall, widgeon, merganser. I logged twenty-nine life birds—species I was identifying for the first time—and recognized another dozen from the canoe trip. All this in one of the country's fastest-growing counties.

I watched an osprey—a brown and white fishing hawk—land on a fence post six feet from my car window, rip up the catch of the day, and gulp it down. The osprey jerked its crested head in my direction and bored into me with its yellow-eyed glare. Its ferocity stole my breath and shook my city-adapted, civilized self.

That night, I told Thor that if this was what watching birds had to offer, I was in. He said he was, too.

A couple of years later, I identified my first yellow-bellied sapsucker in a pine-studded campground near Payson, Arizona. I wrote to Great-Aunt Ardie, *Saw your favorite* picid *today,* and imagined her grinning beneath her curly white hair with the kind of triumph that elders sometimes lived long enough to savor.

Thor and I were involved with animals in other ways. A series of stray dogs found us. I kept looking for the canine equivalent of the hobo code painted on the stucco exterior of our tract house: *nice people, good food, will locate your owner, find you a home, or keep you.*

We rescued birds, too—a red-tailed hawk tangled in a barbed wire fence, and a black-necked stilt (a long-legged shorebird) after a neighbor's cat attacked him. The stilt died of his wounds. Wildlife rehabilitators treated the hawk, and newspaper photographers recorded her release in the coastal hills of El Toro Marine Base.

Birding and animal rescues were satisfying but couldn't cement a crumbling marriage. Thor kept the house and our husky-shepherd dogs. I moved into a one-bedroom apartment and went to work as a secretary.

My job provided an unexpected benefit. I still thought of birds as binocular-distance animals until a computer consultant brought in a little gray-cheeked parrot. She nibbled his lips and eyebrows. When he left her on his desk, she fluttered to the carpet on clipped wings and toddled down the hall after him.

I got up from my typewriter and went to the ladies' room. In the mirror, I stared at the emptiness of my life. It didn't occur to me to question where parrots came from. For my thirty-fifth birthday, I scoured the Orange County pet shops for birds of the same species. That was when Feathers chose me.

After Feathers died, Perry helped me bury him on a Jemez Mountain slope I could see from my apartment. When I could look at parrots in pet shops without crying, I knew I was ready for another.

* * *

I had time to ramble though these memories because Dr. Ramsay was operating on a pygmy owl. According to the receptionist, the bird had been at the side of the highway in Pojoaque, perhaps trying to catch a mouse feeding on fast food garbage, when an approaching pickup alarmed him into flight. The headlights blinded him, and he collided with the windshield. The driver wrapped the bird in his jacket and called Game and Fish, who directed him to their go-to rehabilitator.

When Dr. Ramsay finished the surgery, she summoned Peaches and me. She brought the owl into the exam room, still sedated and wrapped in a towel to keep him from flailing and re-injuring his casted wing and leg.

She caught Peaches with another towel, exposed and examined his eyes, beak, wings, feet, and vent—the common exit beneath his tail for waste and either semen or eggs—and said he looked sound, aside from his dull feathers.

She was just putting him back in his cage when the owl stirred. With her usual good-natured smile, she turned back the terrycloth to reveal the tiny raptor. Full grown, he fit in her hand. He was all soft-looking brown feathers and intense yellow eyes. It was hard to believe that such a death-dealing terror of rodents and birds throughout Santa Fe County could be so cute.

Cute was not how the owl wanted to be perceived. He turned his head, took in the unfamiliar surroundings, and surveyed the humans. He did a double take at the parrot in the cage: *Can I kill it?*

Owls snap their beaks to make a sound all out of proportion to their size, intended to discourage other predators—and nosy humans. The pygmy owl made several staccato pops, flexing the talons on his uninjured foot. *I'm a big, tough owl. Check out the killer equipment.* When I laughed, he went off like a bag of microwave popcorn.

Peaches jerked his head back and stared into the face of would-be death. He fluffed up and flashed his eyes. When this failed to intimidate the owl, he crouched in launch stance, wings out to his sides and quivering. Then he stood up, apparently remembering that he couldn't fly away. He made himself as tall as he could and ruffled his feathers.

The pygmy owl only blinked.

Assured that the owl was recovering, Dr. Ramsay had an assistant take him to the bird room so she could perform the last part of Peaches' exam. With the wooden end of a swab, she teased up the tar-like matter on the floor of his cage.

"This is blood," she said.

I knew what that could mean in humans—rectal or colon cancer—and white-knuckled the edge of the exam table. Peaches might have just begun to bond with me, but he had already lodged in my heart.

Dr. Ramsay ran a test. "Peaches has psittacosis. It's caused by bacteria. A lot of birds in South America have it, especially conures."

"How do we treat it?"

"You want to leave him for at least a week so we can dose him with antibiotics. It might take some experimenting to find the best one for this particular strain. We can treat him right away if he shows any dire symptoms."

"Dire symptoms?"

"It's an insidious illness. Peaches could seem fine, and just like that"—she snapped her fingers—"he could come down with debilitating fatigue, respiratory distress, muscle cramps, and lameness. Even if he recovered, he might never walk or stand again." She leaned across the exam table. "You'd wake up one morning and find him dead."

My resistance to leaving Peaches collapsed. I leaned close to him, kissed, whistled, and tried to sound mature: "A week of separation is a small price to pay." When the assistant carried him away to the bird room, though, my hand flew over my heart.

Dr. Ramsay, who was as good with human animals as she was with pets and wildlife, distracted me. "I see he has a quarantine leg band."

Recovering a little, I asked, "Do you think we should take it off?"

"Does he fuss at it?"

"Not often."

"Then let's leave it on. There's talk about making it illegal for vets to treat birds without either a quarantine band or a breeder band. The assumption is that a bandless bird is illegal. They're worried about diseases."

"Like the one Peaches has that wasn't caught and treated in quarantine," I snapped.

"Right. I'm just surprised that you have another wild-caught bird."

I described the pet shop, the beams of light shooting out of Peaches' eyes—and my worry, now confirmed, that he had a serious illness.

"I don't know what the light beams are about, but I appreciate your motives."

"Buying him creates a market for one more wild-caught parrot, but I just couldn't leave him there."

Dr. Ramsay patted my arm. "You can't save them all, but we can save this one—if we're lucky."

SICKBAY

Two nights later, I inhaled sharply and sat up in bed, breathing in short gulps. What had startled me? The apartment building was quiet. Not a single vehicle moved within earshot, and no wonder. The red numerals on the clock read almost three in the morning. The only sound that reached me was Perry's regular breathing.

It wasn't a noise that had roused me but the absence of Peaches' feathers rustling as he stretched, settled his wings, and sighed back to sleep. I'd become like a mother with a new baby, waking every time he stirred. A friend described her child as the heart outside her body. Animals were like that for me.

I lay down and spooned against Perry's back, thanking the Green Parrot Goddess that Peaches was safe and healing. Earlier, Perry had told me how moved he was by simple intimacies—long embraces, foot massages, my waking at night and laying a hand on him. This was how he could be: thoughtful, touching, safe. Since early childhood, I'd reacted to men's angry voices by looking for the nearest piece of furniture to hide under. Perry rarely raised his voice.

And this was how he could be: One day, he accepted my dinner invitation. After work, I prepared the fixings for stir-fry. I set the table and lit candles—things I never did for myself alone—and turned on some relaxing music.

Perry didn't show up, didn't call. I began to worry and phoned his house, where I got his answering machine. I paced and nibbled at the chopped carrots. Was he all right?

At ten o'clock, I was scooping the food into storage dishes when the phone rang. Perry was at his ex-wife's house. They and their three teenage children had had a nice dinner together.

Had he forgotten our date? No, he'd just decided to eat with them instead. Had he thought to call me? Uh, well, no.

It wasn't Perry's dining with his family that bothered me; I'd encouraged him to keep up relationships with them. What hurt was being stood up and disrespected—feeling unimportant.

It was easy not to look at my choice to keep seeing him—especially now, as he rolled over in his sleep and pulled me close. I felt I was my best self in a relationship. Though I hadn't verbalized it, having a lover made me believe I was lovable; I was all right.

Even if we moved into the deeper commitment I hoped for, I would still need Peaches the way Perry needed his dog—the way all animal lovers found that human contacts weren't enough. I'd known that since childhood, living my first five years in the Berkeley Hills of California. Owls called from the bay-tree canopy at night. During the day, squirrels ate peanuts from pie pans my father nailed up. Stellar's jays hammered at the dining room window, trying to reach the baby box turtles in their plastic pond. Wild animals' ways fascinated me.

Then there were the dachshunds, Chris and Trudy. They accepted me as one of their own, a mostly hairless mammal who crawled around on the hardwood floors and curled up to nap with them in the green overstuffed chair. Together, we made up the Clan of the Underdogs. No matter how arbitrary and confusing my alcoholic parents and the other adults in my life might seem, the dogs were always a refuge.

So was Perry. Our biggest problem was that I was ready for a life partner, while he was giving me the new divorcé's slow-down message: "I need time and space to sort out my life."

Lying in his arms, I thought about a recent public reading, where I'd heard New Mexico writer Judyth Hill recite her poem about wanting to be the woman her lover needed space from. I burst out laughing, along with a lot of other women, but it was the kind of laughter that kept us from crying. The intimacy and everyday give-and-take I hoped for seemed beyond reach, even now, as Perry's body heat and rhythmic breathing lulled me back to sleep.

* * *

After work the following day, I drove down the Main Hill Road to visit Peaches. He was standing in an Isolette, its heater warming him so his body could direct more energy to fighting the infection. I pulled up a rocking chair and told him how much I missed him, adding the best parts of my birdie repertoire. When he cocked his head and looked at me with bright eyes, my heart brimmed. He was *there* in a way he hadn't been before.

Peaches had some interesting avian company. The pygmy owl stood in a nearby cage. A kestrel—the smallest of the falcons—occupied another, his strained wing strapped to his side.

A little gray-cheeked parrot peered from behind bars, looking so much like Feathers that my breath caught.

"The four year old in his family got a plastic Jedi light saber for Christmas," the assistant told me. "He was battling Darth Vader for the fate of the galaxy when he hit the parrot by mistake. Cracked his skull."

I winced. A parrot's life in a human home could be as fraught with danger as a wild existence. The risks were just different.

Dr. Ramsay was also rehabilitating a screech owl, another victim of a collision with three thousand pounds of fast-moving sheet metal and glass. The owl stood at the back of her cage, clenching a rabbit's leg, part of a road kill someone had brought in. She popped her beak and drew her treasure close, then lowered her head and snaked it from side to side, giving me a fierce-eyed glare: *This is my rabbit's leg. Go get your own.*

Dr. Ramsay finished treating her last patient and joined us. "I called that Noah-count pet store. The manager tried to weasel out of the health warranty. He said it was good only if the problem was diagnosed within three days."

The humor that kept her spirits up in the face of the sickness and injury she saw every day went right by me. "We got the first available appointment."

She nodded. "Anyway, the incubation period for psittacosis is more than a few days. Peaches couldn't have contracted it in the short time he was with you. How would he have gotten it at your place, anyway? He had it when the guy sold him to you."

"Of all the . . . I'm going to drive to Albuquerque, wait for the shop to be full of customers, and raise hell. Meanwhile . . . " I dug in my purse for my checkbook.

"Quit hissing and spitting. I've seen this before, and I know how to handle it."

* * *

On the sixth day of Peaches' treatment, an assistant met me at the front desk and told me they had transferred him to a regular cage, where he liked to hang upside down when he thought no one was watching. I peeked around the corner and saw him dangling like a green bat. I ducked back, called his name, and waited for him to regain his dignity. For the first time, he squawked a greeting and sounded excited to see me.

* * *

When I picked him up on day ten, I asked the receptionist how much the bill was.

"Doesn't matter to you," Dr. Ramsay said, emerging from an exam room with a man and woman and their big-pawed rottweiler puppy. "The pet store paid—gave me their credit card number over the phone."

My eyebrows rose. "Who'd you invoke? The Department of Agriculture? The Better Business Bureau? The God of the Old Testament?"

Dr. Ramsay just grinned and called her next patient.

In the bird room, an assistant and I transferred Peaches into his travel cage.

"You know how parrots are with noise, right?" she asked. "He had a pair of sun conures for company."

Perry and I had met a sun conure on our pet-shop rounds—a stunning adult bird, orange and yellow with green and purplish blue on her wings and tail. She was so sweet that I couldn't imagine them being raucous.

Then I gave myself the mental flat-forehead salute. They were parrots.

"I could tell Peaches was healthy," the assistant went on. "He spent most of yesterday and all of this morning trying to out-scream them."

I laughed as I secured the cage exits with twist ties. Sick as he was, Peaches had yelled his head off every time the refrigerator came on, a car backfired, or one of our neighbors knocked on the door to ask if I would water her house plants while she was out of town. And the vacuum cleaner! Nothing was going to out-volume Mr. Last Word.

I held the cage up at face level so I could kiss and whistle at Peaches. "Did you make a great big giant pain in the backside of your little green self?"

He held my gaze and made some raspy chirps: *Sure did. Isn't that part of my job description?*

I remembered the rest of the avian patients and swept my hand around the room. "What about these guys?"

"The owls and the kestrel are going over to The Wildlife Center for rehab. If they can't be released, they'll be used as education birds in the public programs."

An empty cage caught my eye. I had that stomach-dropping sensation I got from movie scenes where the patient wasn't in the hospital room and a nurse was making the bed. "What about the gray-cheek?"

"Oh, he went home. He's going to be fine. Your little guy, too, I hope."

I thanked her and crossed my fingers.

HOME AGAIN

Now that he was healthier and more confident, Peaches was determined not to be a perch potato. The morning after he came home—a Saturday—he woke me up, clambering around in his cage. I pulled off the cover. He looked out the window at the falling snow and around the apartment with new interest.

I opened his cage door. Peaches hopped to the threshold, squawked at the escape opportunity, and flung himself into the air. The flight feathers on his left wing had been clipped before I found him, to keep him from flying and to make him dependent on humans. He could only whirligig to the rug.

His eyes widened as he checked his wings with his beak. Uneasy, he *raaawk*ed, then dashed in a mad, pigeon-toed toddle across the floor. The friction between his feet and the rug slowed his lower half, and he pitched forward onto his chest.

I covered my mouth to keep from saying, *Aw, poor baby.*

Peaches shook himself and hustled under the radiator. I bent down to pick him up. He charged across the room, pausing amid the forest of table and chair legs. The space beneath the wicker bookcase offered better cover. As I knelt down in front of it, he jerked his head around, ran under the dresser, and crouched against the wall.

Then he discovered an even better hiding place. He feinted, faked me out, and sprinted for the shadowed space between the back of my desk and the white brick wall, created by the desktop's six-inch overhang.

How was I going to get him out? Lying on my mattress on the floor, I edged the broom past the filing cabinet and along the wall. Peaches screamed and ran to the other end of the desk.

The broom wasn't long enough to force him out. Back and forth I scurried, poking the broom behind one end of the desk and trying to grab Peaches at the other. I took it in earnest until it occurred to me how cartoonish we looked. *Over here,* I imagined him taunting, while I took the bait. *No, over here.* I collapsed on the bed, arms flung wide, and guffawed.

Then I sobered. Chasing Peaches only reinforced his fear of people.

I wished for a clever way to beat him at his own game, but all I could muster was an ounce of low-tech prevention. He allowed himself to be enticed to a dish of sunflower seeds. After locking him in his cage, I taped some heavy cardboard across the openings between the desk and the wall. It would take a while for him to chew through, perhaps long enough for me to shoo him away and repair any damage.

* * *

Before his stay at the clinic, Peaches had refused to do anything while I was around that a bird at ease would have done without concern—scratch, stretch, preen, or nap. More self-assured now, he let me watch him eat, though not without caution. He positioned himself on a perch to one side of his dish so he could keep his back to the wall and the rest of the room in view—especially the human sipping split pea soup at the dining table. He ducked his head into his dish and pulled out a beak full of food.

Within days, he was bathing in his water dish, singing a special melody I called his water song. He sounded more like a warbler than a parrot as he dipped his head, sluiced water down his back, and flapped his wings, spraying drops in all directions. I had to protect the computer and printer with his cage-cover towels.

The pet shop had fed Peaches an inexpensive seed mix. To stay healthy, he needed a wider variety. I'd brought home a bag of high-quality kibbled food from the clinic, which Peaches was now strong enough to crumble. He liked rice, quinoa, millet, pasta, beans, fruits, and vegetables. Corn and apples became his favorites. He gobbled cooked eggs. I patted myself on the back for not making any snide references to cannibalism.

Like any human, Peaches found different foods appealing on different days. The first time I microwaved frozen mixed vegetables, he picked out the cut green beans and scattered them across his cage floor—except for the ones he hurled out.

I was late leaving for work the first day he did this, and made up time by leaving the bedcovers piled against the wall. That night, when I turned out the light and got into bed, my legs landed on half a dozen clammy objects. I yelped and scrambled out, grabbing my flashlight. "Beans!"

Peaches made creaky grumbling sounds: *It's dark. Decent creatures are asleep already.*

The following day, Peaches showed me how he did it. He stood on the cage floor with a bean in his beak, turned his head, then hurled with an energetic snap. About one time in ten, he released at the right instant and angle, and the bean sailed clear. I started to copy the move but realized the whiplash would land me on the chiropractor's table.

Some days, Peaches ate everything except carrots, which dotted his cage floor like orange pebbles. Or he might pick around the lima beans. He liked chopped green chilies, which I offered because of their vitamin C and beta carotene.

"No gringo wimp," Perry remarked one evening as he watched Peaches chomp into a chili slice. My boyfriend and my parrot ate chilies that made my eyes water and my tongue ignite. If there was a gringo wimp, it was me.

The following morning, I served corn grits for breakfast. Peaches gobbled his as if he hadn't eaten in days. I dropped another dollop into his dish. He wolfed it. I kept spooning. By the time he was sated, his crop—the elastic pouch in his throat where he stored food to be digested—bulged like a ping-pong ball.

Perry chuckled. "I guess you don't have to worry about his appetite."

I nodded, thinking about the things I did have to worry about. Pretty soon, I'd have to train Peaches.

I suspected he'd already figured out how to train me.

TRAINING YOUR PERSON

The following Saturday morning, I stood in front of Peaches' cage, trying to sound like a drill sergeant. "All right, you, it's training time. Perry's on travel, and we've got the whole weekend. Let's get to work."

Peaches glanced up from the cuttlebone he'd been nibbling and cocked his head: *You talkin' ta me?*

I straightened, trying to convey more confidence than I felt. There were no bird owners' groups in the area, and I didn't know anyone else who had trained a wild-caught parrot. I'd found books about parrot care but none about training. The Internet was still in its military-industrial infancy. I would have to rely on my experience with Feathers and on what I'd read in magazines.

As a novice, I had made mistakes with Feathers. I'd tried getting him to step onto my hand from his cage, assuming that he hated being confined and would take any opportunity to get out. I didn't understand that the cage had become his territory, his safe haven. Our eventual success owed more to Feathers' willingness to make friends than it did to my inept techniques.

I opened Peaches' cage door, stood back, and let him spiral to the floor. He'd already discovered that he couldn't hide behind the desk and that I could reach him under the rest of the furniture. He leaped and flapped toward his cage, getting about eight inches of altitude before falling back to the rug.

Peaches' desire to return to the high safety of his cage was central to my plan. I leaned over and put my right index finger in front of him, while I swept my left hand toward him from behind, saying, "Peaches, up."

He jumped right onto my finger. Thrilled, I was about to praise him and give him a sunflower seed when he administered his own training technique: He bit me, leaped off, and dashed under the radiator.

I sighed and sucked at the blood. "Oh, well, it's a start."

Finger training Peaches in a weekend was overly optimistic—not because he wasn't smart enough but because I had underestimated his natural fear. By the time Perry flew home from the East Coast the following Friday, Peaches and I had progressed to a seesaw of *almosts*. He *almost* climbed onto the proffered finger, then bit and dashed under the dresser. He got on and *almost* accepted a ride back to his cage, then bit, leaped to the floor, and darted under the dining table.

I wished I could use gloves. Three days after Peaches came home from the clinic, I had dug out the pair I'd used when I was taming Feathers. Peaches jerked his head back, squawked, and pressed against the farthest cage bars. I drew the second glove on. He screamed and flapped, dislodging feathers, until I tucked the gloves back in the drawer. No doubt his captors and the quarantine staff had worn something similar. Gloves reminded him of the horror of confinement.

* * *

Stubbornness turned out to be my biggest training asset—that and an understanding of the future awaiting birds that people gave up on. Confined to their cages, bored and miserable, they might scream, pull out their own feathers, attack people or other animals, and numb themselves with ritualized behaviors. I couldn't stand the thought of Peaches living the next twenty years neglected and neurotic.

So we kept at it. It took Peaches two weeks to stay on my hand. He had learned to get on the first time, of course, but did so now only because I kept insisting—and rewarding him with sunflower seeds.

ROUTINE

With training basics accomplished, Peaches and I settled into a routine. I was working Monday through Thursday and half of Friday at Dr. Nelson's dental office. My job description included answering phones, making appointments, and billing insurance companies.

And comforting anxious patients. Even the toughest-looking

ones—the biker-physicists who wore black leather and rode motorcycles to work—claimed they would rather endure a beating with a rusty pipe, their annual performance review, *and* a two-week visit from their mother-in-law than sit through a root canal.

I often drove home to eat lunch with Peaches. He had a few toys, and I left the stereo or television on, but I didn't think these were enough to keep him occupied.

That was more true than I realized. I later learned that birds' eyes and brains registered faster than a TV's refresh rate. The sound might be continuous, but to Peaches, the picture must have appeared fragmented and jumpy.

Perry and I divided our time between his house in the North Community, my downtown apartment, and the local landscape. To celebrate his singlehood, he had bought a motorcycle. I enjoyed riding on the back so much that I bought a scooter. We had great fun, two-wheeling the mountain roads. When I leaned into the pine-margined curves, I forgot about the conflict between my long-term longings and his friends-with-benefits attitude.

We hiked and skied cross country, though I had trouble keeping up because of my weak left knee. I'd broken the kneecap twice. It had been removed and my quadriceps transplanted to compensate for a congenital defect. Post-surgical arthritis was decaying the bones. I was limping down the road toward joint replacement.

To round out my life, I took creative writing classes at the University of New Mexico, taught by award-winning bilingual author Jim Sagel. I'd had a few poems published. I was proudest of the one in *Writer's Digest* called "What It's Like to Be a Poet." I was working on some short fiction and tinkering with an unfinished novel.

* * *

Less enjoyable were the regular trips Peaches and I took to Dr. Ramsay's office for nail and wing trims. No matter how tame Peaches was becoming with me, he struggled, screeched, and tried to bite the vet and her assistants.

"No gratitude," Dr. Ramsay would say, "for the people who

saved your green feathered butt."

Living wild, Peaches would have worn his nails down on trees and rocks. I'd considered sandpaper perches, until I met a woman whose budgies' feet had been inflamed by them. Perches that were smooth on top and rough along the sides hadn't come on the market yet.

When Peaches' clipped flight feathers grew out, Dr. Ramsay gave him a better trim. She splayed each wing and cut the shafts of the secondaries, the ones closest to his body. She left the primaries at the ends of his wings untouched, giving him a more natural-looking line and better gliding control.

Afterwards, he always flashed his eyes, ruffling his feathers—and his dignity—back into place: *Hmf!*

My greatest concern wasn't that Peaches might wing into a window, thinking it was open air, and injure himself. With his beak, he had tested the hard barrier that he could see through but not cross and had accepted it. What worried me was our apartment door, which opened into the upstairs hall. If Peaches got out of the building, he could be gone for good in a place without familiar food and with sub-freezing and sometimes sub-zero winter nights.

Every time we drove home from the vet's, I promised Peaches that if we ever lived where he could fly free, I'd let his flight feathers grow out. The vow felt sacred.

OUNCE OF PREVENTION

It was a good thing Peaches couldn't do more than break his fall and glide to the floor. One evening when I opened the apartment door, I noticed the absence of that yucky smell from my clogged bathroom drain. The plumber had finally come.

Then I noticed that Peaches' cage door tie had been tossed on my desk. I always twisted it onto a cage bar. The cage door was closed, and Peaches was clinging to it—on the outside.

My stomach lurched. The plumber or his helper had let Peaches out. My face burned with protective fury. When I opened the cage,

Peaches darted in and gobbled all his food. He drank and drank.

I took several slow breaths, called our landlord, and registered my complaint. He claimed he'd never had a problem with this plumber. Helpers came went; nothing to do about that. His dismissive tone told me he didn't want to be bothered.

I thanked the Green Parrot Goddess for Peaches' safety, dropped corn and apple chunks into his food cup, and watched him eat. He was afraid of strangers and might have hidden under the furniture until the men left. Then he'd probably scrambled up the wicker chair and jumped to the filing cabinet, only to find his cage door closed.

After my own dinner, I began to relax. Peaches was healthy and safe, and our training was progressing. It looked as though our lives together would be peaceful and friendly after all.

I knocked on wood.

MIDNIGHT FLYER

A few nights after finding Peaches outside his cage, I was startled awake again. It sounded to my sleep-hazed brain like a tornado whipping the Sunday *New York Times* around inside a metal trash can, accompanied by banshee screams.

I bolted upright, wished Perry was there, and finally realized the noise was Peaches, thrashing and shrieking. I clambered up, switched on the desk lamp, and whisked the towels off his cage.

Peaches' left wing was hooked over his lower perch, his right caught on a horizontal bar. His toenails barely touched the cage floor.

Before I could get his cage tie off, Peaches pulled his wings free and folded them over his back. His chest heaved, and his eyes widened. He didn't seem to register me or the apartment.

I sat down in my desk chair, my face level with him, trembling. Things that happened in the middle of the night seemed especially nerve-wracking in Los Alamos's roll-up-the-sidewalks quiet. As far as I could tell, no noise had startled Peaches; all I could hear were the wooden building's normal creaks. Our apartment was high enough and far enough from the street that a car's headlights couldn't sweep our window and alarm him.

Maybe Peaches had had a nightmare. What would a wild-hatched bird dream about? Probably every predator in South America, from anacondas to harpy eagles to ocelots to anteaters ripping open the termite mound that held his nest.

"You're safe now, Peaches; you're home. Did you have a bad dream? Was something chasing you?"

Peaches shuddered and looked straight at me, present at last. His breast feathers rose and fell as he took a deep breath, climbed to his top perch, and fluffed himself all over. He met my eyes again, perhaps reassuring himself.

Another idea struck me. "Was it the people who caught you, Peaches? Were you trying to fly away from them?"

He held my gaze before sighing and tucking his beak into his wing. He was asleep in a couple of minutes.

I covered his cage and doused the light but couldn't switch off my mind. I lay in bed, remembering a bit of avian physiology. Birds had tendons running down the backs of their legs that pulled their toes into a tight curl as they settled down on a branch and fell asleep. That was why they didn't fall out of trees.

So Peaches hadn't fallen; he'd actively flown. But why? Did some birds sleep-fly the way some people sleep-walked?

Peaches' dream, if that was what caused his flight, might not have been a nightmare. What if he became a free parrot in his sleep, flying with his flock among his native trees? What a rude awakening to sail into the cage bars.

Some jumble of guilt and imagination took a late-night leap. I'd let Peaches' wing feathers grow out, fly him to Brazil, and set him free into a flock of his own kind. He'd live out his life naturally, free of human ego and greed, including mine. It wouldn't make a dent in the damage done by the wild bird trade, but it seemed a righteous thing to do.

I sighed and rolled over, thinking, *Right, in a part of the world where the human population is skyrocketing. Where miles of natural habitat are being ruined every day. Where Peaches might contract psittacosis again. Where he might be captured again.*

And I was going to do this on my extensive salary and savings? Who was I kidding? The tradeoff for life in the mountains was the local pay scale.

I wasn't about to let reality spoil a good fantasy, though. In my mind, I lifted Peaches from his cage as a hundred wild peach-fronts winged past and called to him. I kissed his black beak and tossed him into the air. Watching him wing away in my imagination was so triumphant that it brought a surge of real tears.

REWARDS

It wasn't just Peaches' occasional night flights that made me realize he should have larger lodgings. A parrot needed a cage at least one-and-a-half times his wingspan wide and deep. The one that had worked for Feathers was too small for Peaches.

I kept an eye on the classified ads. One Friday after work, I drove down to White Rock, Los Alamos's bedroom community above the Rio Grande, to see a boy who raised canaries. His flock had expanded, and he was selling their original cage.

I drove home with the cage on the seat next to me, thinking about how to introduce it to Peaches. Any change in his environment could make him anxious. Maybe I would leave him in his old cage and keep the new one on my desk for the days or weeks it might take him to get used to it.

Perhaps because Peaches had gone through so many radical changes, the new cage didn't faze him. He climbed right in and scrambled around, eyes wide, chirping like an excited sparrow. The manzanita branch I'd angled across the cage was a big hit. How wild and natural he looked, clambering across the twisted, reddish wood.

When I transferred his bowls and toys, he touched each one with his beak. With that simple ritual, he accepted his new home.

* * *

The new cage had one drawback: It had three doors, two at the bottom and one half-way up. They were big enough to accommodate Peaches, but he refused to use them. Perhaps, after the wide opening in Feathers' cage, these smaller doors felt claustrophobic.

Fortunately, the top was easy to remove. Peaches approved by climbing up the manzanita branch to the uppermost dowel perch and launching, *aak aak aak*ing with excitement.

This time, I didn't pick him up off the rug, as he'd learned to expect. I pushed the wicker chair to the other side of the room so he couldn't climb it and jump to his cage. He looked up, making worried-sounding calls. That was when he spotted the long wooden bird ladder I'd set up. He climbed beak-over-claw to safety.

Peaches liked this game. He sailed to the floor again and started up the ladder. I sat down and propped the ladder against my knee. He hesitated, then climbed into my lap, up the front of my blouse, and out my extended arm to his cage. I gave him a sunflower-seed reward.

After several repetitions, I stood up when he reached my shoulder, and walked across the room. Peaches flashed his eyes and fluttered to the floor. I let him climb back to his cage while I chopped some apple. The next time, I offered him a piece as an incentive to stay on my shoulder. He was caught in a conflict of impulses. He crouched to fly, paused, reached for the fruit, turned away, and reached again, over and over.

Every time he stayed, I gave him a treat and told him what a good and brave parrot he was. I meant every word.

* * *

The issue of food treats sparked a question among my human acquaintances that amounted to: "When you reward Peaches for doing something you want, aren't you using food as a bribe?"

The first time this came up—with a woman who lived down the hall—I said, "Of course."

"Shouldn't the bird do what you want because he loves you? Shouldn't he love you for who you are, not for something as crass and material as food?"

I had to think about that. "Peaches may do that someday, but he doesn't love me yet. He's still afraid of people. Because I feed him, he's learning that I'm safe and that I care about him.

"Besides, his head is still in the South American forests. If he's going to lead a satisfying life, he needs to learn what will work in a human home. Food's an important reinforcement. In the wild, parrots spend hours every day searching for things to eat."

That night, I gave Peaches a piece of apple for the delight of watching him hold it with one foot and eat it. As he swiped his beak on a perch to rub off the "food beard" of excess apple, I realized that the opposite of what I'd said to my neighbor was also true. Would Peaches love me if I ignored or abused him? Of course not. How would he know I loved him if I didn't show it?

I wondered if my neighbor had ever had pets—or children. Would she have kept going to work without the reward of a paycheck?

LUNCH MUNCH

Having a parrot was like having a baby: I celebrated all the "firsts." The best were the ones Peaches did of his own accord.

One noontime, he fluttered from his cage to the floor, toddled to the dining table, and scrambled beak over claw up my pants leg and blouse to my shoulder. He surveyed the room with a wild bird's head-swiveling vigilance, then hiked down to my wrist. He hesitated and cocked his head, right eye considering my rice and beans, left eye gauging how proprietary I was about my food.

I told him to help himself. He leaned over, grabbed a grain of rice, and dashed up my arm. He continued this charge-and-retreat tactic until his crop bulged.

Things I put in my mouth were not always to his liking, however, and that confused him. I drank a medicinal tea at bedtime. Peaches clung to the front of my bathrobe, wedging his beak between my lips and the cup. He shook his head at the bitter taste, yet he was determined to shove in for another sip.

He was even more fascinated by the motions of my toothbrush and nibbled at the corner of my mouth until I let him chew on the bristles. I was certain toothpaste wasn't good for him but thought that one taste would discourage him.

Sure enough, he pushed it out with his tongue, wiped his beak on my shoulder, and shook his head. Before I could say, "Told you so," he leaned back in for more. I had to lock him out of the bathroom.

Why did Peaches keep coming back for bad-tasting substances? Wild parrots depended on spotting others eating. Anything that one ate would taste good to another. Perhaps Peaches couldn't conceive of something in my mouth being unappealing to him.

CLEANUP

Of course, the remains of the food that went into the parrot came out as waste. Peaches had the run of the apartment for a while almost every day, so cleaning up after him became part of my routine.

A bird magazine article on housebreaking seemed timely, so I sat down at my desk one evening, rewarded Peaches for staying on my shoulder, and read. The idea was to watch the bird until he looked as though he was about to drop, hold him over a wastebasket, and say a trigger word such as, "Poop." Then, every twenty minutes or so, hold him over the wastebasket and give the command.

I nearly fell off my chair, laughing. Potty training a parrot was too compulsive, even for me. Peaches reacted, too, squawking and fluttering off my shoulder. He stood on the wicker chair and made screechy mimics of my hilarity.

All right, I admitted, potty training made sense for a big bird like a macaw, who could eject a veritable river of fruit and seed waste. But a four-ounce conure? I decided to do what I had with Feathers: deal with the mess as best I could. Besides, Peaches backed up before he let go, a warning I could use to get him off my shoulder in time.

These habits could be tenuous, though. Feathers had bobbed his head before he relieved himself—until I started giving Perry a lot of time and attention. Feathers' protest was to stop warning me.

There was one thing I did have to pay attention to with Peaches. He would drop anywhere: my shoulder, the dining table, the outside of his cage.

The rim of a glass, unnoticed, vent squarely over the water.

Parrot poop, in case you're wondering, tastes salty.

MOLT

As snow melted on the mountains above Los Alamos, the dull, frayed feathers Peaches had worn through his capture and quarantine carpeted his cage floor. Pinfeathers emerged—little spikes covered with white keratin that made him look like a porcupine.

My feathered companion was as uncomfortable and cranky as a teething baby. He was preoccupied with the his new plumage, nibbling off the sheaths he could reach, scratching off what he could with his claws, and working others against his cage bars and food cup. Hard-cover book corners became his favorite head rubs.

No doubt Peaches would have preferred a mate or other flock member to exchange grooming favors with. Because I was his only option, he would walk across the desk, lower his head, and push it against my fingers.

I rubbed the sheaths between my thumb nail and index finger, telling him what a beautiful green parrot he was. He sighed or answered with an excited call I dubbed *squabble-dee-wobble*. If my attentions were uncomfortable, he cry-squawked and gave me a gentle but firm bite. Usually, he lowered his head again.

His new feathers unfurled sleek and bright, especially the orange ones on his forehead. He looked like a different bird, shiny with new life.

Even after his molt had ended, he let me groom him with my fingers. He reciprocated by nibbling my hair, eyebrows, ears, lips, and nose. He worked a hole in the shoulder of my terrycloth bathrobe and ran the threads through his beak over and over, eyes closed with pleasure. His intimate ministrations stopped time for me and held the rest of the rushing world at bay.

These moments were so perfect it seemed that nothing could interfere with our happiness. I continued to believe that, even when the first signs of trouble floated to the bottom of Peaches' cage.

PICK, PICK, PICK

The aspens leafed out on Pajarito Mountain, greening the horizon and urging Perry and me outside. One Sunday, we doubled up on his motorcycle and bounced up Los Alamos Canyon, splashing through the stream to the reservoir. The air, shadowed by pines and steep tuff walls, smelled newly born.

Perry dropped me off at my apartment afterwards and went to his office to prepare for a Monday meeting. I climbed the stairs, mud-splattered, exhilarated, and ready to play with Peaches.

What I saw stopped me at the door. The rug and the bottom of his cage were littered with feathers. It was too soon for him to molt again. Gray down feathers had sprouted through the sleek plumage on his chest, back, and wings.

I tossed my helmet and jacket on the bed and grabbed my companion-parrot books and magazines. Was this some kind of abnormal molt that signaled another health crisis? I found nothing useful, so I fell back on a bit of advice I'd gleaned somewhere in my childless life: Put down the book, pick up the baby.

When I opened the top of his cage, Peaches jumped to my shoulder and accepted a head scritch. Then he did something that would send me to the phone the following morning to make an appointment with Dr. Ramsay.

* * *

Late Monday afternoon, Peaches stood in his travel cage in an exam room and did the same thing. He arched his neck and tugged at a breast feather. He worked it out, chewed on it for a few seconds, dropped it, and started on another.

"See what I mean?" I said, failing to keep the shrill of alarm out of my voice. "Why is he doing that?"

Dr. Ramsay sighed. "Compulsive, habitual feather picking. Some birds do it out of boredom or frustration or to use up nervous energy. He may stop of his own accord, or he may ritualize the behavior and never quit."

I pressed my lips together. Feather picking meant that despite all my efforts, Peaches was unhappy. It also suggested that I wasn't just the heroic rescuer of a sick parrot. I was an inept bird mom, and he was paying the price.

Dr. Ramsay cocked her head at him in the most birdlike way and asked, "Have you changed anything around your apartment that might worry him?"

"He did fine with his new cage. The only other thing I've changed is the bedding."

Then I remembered, "I just started feeding the sparrows and finches on the window sill to attract company for Peaches."

"We've thought he was a youngster, but he may be older. If he's breeding age, the wild birds' mating behavior could trigger his sexual instincts. He might be frustrated by the lack of a mate. Parrots are flock birds, remember, and he's alone a lot."

I wrung my hands. "Should I get another bird?"

"If you do, and they bond, he won't be as friendly with you. If they don't bond, you'll have two antagonistic parrots in a small apartment. Remember what that was like?"

I did. Feathers and I had suffered through a dreadful few weeks with a blue budgie named Chamisa. From his cage on my desk, he screeched at Feathers for hours on end. I had to let them out in shifts.

Feathers learned to stay off Chamisa's cage when the budgie bit his toes. When Chamisa was loose, his only interest was in clinging to Feathers' cage and taunting him. He was quicker, leaping away when Feathers charged.

Finally, an acquaintance who kept a flock of budgies in a large cage offered to take Chamisa. He was so aggressive that within days, he had appropriated the dominant male's mate.

"If you got another bird that Peaches didn't like," Dr. Ramsay said, "it could aggravate his feather picking."

"What can we do?"

"Let's start with the most conservative measure: female hormones."

"But Peaches may be a male."

"This works in about ten percent of feather-picking cases, whether the bird is male or female."

The hormone shot cut Peaches' picking in half, but the improvement wore off in a couple of weeks. I came home for lunch every day, left the television on, and played radio stations from classical to country to jazz. When I was home, I gave him a lot of time out of his cage and plenty of attention.

More gray down feathers appeared, along with a patch of pink skin on his chest.

"Next step," Dr. Ramsay said, "break the habit." She opened a drawer and whipped out a little white plastic collar shaped like a cone with the point cut off. I'd seen larger ones used on dogs and cats. She slipped it over Peaches' head and released him into his travel cage.

Feather picking took second place to getting the hated collar off. Peaches rolled his head, trying to reach it with his beak. He lodged it against his food dish and tried to back out of it.

I shook my head. "I don't know."

The ride home distracted him. Once there, he learned to get the collar off in less than a minute. It took me five minutes to catch him in a towel, hold him between my knees, and work the collar over his head—only to watch him stand on one foot, grab the narrow end with the other, and wiggle it off.

After a few days, I gave up. How bad could it get? Maybe if he plucked enough to get cold, he would let new feathers grow in.

The next issue of my pet bird magazine horrified me with photos of parrots who had pulled out every feather they could reach. They were naked except for their heads.

PLAY

That same bird magazine informed me that playthings could prevent boredom, thus reducing or even eliminating feather picking.

One problem was that I'd found few toys for birds Peaches' size. Those made for budgies—with mirrors and bells and beads on thin wire—he ripped apart in seconds. Stouter toys made for Amazons and cockatoos were so tough that he gave up.

The other problem was that while Peaches might tear things up to work out his frustrations, he didn't understand play. Baby conures loved roly-poly and handling objects with their beaks and feet. Adults played, too, chasing one another on the wing and hanging upside down.

Had Peaches been taken from the nest before his instinct for play had developed? Had the traumas of captivity extinguished his ability to have fun? Or was it the absence of other birds?

It took weeks to trigger Peaches' play instinct. First, I had to get his attention. I handled objects I wanted him to recognize as toys, moved them around on the desk or dining table, or rubbed them under his beak while I spoke in an excited voice: "Hey, Peaches, look at this great piece of balsa wood. Isn't this the coolest thing you've ever seen? Check it out. What do you think?"

It wasn't always bird toys that caught his interest. He loved anything he could dig his beak into, including the torn-off strips of tractor paper from my printer. He discovered sponges when he started exploring the kitchen, and I added one to his toy collection— after rinsing out the soap the manufacturer had laced it with. Phone books were a hit, too—soft on the inside, crunchy on the outside.

If Peaches tugged at an intended toy, I wiggled it back and forth to make him work for it. Or I tossed it to the other end of the table and raced him to it with my hand. He was more interested in something he could snatch and keep from me than in something I didn't want.

He went through a phase where pens were the most attractive

objects in our apartment. He would stand on my hand when I wrote a letter, grocery list, or rent check, gnawing on the top of the pen, eyes closed. My handwriting sometimes looked as if I'd hiccuped mid-word.

Unfortunately, Peaches found the writing ends of pens as fascinating as the caps. I didn't think he could pry out the ball, tiny and well fixed as it was—until I noticed him shaking his head and pushing at something with his tongue: a beak full of ink. I grabbed him with a towel, pried open his beak with a cotton swab, and cleaned out the ink, praying to the Green Parrot Goddess that he hadn't swallowed any.

Then the ultimate pen came home with me from a drug store in Santa Fe. Its fat barrel contained black, red, blue, and green cartridges. Each was activated by its own button. Peaches made so many failed attempts to extract the buttons that I assumed the pen was safe.

When Peaches got one out, he wasn't about to give it up. I chased him all over the apartment. His exaltation was his downfall. He opened his beak to squawk in triumph and dropped the button. I snatched it. He ran at my foot, then looked up at me, towering over him. Instead of attacking, he complained in his most annoyed voice, *AAAaaa, AAAaaa, AAAaaa.*

Fortunately, more toy ads were showing up in the bird magazines. Peaches' favorite had a large wooden bead and long bristles. He also liked a piece of untanned leather that Barbara, a Los Alamos friend who did crafts, came up with. Peaches groomed these and snuggled up to them at night.

* * *

The initial need for dependence was ending. The new cage's top perch put Peaches at eye level with me when I was standing up, and he took an equal's advantage. By mid-spring, he was jumping on for rides. Beak over claw, he would climb my hair to the top of my head, flap his wings, and scream in triumph.

He enjoyed this king-of-the-mountain game so much that I

started lifting him to the valance over the window. After an ecstatic wing-flapping display that I named Peaches Wind Machine, he would leap off and glide to me.

That gave me another idea. I got him on my finger, walked to the farthest corner from the bed, and tossed him. He sailed and fluttered to a soft and safe landing, *awk-awk-awk*ing all the way. He ran across the rug and climbed up my clothes, ready to do it again.

About that time, the morning screech became one of Peaches' favorite rituals. I sang "Morning Has Broken" as I opened the Venetian blinds, substituting *parrot* for *blackbird*. Peaches squawked, creating an unusual and exuberant duet.

I didn't tell him the song was popularized by *Cat* Stevens.

* * *

Now that Peaches had accepted me, it was a small step to accepting our most frequent visitor. Perry had been chased by chickens as a toddler and was nervous around birds. That he had made friends with my previous parrot owed more to Feathers' initiative than to Perry's.

One evening, as Perry and I passed in the small space of my apartment, Peaches hopped from my shoulder. The enticement was obvious: Perry's short-trimmed beard. Perry sat down and slowly relaxed as Peaches groomed him.

Perry ignored my description of conures as poor talkers and spent a lot of time trying to get Peaches to say, "Awwk, my name is Ralph." He said it over and over, to my distraction and possibly Peaches'. Peaches always had the last squawk.

When Perry finally gave up, I suggested, "Maybe he knows his name isn't Ralph."

"Maybe in his language, it is."

* * *

Did play and socializing eliminate Peaches' feather-picking? No, but they did reduce it. He picked sporadically. It wasn't a perfect situation, but it was an improvement.

I kept looking for ways to make my parrot's life more

interesting, never suspecting that life would give us more interest than we wanted.

FIRE ALARM

Our aging apartment building provided Peaches and me with some Thanksgiving excitement.

Perry was visiting family in another state. To take my mind off the possible reasons why he never invited me to meet them, I had planned a fall housecleaning. I stripped off the bed linens, took down the curtains, tossed the towels into the basket after them, and left Peaches protesting in his cage. I sat outside the first-floor laundry room in the cool sunshine, reading and soaking up some rays.

About the time the washers' rinse cycles kicked in, I smelled smoke. Our building didn't have fireplaces. It must have come from a house in the next block.

The smell grew stronger, and I got up to look. Brownish-gray smoke was pouring from a second-floor window on my side of our building. I hobbled up the inside stairs and found it seething out around an apartment door. I headed for our place, slamming both fire doors behind me. For the first time, I noticed they were made of wood.

Peaches' eyes widened as I dashed in, grabbed the phone, and dialed 911. He squawked and swiveled his head, searching for the threat, while the operator told me I wasn't the first to notice the blaze.

As I hung up, footsteps rumbled up the outside stairs. There was a knock on our door, and a muffled male voice called, "Fire Department."

Several firefighters, clad in brown suits, yellow vests, and rebreather masks, were ordering people to evacuate. When I turned away, the nearest one said, "Now! Don't stop for anything."

"I'm not going anywhere without my parrot."

"Leave the damn bird. Get out!"

I unclenched my teeth long enough to say, "Not in this life or any other."

The firefighter started to say something about leaving my handbag as I swung it to my shoulder. I appreciated that he was doing his job but gave him a look that conveyed the foolishness of telling a woman to abandon her purse.

As Peaches and I headed toward the near end of the building, a firefighter flung open the fire door. Smoke surged into the hall and pursued us out the exit.

I set Peaches' cage in Macha's passenger seat, got in the other side, and watched firefighters drag a hose to the stairs at the far end of the building. Steam poured out the window of the burning apartment.

It was all over in minutes, but firefighters kept tenants out while they shut off the electricity and made certain the fire hadn't crept into the walls, sub-floor, or ceiling, where it might spread unseen. One of them told us that somebody had left bedding and newspapers piled against an electrical outlet. A short in the old wiring had ignited it.

I sat in Macha through the afternoon, reading the book that had been in my purse and talking with Peaches. He cocked his head every few minutes and squawked a question I interpreted as, *How come we're in the truck, but we're not moving? Isn't the light ever going to turn green?*

* * *

The fire marshal let us back in at sunset. Every upstairs apartment door and window was open. The apartments reeked, and the residual smoke triggered a lot of coughing as a dozen of us gathered, shivering, to wonder why opening the fire doors had seemed like a good idea.

Tom, who had been skiing at Taos and had arrived home as the firefighters were packing up their hose, voiced what we were all thinking: "I wonder if we should move." His *we* included a pair of cockatiels, who had sat through the excitement in their cage, safe until someone opened the door, and smoke rolled in.

"All the apartments I can afford are the same vintage as this one," I said.

"Right," said Suzanne, the woman whose plants I tended when she was out of town. "We could as easily move *into* a firetrap as *out of* one."

Squabble-dee-wabble! Peaches agreed.

Everyone looked at him, sitting in his cage on the floor. It was the first time some of us had smiled all day—a reminder that we had a lot to be grateful for. All but one of he building's residents had an apartment to come home to.

* * *

Someone asked the owner whether he or his insurance company would compensate us for having to launder our clothes, bedding, curtains, towels, and rugs, but nothing came of it. Despite our gratitude, we did a certain amount of griping as we lined up in the laundry room.

We weren't the only ones. Peaches had developed the habit of pacing back and forth across the windowsill, squawking. He looked like a tiny orator, hands clasped behind his back, spreading his wings to emphasize a point. His rhetoric the day after the fire probably revolved around the risks of aged electrical systems, the careless storage of combustibles, and the mysterious motives of firefighters.

A few days later, I caught myself pacing in front of the window, talking on the phone, and gesturing. How often had Peaches watched me do that? I stopped and looked at him looking at me.

Sure, I imagined him saying, *learned it from my mom.*

LOST LOVE

That winter, the window put Peaches in touch with an unusual avian *inamorata:* a glossy black raven, who perched on the chain link fence around the tennis courts next to our building.

The first time Ravena swooped up in front of the glass, Peaches screamed and soared off my shoulder. Ravena landed on the roof above the window, leaned over, and *tap-tap-tap*ped on the metal drip cap, perhaps trying to find a way in.

Peaches huddled under my desk. But when Ravena made that

41

coruscating call like water tumbling over river-rounded stones, he came out and gazed up at her, seduced by her song. He called back in his own tongue, apparently not sensing that her enticements sprang from deadly intent.

I told him, "She wants you in the worst way: for dinner," but it was like telling Romeo not to long for Juliet. How could a prey bird fall in love with a predator-scavenger? The attraction suggested how unnatural Peaches' life in a human home was.

Their love affair went on for a couple of weeks. Then a three-day snowstorm blew in, and Ravena stopped coming around.

"She's flown south for the winter," I said, as Peaches stood on the window sill, searching for her.

Was I telling the truth? We saw ravens all year. She might have died or given up trying to nab the little green feathered morsel. Maybe the pickings were better in the Western Area, on North Mesa, or at the downtown restaurant dumpsters.

For three days, Peaches pushed his food around, scarcely ate, and didn't hurl a single green bean onto the bed. He rejected offers to ride my hand out of his cage and have his head scritched. Instead, he sat on his manzanita perch, eyes closed. He didn't even pick his feathers.

On day four, after a little "Morning Has Broken," Peaches was bright-eyed and ready to dig into my breakfast. He had loved, lost, and let go.

At least that was what I told myself. Did Peaches daydream about Ravena as I did about Perry when he was gone on weekend hikes with friends and visits to family? I always wished him a great trip and never acted hurt, but I felt the pain of exclusion more and more.

ROAD TRIP

I decided the next trip would be mine, and not to get back at Perry. Northern New Mexico felt like home, but I couldn't minimize the impact of leaving my native California. A lot of friends still lived there. We remained emotionally close, but the air gap sometimes felt greater than the nine hundred-plus driving miles.

Dr. Nelson's office closed for two weeks in the summer. As the hygienist and I hung a sign in the window, directing patients to the other dentists in the building, I said, "Peaches and I have friends in California who'll put us up. Macha can pass a lot of gas stations."

"Does she have air conditioning? You're going to need that off The Hill."

"No, but I'm a pro at the four-sixty kind."

Her expression went blank.

"Roll down all four windows and drive sixty miles an hour."

Perry stayed over the night before Peaches and I left. He made all the right noises about missing me, but the undercurrent of relief was impossible to ignore. All I could do was hope that a couple of weeks' absence would make his heart grow fonder.

* * *

The first leg of the trip was a two-hour sprint to Albuquerque, where we visited Barbara, my craft friend, and her husband Daniel. I slept on their living room futon ("Japanese," Barbara told me, "for 'uncomfortable bed'"), with Peaches in his cage on the floor beside me. Covered, he couldn't see the two cats nosing around, but he made anxious creaks when he heard them. I woke up several times, shoved the cats away, and told them to quit shopping.

We were on I-40 at five the next morning. Peaches watched the scenery with cheerful squawks. Only eighteen wheelers made him edgy. He reacted with the low, uneasy growls he usually reserved for curious waterfowl at Ashley Pond on evenings when it was too hot for us to stay in our apartment.

He might have been mirroring my anxiety. When big rigs rumbled by at seventy-five or eighty miles an hour—tarps flapping, chains jangling, retread tires hurling off pieces that thumped against Macha's flanks—I tightened my grip on the wheel and had to work at breathing.

We took an hour out to nap beneath the pines east of Flagstaff and pulled into Kingman about four in the afternoon. A time-and-temperature sign read an even hundred degrees.

"We can stop here for the night," I said, "or, in less than an hour, we can cross the Colorado River and sleep in California. What do you think?"

Mr. Last Word didn't respond. I lifted the wet towel draped over his cage and saw that he wasn't even panting in his own personal evaporative cooling chamber.

Half-way to Needles, I remembered how far the highway dropped and how much the temperature could rise. I was sweating so heavily that I didn't need to douse myself. I just kept drinking water.

Peaches panted and pressed his feathers against his body to keep internal heat from building up. I soaked his towel and spritzed him from a spray bottle. "Should we turn around?"

I didn't wait for an answer as the wrong decision leaped to my heat-muddled mind. "I hate retreating. If we're going to bake, we might as well go forward. It can't get much hotter."

Was I ever wrong. At the produce inspection station on the California side of the river, the thermometer in the shade read a hundred and twenty-one degrees. Peaches was panting as though he'd run a footrace. His eyes were dull. He wasn't dumping heat fast enough, so I soaked him from the spray bottle and asked the produce inspector for directions to the nearest motel.

I was relieved to see air conditioners protruding from the motel's cinder-block walls. They were running only in the occupied rooms, however, so it was the same temperature inside as out. At least we were out of the sun. I cranked up the AC and covered three sides and the top of Peaches' cage with pillows. A sudden chill could be as dangerous as heat prostration.

Without peeling off my sweat-soaked clothes and rubber sandals, I stepped into the shower and twisted the cold handle. By the time I stepped out, the air temperature was down to a hundred, and Peaches was snacking from his food dish.

His survival was a gift and a lesson. As I stripped down and dried off, I committed aloud, "No driving in temperatures over a hundred. If we have to travel like vampires and hole up in motels during the day, so be it."

KEEPING GOING

Peaches and I were fine the next day, after sleeping for ten hours behind the motel's light-blocking curtains. I let him out of his cage about five in the morning to share fruit and hard-boiled eggs, then locked him up and started loading the truck.

According to the thermometer in the shade at the motel office, the temperature was eighty-five degrees. It climbed a degree every time I carried out a load. I could see another scorching day coming and drove away from it as fast as I legally could.

* * *

Three hours later, we were cruising south on Interstate 215 toward California 91 and Orange County. The air had that smoggy smell like a fire in a dumpster. This was the point at which Thor and I had always talked about hanging a U back to Deerskin Lake in the North Woods of Wisconsin, where he had grown up.

"I hate breathing air I can see," I grumbled. I lifted my foot off the gas pedal and shifted into neutral. "It's not too late to turn around."

Peaches answered with an ambiguous mutter.

We coasted while I considered spending our vacation in Sedona; we'd passed the exit on I-40 the day before. I weighed blue sky, green shade, and Oak Creek flowing over red rocks against the people waiting for us: Elida, my closest friend since high school (we called ourselves sisters without papers); Rod, her firefighter husband; folkdance friends Anita and Logan; Dianne, crippled by juvenile rheumatoid arthritis but still one of the most able people I knew; Sheri, a coworker from my library days, who had a canary named Tom Selleck; Thor, scheduled to come up from San Diego for some bird watching; and, of course, my parents. I shifted back into fifth and kept going.

Keeping going was a challenge. The lower we drove, the more Macha sputtered and cut out. We got off of I-5 in Mission Viejo, where she lugged away from the traffic light. At the last intersection before Elida and Rod's house, she coughed and died.

"Come on," I begged, jamming the gas pedal to the floor and cranking the starter. Drivers honked and dodged around us. A man in a business suit and a red tie that matched his car tossed an obscene gesture. Against my rule not to react to other drivers, I yelled, "Yeah, I guess your Audi never breaks down."

Peaches leaped to his front perch and squawked, *Squabble-dee-wobble!* as if to let the rude man know whose side he was on.

CAN'T GO HOME

Macha ran better after I crossed a mechanic's palm with plastic. I drove back to Elida and Rod's, where I jotted a note in my appointment book to have the carburetor adjustment reversed when we got back to New Mexico. I grumbled to Peaches that while that would make Macha run better at high altitude, it wouldn't reverse the flow of money out of my checking account.

Peaches' *Squawk, squawk, squawk* sounded like *Bitch, bitch, bitch.*

* * *

Thor and I met the following day at the Back Bay in Newport Beach. Many of the birds that had wintered on the saltwater estuary had flown north to nest, but there were enough to make us point and jot down their names. The most memorable were three Forster's terns, diving one after another into a school of fish. They reminded me of circus roustabouts, hammering in a stake for the big top.

The smells of salt water, low-tide mud, and native plants made my heart open again to this place where bird watching had first taken hold of me, leading to my life with Feathers and then Peaches (I begrudged including Chamisa the budgie). Despite the apartment complexes and the traffic on the four-and six-lane streets visible from the bay—despite the private and commercial jets roaring off from John Wayne Airport—the Back Bay still felt like home.

So did my friendship with Thor. We might not work as a couple, but our camaraderie sustained us both.

* * *

I set aside the following morning for poking around downtown Huntington Beach. Over Rod's delicious omelets, he and Elida offered to chauffeur me. He had the day off. She happened to have no massage clients—or maybe she'd scheduled it that way.

"Don't trouble yourselves," I said, wanting to be an easy guest.

"No trouble," Rod said, his tone shifting from offer to insistence. "We'll take you."

"You want to go with us," Elida added. "Trust me."

"Always," I said, as an uneasy ripple started in my stomach.

* * *

As we approached the pier an hour later, my breath stuck in my chest. The fun, funky downtown area had been leveled. In its place stood two- and three-story, *faux* art-nouveau shops and office buildings, painted pink, the kind that had become popular in the high-end sections of Newport Beach.

The Golden Bear Theater had been demolished. Everyone who was anyone in the sixties, seventies, and eighties—comedians, rockers, and country musicians alike—had performed there. The lengthy list painted on an outside wall had included Janice Joplin, Jimi Hendrix, Hoyt Axton, Linda Ronstadt, John Mayall, The New Riders of the Purple Sage, Steve Martin, and Robin Williams.

I dabbed away tears, blew my nose, and thought that while change might be the only constant, this one was going to take a while to accept. A part of my past had been bulldozed. I hadn't seen the evolution but was experiencing the shock all at once.

"I understand," I said, "why some people never return to their favorite places."

Elida nodded. "'You can't go home again.' There's a reason for that cliché."

* * *

Huntington Beach hadn't finished disappointing me. I was

driving to the Bolsa Chica wetlands the following day to see a flock of black skimmers when I decided to detour a mile to the house Thor and I had lived in.

Things had changed there, too. A tall, black-windowed office building walled in one side of the neighborhood, and a monolithic apartment complex loomed beyond the end of our cul-de-sac. The house Thor and I had put so much love and color into was now painted a nondescript shade I thought of as rental beige.

The real shock was the police cars blocking the street. Half a dozen black-uniformed S.W.A.T. cops jumped out of a van in front of the house, rifles at the ready. A policeman called through his megaphone, "Throw out your weapons and come out with your hands up."

The *thump* I heard wasn't the shotgun landing on the lawn. It was my heart hitting my hip bones. A man in his late thirties, wearing jeans and a tattered gray T-shirt, stepped out with his arms in the air. The police swarmed him, handcuffed him, and shoved him into a black-and-white. The S.W.A.T. team stormed inside the house.

Had our lovely home been turned into a meth lab or a hole-up for bank robbers, car thieves, or murderers? I didn't stick around to find out. The instant I could breathe, I cranked the wheel and stamped Macha's gas pedal to the floor.

CLIP JOB

Watching the skimmers at Bolsa Chica sopped up some of my adrenaline, but I was still shaken enough to need a long soak in Elida and Rod's hot tub.

Next was a grooming session with Peaches. I stepped into the guest bedroom and closed the door to keep out the resident predators, seal-point Balinese cats Pandora and Sushi Samurai and tuxedo kitty Gremlin. They awakened me at night, snuffling around the bottom of the door. *Parrot fricassee,* I could almost hear them purring. *Parrot à l'orange. Parrot under glass.*

I double-checked the door and opened Peaches' cage. He

climbed onto my finger and crouched as if to offer his head for grooming. Instead, he took off flying. He circled the room several times before landing on the framed mirror. He caught his breath and flew a few more laps, squawking and screaming.

My heart lifted as I watched him wing around the room. "Someday," I promised him again.

Several thumps at the bottom of the door and the sound of claws on wood made me check the latch again.

* * *

For breakfast the next morning, I had an omelet with a side order of yellow pages, then phoned the nearest vet. Peaches' safety won out over the joy of flight.

The familiar smells of animals and cleaning solutions at the clinic reassured me until an assistant picked up Peaches' cage and headed for an exam room. When I followed, she said, "Oh, no. The doctor and I will do the wing trim by ourselves. We find it goes easier."

I didn't like a single thing about that—not her haughty tone, not the suggestion that I would be in the way, and not the idea of allowing strangers to take Peaches out of my sight. As I sometimes did, though, I wimped out and avoided a confrontation.

My stomach churned until the assistant set Peaches' cage back on the counter. Then it roiled. Peaches was frantically checking his wings with his beak. The vet had clipped all his flight feathers, primaries and secondaries, back to the limbs. It wasn't even an artful job. They looked hacked and butchered.

The assistant cooed, "Don't worry, he'll still be able to break his fall."

"With *what?*"

It was too late to do anything about the hatchet job, and the receptionist had run my credit card. I grabbed Peaches' cage and stormed out, more angry at myself than at the inept vet and his staff. As I drove away, I told myself, *I'll never make this mistake again.* I hoped I would muster some courage the next time something like this confronted me.

A few minutes later, I was telling Elida, "I assumed Peaches would get the kind of trim Dr. Ramsay gives. No one asked, and I didn't tell them."

Elida patted my arm. "I presume a bad wing job is like a bad haircut."

"Yeah, it'll grow out."

"Everybody lived, so quit beating yourself up."

I didn't mention how hard that good advice was for someone with my shaky self-esteem to follow. Fortunately, I didn't have to.

FAMILY

I thought of Elida and the other people I was close to as my real family. One day, I left Peaches with my "sister," Dianne, in Long Beach, while I overnighted with my biological family, the one I didn't have a choice about.

Things had changed in Palos Verdes, too, of course. The once-open hills were now built solid with houses.

What remained the same was that my parents still smoked four packs of Camels a day between them. The second-hand smoke stung my eyes, irritated my sinuses, and triggered the pain in the middle of my chest that I had had for years, living in the smoggy inland cities of Orange County. I could only imagine what it would have done to Peaches' delicate respiratory system.

My parents had stopped drinking in their early sixties, before I moved to New Mexico. Sobriety had come soon enough for Dad. Mother, plagued for decades with depression, had succumbed to dementia. She served the foods I told her I was sensitive to and huffed when I rummaged in the pantry. Over and over, she interrupted conversations to tell me, "We're so proud of your brother."

The pain in my chest was aggravated by the sadness of listening to Mother ask her standard questions: Why had Thor and I divorced, why hadn't we had children, why had I had a hysterectomy? Without going into detail, I gave her my stock answers. Mother forgot them and asked the same questions a dozen times during the evening.

When I got back to Long Beach, I greeted Peaches but didn't let him out of his cage until I had stripped off my smoke-fouled clothes, stuffed them into my plastic laundry bag, and tied it shut. I showered, scrubbing off the bad smell of a relationship that was never going to be easy or satisfying.

* * *

On our way home, Peaches and I had a different kind of parental visit—with Elida's mother in Prescott, Arizona. Irene was a gracious and spiritual woman. The first thing she did was to clear a small table by a window so Peaches could watch the wild birds.

As Irene and I talked, I realized that my experiences in Huntington Beach had served a useful purpose: They had disconnected me from Southern California. How easy it had been, from the uncrowded, clear-aired perspective of New Mexico, to think of my long-time former home as a fallback position.

Irene helped me crystallize what had been building in the back of my mind the whole trip: I could treasure my West-Coast experiences, visit my real family and my family of origin, and enjoy the beach and the wild birds. My home, however, was with Peaches on the Pajarito Plateau.

* * *

The rest of the trip was uneventful except for big trucks, which Peaches continued to comment on in uneasy tones. They didn't slow us down. I couldn't wait to get back to the pines, junipers, our little apartment, and Perry.

If I'd known what awaited, I might not have been in such a hurry.

I'M THE ONE

The last day of vacation, I stood in front of my dresser, putting away my clean laundry. Perry had spent the night and left.

Peaches was so aware of the radical wing clip the California vet had given him that he refused to glide off his cage and had called until I picked him up. He perched on my shoulder now, murmuring what sounded like my own thought: *Glad to be home.*

As I tucked my bathing suit into its drawer, my fingers came across the pin Dianne had made for me before I moved to New Mexico. It was emblazoned with a red heart. Bright yellow letters, outlined in black, proclaimed, *I'm the one you've been looking for!*

I'd kept the pin on my purse until Perry and I had started dating, partly for fun and partly because Mr. Right might spot it and be intrigued. Now it occurred to me that it might be read as *desperate* by Mr. Right—and any number of Mr. Wrongs. I wondered which one I was sleeping with.

I turned the pin over and over, so distracted that I barely noticed Peaches nibbling my earlobe. Had Perry been looking for someone? He might have denied it, but his actions showed that he was at least willing to leap at the chance.

I had to admit that my relationship with Peaches was on a more solid footing than the one with Perry. All right, Peaches couldn't leave me, but he could have chosen to sulk, scream, and bite for the rest of his life. Even after I subjected him to the awful wing trim, he initiated conversations and climbed up my clothes to snuggle against my neck and peek out from under my hair.

Peaches made choices that brought us closer. I couldn't say the same for Perry. One night before I'd left, he'd insisted he didn't know whether or not he loved me.

"Are you that confused?" I asked. "That cut off from your feelings?"

"I just don't know how to tell."

"What do you feel in your body?"

"I've shut down my emotions for so long that I don't know what I feel."

I was still trying to bear in mind that he was going through post-divorce upheaval. It didn't help me feel better.

At least Perry and I were both willing to look at our histories and attitudes. The downside was that self-examination and change kept our relationship in flux and off balance. That made me anxious, and *that* made it hard not to come off as needy and hungry for reassurance.

I'd told my California friends that the uncertainties would smooth out over time and give Perry and me a better chance to be happy together in the long run. A couple of people had asked who I was trying to convince.

Now, I tucked the I'm-the-one pin back in its drawer and mechanically continued putting laundry away, my mind elsewhere.

No amount of attraction compensated for the tension our differences created. The most obvious was the conflict between his needs as a recently divorced man and mine as a years-single woman, but there were others. Perry described himself as a recovering Catholic. I'd swung from my vaguely Protestant upbringing to atheism, settling in a Hindu-Buddhist-universalist-humanist-twelve-step middle ground.

Perry was avid about his other religion: sports. Who won and lost affected his mood in a way I couldn't fathom. I rooted for his favorite teams but watched soccer, basketball, and football on TV mostly for the chance cuddle with him.

Then there was the matter of diet. I'd been a vegetarian for a couple of years when I met Perry and hadn't realized what a personal path it was. I was vocal against his hunting. I couldn't stand the thought of him dragging a gutted buck into my kitchen in a clatter of antlers. He didn't need a deer in the freezer to get through the winter, as his childhood family had, so wasn't hunting bad karma?

It hadn't occurred to me that it might be bad karma to try to change someone else who had his own path—or that he might not appreciate my efforts.

NIGHT OUT

At least Perry was comfortable with the nudist lifestyle I'd enjoyed in California and had found thriving on a smaller scale in Northern New Mexico—until we spent a summer afternoon at

McCauley Warm Spring, a remnant of the Jemez Mountains' volcanism. We rendezvoused at Redondo Campground with friends of mine who had already been to the pools, then parked Perry's truck at Jemez Falls and hiked down the trail.

I sank into the clothing-optional pool. Perry stepped into an oak thicket to take a whiz. When he came out, his naked forty-something girlfriend was shaking hands with his naked seventeen-year-old son, who had come down another trail with friends. Even if I hadn't seen pictures, I'd have known Ed for a younger version of his father.

Perry clamped his fallen jaw shut and pulled off the encounter pretty well, chatting with Ed and his friends about what they were doing during the summer. It was obvious, though, that the conflict between his previous and current lives had hit critical mass. He was so far out of his comfort zone that he sat on a rock, fully clothed, arms and legs crossed. He didn't even take off his shoes and dangle his feet in the water.

When I had dressed and was ready to leave, Perry insisted, "I'll hike up the trail and get my truck. You walk down to Battleship Rock Picnic Area. I'll pick you up there."

I tried to calm the panic in my voice. "You *never* abandon your hiking partner, no matter how you feel. It's a basic safety rule."

"With your weak knee, it'll be easier to go downhill."

"Downhill is harder on my knee. You know that. I've never hiked this trail. What if I get hurt? What if you do?"

"Other hikers will come along." The rapid tumble of words suggested how desperate he was to run away. "If you have trouble, sit down. I'll hike up the trail and meet you."

He took off at a pace I couldn't match and was out of sight in half a minute.

In a welter of hurt, fear, and anger, I cast around for the path to Battleship Rock. What I found meandered through pine forest above the East Fork of the Jemez River, so breathtaking that it almost made up for Perry's shabby treatment.

It didn't occur to me how rough the trail was getting or how steep the slope it crossed until a rock rolled under my foot. My weak knee collapsed, and I tumbled and slid ten feet. I scrambled back to the trail, dusted myself off, and rubbed at the scratches on my arms and legs from the volcanic cinders. Shaky, I hiked on.

Two or three miles from McCauley, on a sloping ledge, I came to a washout six feet deep and twenty feet across. No wonder I hadn't seen other hikers. This was an abandoned trail.

Loose cinders rolled under my feet when I tried to climb up and then down. To get to the ledge, I'd edged across a narrow, slanting portion of the trail. Going back, leading with my weak knee, looked more dangerous than doing what Perry had suggested. I sat down and waited.

I was still waiting when the sun sank behind the canyon wall.

To still the fearful shiver that ran up my spine, I did what expert hikers suggested: I took stock. I was wearing shorts, a sleeveless blouse, tennis shoes, and socks, and was carrying a beach towel and a hiking stick with a wrist cord about a foot long. No food. More important, no water. Perry had taken the canteen.

My biggest problem, besides keeping warm in the mountains on a clear-sky night, was where I was stranded. What would keep me from falling asleep, tumbling off the ledge, and plunging to the boulder- and tree-strewn river a couple of hundred feet below? That fear seemed enough to keep me awake, but would it work until dawn?

Luck was with me. A ponderosa pine clung to the slope about ten feet above me. One of its roots, an inch in diameter, looped out of the ashflow wall behind the ledge. I took the cord off my hiking stick and, in a contortionist's maneuver, ran it through the loop, then under my bra strap, tying as many knots as I could.

As darkness fell, and a chill breeze wafted down the canyon, I leaned forward and gave my lifeline a test tug. Then I drew up my knees and huddled under the beach towel.

My lifelong affinity for poetry served me well that moonless night as I dozed and jolted to heart-pounding wakefulness at the end of my cord. To calm myself, I recited every poem I could remember, including the Twenty-Third Psalm, part of the prolog to Chaucer's *Canterbury Tales,* Shelley's "Ozymandias," Frost's "Mending Wall" and "Something Like a Star," and part of Byron's "Childe Harolde's Pilgrimage."

Peaches came to mind over and over. I imagined lying in my own safe bed, hearing him grind his beak and fluff his feathers as he settled in. Knowing he was there in our little home anchored me.

I thought of Perry, especially when I started shivering. That was when it dawned on me that he might never have gotten to Battleship Rock. The winding two-lane road through the Jemez was infamous for metal-mangling accidents.

My heart flip-flopped. "If that's happened to Perry, then no one knows I'm here."

To distract myself, I checked for numb spots and tried to think of another poem. What came to mind instead was an article I'd read about hypothermia. You were in trouble when the shivering started, as muscles tried to generate heat. You were in *serious* trouble when it stopped. Blood vessel constriction could fail, causing a rush of heat that made people strip off their clothes. My first winter in New Mexico, a man had been found dead after shedding everything he was wearing.

I shook my head and peeked out from under the towel. The sky was spangled with constellations I didn't recognize, suggesting it was after two in the morning. I licked my dry lips with my parched tongue. It would be light in two or three hours. Maybe I could edge across that iffy place in the trail. Even if I could have reached it, the Jemez River was contaminated with the intestinal parasite *giardia.* Maybe I could get some water from campers at McCauley, trek up to Jemez Falls, and hitch a ride to Redondo Campground.

It took me a moment to realize that not all the lights I was seeing were stars. Three of them bobbed against the black canyon wall half a mile upstream. I couldn't blink them away, but I still didn't trust them. I'd been in a sensory deprivation tank and knew that my mind could create imaginary lights. I pulled the beach towel over my head.

The lights were closer when I looked again. Another set approached from downstream. Several men and a woman called my name. I called back, my voice hoarse. Headlines like *Search Called Off Until Morning* or just *Called Off* had run through my mind. I'd even wondered whether Perry, in the throes of anxiety, had failed to report me missing.

Within minutes, a three-person team from the nearby community of La Cueva stood on my ledge. Another team, with good knees and lug-soled boots, crossed the washout. These rescuers—the most wonderful people in the world just then—untied me from the pine root, bundled me up in a goose-down jacket, and gave me all the water I could drink.

They were thrilled to find me in such good shape. I'd done the right things, they said, adding that I wouldn't believe how often they found people injured or dead because they had panicked.

The leader radioed headquarters about their find. His wife later told me that she had just stepped outside and stood in the quiet dark, praying that I would be found alive and well. She'd just said, "Amen," when her husband's call came in.

Two of my rescuers buckled me into a climbing harness. A third roped it to a tree on the other side of the iffy section of trail. I walked across it as if it was a level sidewalk. We angled up the face of the mountain, clambering over fallen trees and detouring around obsidian boulders the size of SUVs until we intercepted the real trail. Compared to the one I had been on, it looked like Interstate 25.

Around sunrise, we trudged into Battleship Rock Picnic Area. A state police cruiser idled in the parking lot, exhaling the gas-exhaust smell of civilization. Upwind of it stood my nudist friends. I hugged them and my rescuers, and shook hands with the policeman who had coordinated the search and with the handlers of two dogs teams who were about to set out looking for me.

Perry ran to meet me, tears streaming down his cheeks. "There were so many trails, so many dead ends. I couldn't find the right one."

I fell into his arms, certain that this ordeal would prevent him from ever hurting me again. I was so afraid of alienating him that I never spoke an angry word.

FREE FALL

My nudist friends later said they had been ready to tell Perry off at Battleship but had taken their lead from me. I wrote an account of my adventure and read it in class, where a dozen outraged writers wanted to drag Perry behind the woodshed. People at work looked askance when I told them how I had gotten stranded.

I ignored everyone's skeptical remarks. Survivor euphoria left me more in love than ever.

My denial and misplaced optimism took a gut-check a few weeks later, when Perry decreed a six-month separation to sort out his life. Most stomach-lurching was the last thing he said: "If you find someone else, you should forget about me."

We exchanged a few letters and phone calls but didn't see each other, even by accident in our small town. It took me a while to admit that he might have planned it that way.

A couple of months later, Perry broke the separation, inviting me on a combination business and pleasure trip to the spectacular Monterey coast in California. We could hardly stay out of bed. I hoped that meant a permanent thaw, but when we returned to Los Alamos, it was to the chill of isolation.

The up-and-down swings kept getting bigger. I broke up with him because I couldn't stand the strain of uncertainly. A few weeks later, I showed up on his doorstep, insisting I would take whatever I could get.

The final breakup came over a job offer Perry received. It meant six months in Washington, D.C., after which he might or might not return to Los Alamos. Much as I didn't want to live in a city again, I'd have packed up Peaches and moved to be with Perry. But, of course, he wasn't inviting me.

* * *

My emotional free fall lasted for months. When Peaches was asleep, and late-night TV movies couldn't keep me distracted, I drove Macha along the dark Jemez Mountain roads, sobbing and beating on the steering wheel. The thought that twisted through my mind was that if Perry didn't want me, how would anyone else?

In our final conversation, Perry had called me a drug. I was horrified that he thought of me as an ugly, addictive substance that brought him pain. For weeks, I was too swamped by anguish and confusion to realize that he had never spoken about his own emotions. Had he had grown uncomfortable with the exposure of his feelings and the intensity of his needs? He never took responsibility for his choice to begin and continue the relationship.

Perry was clearly in pain, but any possibility of compassion evaporated when I received the letter that announced his upcoming marriage. The timing made it impossible to avoid the conclusion that he had been seeing his future wife while he was dating me.

* * *

That I might have deserved better treatment didn't occur to me for a long time. When the idea surfaced, so did fury. I prayed that Perry wouldn't step in front of Macha in a crosswalk—and that he would. If I loved him, I should wish for his happiness, even if it didn't include me. That kindness was as out of my reach as the far side of the moon. I was glad for the everyday distractions of work, shopping, and trying to look normal, the way a sick bird would.

Peaches may have saved my life. I thought about suicide, not for the first time in my life, but for the first time over a man. My friends would go on without me. Dr. Nelson would find a new receptionist. But who would feed my beloved parrot, toss him on glides across the room, chat with him in some semblance of his own language?

The self-destructive thoughts subsided when I remembered how little I respected women who killed themselves over men. Besides, I didn't really want to take my life. I wanted to not feel the pain of loss and inadequacy.

* * *

While I was edging uncertainly toward healing, I spent an evening with Rob and his girlfriend. I ran a riff about what I would do in my next relationship, if there was one: choose a man who was available, one who wasn't just out of a long marriage, someone who was looking for a life partner. I would be less needy, stronger, smarter. I would protect myself.

The gleam in Rob's eyes told me he had spotted the flaws in my wishful thinking. He pointed out that I couldn't control who I was attracted to. All I could do was stay or leave and deal with my emotions. "So you can throw away the questionnaire you're thinking of administering."

"Right," I grumbled, "to the line of men down the stairs and around my apartment building."

* * *

Trying to manage the unmanageable was predictable. Phoning my parents was crazy. I couldn't stand to stay in Los Alamos, I told them, where I might run into Perry while I was pumping gas, eating at a Chinese restaurant, or hiking Quemezon Trail.

On the spur of the moment, I said, "I'm going to quit my job and give up my apartment. Peaches and I can travel around California until we find someplace else to settle."

"Okay," my father said. "So we'll see you when?"

"I don't know. I'll have to work it out."

As soon as I hung up, I burned with humiliation. Turning to my parents for sympathy and exposing my vulnerable emotions placed on a spectrum between weird and self-abusive. So did moving back to California. I couldn't leave my heartbreak behind with the white brick wall and Venetian blinds.

I was sitting in bed later that evening, trying to distract myself with a novel; better someone else's troubles than my own. Peaches, who was usually asleep by then, fluttered down from his cage. He clambered across the rumpled sheets with his wings outstretched for balance, climbed beak over claw up the front of my caftan, and snuggled against my chest.

My heart opened to Peaches' empathy. He snapped me back to the present, to a sensible thought process: "Wouldn't it be better to tough it out here in New Mexico, where we want to live?"

He answered with some drowsy beak grinding and a sigh. In moments, he was asleep over my heart.

* * *

Peaches' natural compassion propelled us to a whole new level of intimacy. Perhaps he was seeking comfort, as well as giving it. Maybe I was helping him heal, not just from losing his friend, Perry, but from the loss of his wild life.

If he could trust and love after all he'd been through, then maybe I could, too.

I'M THE ONE AGAIN

On a late-August Saturday morning, about a year and a half after Perry and I had broken up, Peaches stood on the top perch of his open cage and made an anxious *raawk* as I rummaged in a dresser drawer.

"Don't worry," I said, "I'm not looking for the gloves." I blew him some kisses.

He answered with a sigh that suggested, *Whew!*

I found my *I'm the one you've been looking for!* pin and turned it over in my hands. For months, I'd been crossing my index fingers as a hex against another relationship—as though love, with its risk of heartache, were a vampire I could ward off. Now, I was acknowledging that the only way to deal with my residual heartache was to move forward.

Peaches ran his beak and tongue around the pin as I clipped it to my purse. He grumbled in his throat.

"Don't be offended. If I were a peach-fronted conure, I'd take you for my mate in a heartbeat. I'm longing for someone with hair on his chest. It's a mammal thing."

He lowered his head for a scritch. He had become my knight in shining green armor, spending hours on my shoulders. He groomed my hair, gazed into my eyes, and made the soft little sounds I'd hoped to hear during our first days together.

Feeling a little guilty, I shut him into his cage, interpreting his protest as, *Aw, Mom, it's such a gorgeous morning, why don't we go to the park and watch the ducks?*

I sympathized but hauled my guitar and hammer dulcimer down the stairs and off to the annual Banjo and Fiddle Contest at the Santa Fe Rodeo Grounds. In addition to the competitions, there were bluegrass music workshops and the once-a-year chance to jam with musicians who came from other parts of the country.

That night, a band played for contra dancing, and an instructor showed us novices the steps. One of my partners was a handsome, hazel-eyed man with dark hair and a salt-and-pepper moustache. His eye contact and athletic strength as he twirled me around raised my heart rate as much as the lively music.

On Sunday morning, another hammer dulcimer player and I were jamming behind the stands when a guitar player joined us—my previous night's favorite dance partner. Joe's talent for improvising riffs to tunes he'd never heard before impressed me, but I was disappointed when he lit a cigarette. His accent said New York City, and his attitude—edgy and pushy—left me ambivalent

I'd tucked my purse, with my *I'm the one* pin, behind Macha's driver seat, but it didn't seem to matter. Joe asked for my number and called a couple of days later. We agreed to meet in Los Alamos, at a talk by Taos novelist John Nichols, author of *The Milagro Beanfield War*. I figured that if Joe and I didn't hit it off, I could always walk home.

But I didn't. After the talk, we drove to a café to listen to a local singer. Then we went to my apartment, where we talked and played our guitars. Around midnight, we went out on the landing at the end of the hall so Joe could smoke. When we kissed, I sucked in that tobacco taste because it came with his lips and tongue, and his hand sliding under my blouse.

* * *

Joe was long divorced and said he was interested in a lasting relationship. Despite his sometimes impatient manner, music and physical attraction forged a quick connection.

Peaches stayed in his cage the first few times Joe came around but succumbed to his persistent attention. In a couple of weeks, he was riding on Joe's shoulder and grooming his moustache. Joe was conscientious about washing off any tobacco residue first.

SHREDBETTY

One thing that attracted me to Joe was that nearly everything about him was unconventional, including his ski-bum lifestyle. He taught skiing during the winter. When the snow melted, he took odd jobs, from cashiering to carpentry, to get by until the next season.

I had been on downhill skis once in my twenties and had been lucky to get off the mountain with only bruises and sore muscles. Yet I never missed the annual Warren Miller ski film in Los Alamos. I'd grown up at the beach with Miller's surf movies and found the same excitement in the ski films. That, and the audience's enthusiasm, sent me out of the auditorium on an emotional high that lasted for days.

That year's film showed snowboarding for the first time. I whispered to Joe, "I think I could do that."

After a couple of lessons on rented boards, I was sure. Snowboarding was like the slalom water skiing I'd done with Thor. It was even more like the skateboarding I'd enjoyed as a teenager, when we made boards out of scrap lumber and roller skates.

That winter, I became a confirmed shredbetty, a knuckle dragger. I limped my way through the workweek until I could get back on the snow. The slopes were the only places I could be graceful.

One lift ride proved that more would be too risky. Wind gusts hit the board and twisted my weak knee. My solution was to trudge up the runs, pulling my board with a rope tied around my waist.

Joe saw I was serious and put his creative side to work,

fabricating a brace that clamped to my boot. The garage door spring on each side kept my knee from collapsing. I could ride the lift to the top of the mountain and go anywhere. My teeth ached from grinning in the cold air.

* * *

The brace was typical of Joe's generosity. When a store in Albuquerque advertised one of the first laptop computers, he drove down and bought me one. He recorded my poetry reading at an open mic event in Santa Fe and used his electronic equipment to make it sound as though I'd read at Carnegie Hall.

What woman wouldn't fall in love with such a man? If he got tense and snappy once in a while—even red-faced furious over some small thing I couldn't understand—well, I had to take the bad if I wanted the good, didn't I?

FREE FLIGHT

Before meeting Joe, I'd accepted a job with Dr. Krohn, a local pediatrician and allergist. I was hired to research and write patient medical reports and to fill in at the front desk. I also substituted for the nurse, edited book manuscripts, and learned the new computer billing system so I could teach it to the rest of the staff.

The work kept me stimulated, but the hours were longer than at Dr. Nelson's dental practice. I was also spending time on the slopes and at Joe's place, a travel trailer in a park outside of Santa Fe. The compensation was a more flexible schedule. I could work at home a day or two a week with the stereo playing and Peaches perched on my shoulder or trying to wrestle a pen from my fingers.

Of course, any papers I wasn't working on at the moment had to be covered up because Peaches liked to nip off the corners. Better yet was hooking his beak under staples and ripping them out. "My parrot ate my homework" never failed to spark chuckles when I turned in scalloped pages in Jim Sagel's writing class. For work, things had to look more professional.

* * *

The spring after my first snowboarding winter, I used my job's flexibility to make a Friday afternoon appointment for Peaches' overdue nail and wing trims. We detoured to spend an hour at Joe's beforehand.

Inside Joe's trailer, I let Peaches out of his cage to explore. He took a quick tour on the wing—level flight seemed all he was capable of—and landed on top of his travel cage. That's where he was when I got up to go to the car for something.

Distracted by new love and not used to being mindful of Peaches at Joe's place, I opened the door. Peaches flew *up* to my shoulder. Joe yelled. Peaches shot out and landed in a small Siberian elm.

I stage-whispered to Joe, "Get a towel!"

Peaches perched on a low branch. I stepped toward him, talking and making mock bird noises as if nothing were the matter, while I vibrated inside. With my bare hand in front of him and the towel behind, I grabbed.

Peaches screeched and winged up in a wild spiral, landing thirty feet up in the mature elm next door. Joe charged up the tree while I paced below. Peaches was the same color as the leaves; it was hard to keep track of him as he clambered from branch to branch. I kissed and whistled and called, "Please come back, Peaches. Come on, Peaches, come down," while my heart pounded.

Peaches edged out on a bare branch, craned his head around, and squawked when he saw all those miles of open space. He caught sight of Joe half-way up the trunk and took off, landing in one big cottonwood and then another. I kept up a lame pursuit, scanning for hawks.

Joe climbed down and made for the cottonwood. Peaches didn't wait. He flew back and forth in widening arcs, ever closer to the highway less than a quarter mile away. If he crossed those four lanes, I might never find him. If he tired and tried to land among the cars and trucks . . .

And he was tiring. Every time he perched high in a tree, he

panted, beak open, chest heaving. Ten minutes on the wing was wearing him out.

Peaches landed in a neighbor's cottonwood and stayed put long enough for me to dash into the yard and grab the garden hose. The nozzle shot a steady stream of water that fell on him like heavy rain.

Peaches launched but was too drenched to fly. I threw down the hose and caught him as he fluttered down. He shivered as I tucked him under my shirt.

Like a mother whose errant child had been found safe, I wanted to yell and cry and spank him and hug him all at once.

* * *

As we drove to the clinic, Peaches didn't hop around inside his cage, as he usually did. He stood on his perch, tired and subdued after his first free flight in three years.

I wanted to believe he was glad to be back with me, as I fought that feeling that I was lower than slime mold for letting him out. He might have paid a terrible price.

While Dr. Ramsay trimmed Peaches' flight feathers, I told her what had happened.

"How did you know to soak him down?" she asked.

"When Feathers and I lived in California, I saw one of our neighbors watering his pepper tree. I thought it was strange that he was aiming the spray toward the top until his Amazon parrot fell out." Witnessing that odd event had saved Peaches' life and my sanity.

My guilt and shame subsided over the next few days, and I remembered the awe I'd felt, watching Peaches fly from tree to tree. If I hadn't gotten him back, that image would have haunted me. As it was, it made me more determined than ever to live where he could fly free indoors.

ATE IT ANYWAY

Joe and I had been seeing each other for a little over a year when I got a job offer from my chiropractor in Santa Fe. I turned it down at first because the commute from Los Alamos was too long, and living in the state capital was beyond my means.

Then Joe did what I was secretly hoping he would: He suggested that Peaches and I move in with him. To me, the invitation meant the kind of deepening intimacy and commitment I longed for.

Something chewed at the back of my mind, though. I'd had some exposure to the less-than-generous side of Joe's personality. After being fine for days, he would launch into a weird verbal attack. He blamed me for a muscle pull at the gym. When I crossed out a day in my appointment book, he pitched a fit but wouldn't explain why.

Out of the blue, he would say, "Stop doing that!"

I would stop reading a book, preparing vegetables for Peaches, or washing the breakfast dishes.

"No," he would say, "the other thing you're doing."

"What thing?"

"You should know. You're the one who's doing it."

"Uh, okay," I would say. I tried to sound nonchalant, despite my anxiety.

Like the unwary person finding a rotten peanut—from a childhood camp song—I ate it anyway. Why did I move in with Joe? These double-talk outbursts seemed to be short-term glitches in his mental wiring. I focused on our great music sessions, talks over dinner, and memorable times in bed.

I wanted to prove that I could face down my lifelong fear of men's anger, that I was strong and healthy enough to make a difficult relationship work. Wasn't that what agreeing to disagree and rolling with the emotional punches was all about?

Not once did I question whether this was a mutual approach.

* * *

Joe's travel trailer was too small for two people and a parrot, so we traded it in on an eight-by-forty-seven-foot trailer, fabricated in the 1950s. It reminded me of the old Lucille Ball and Desi Arnaz movie, *The Long, Long Trailer*. It had lovely wooden paneling inside and looked like a fun place to live.

We spent a night lugging my belongings down the stairs from my apartment and stacking them in a rented truck. I swept through the place one last time as the sun rose, making sure we hadn't left anything behind.

Peaches was dozing in his cage on the bathroom floor. As I picked it up, dizziness and disorientation struck me like a wave. Pulling an all-nighter might have contributed, but the big thing was that the apartment had reverted to 1943. It didn't look as if Peaches and I had ever lived there.

It was a burned bridge.

* * *

Not-so-gentle fate wasn't long in pointing out the error of the move. Joe, Peaches, and I hadn't been in the trailer a week when I ran into Rob at the hardware store in Los Alamos. When I mentioned that we were heating water on the stove for our showers because we didn't have a water heater, he said, "Get in your car and follow me."

From his garage, Rob produced a small electric water heater, the kind that fit under a sink and generated enough hot water for one shower before it did a quick recharge. It was so like him to share with a friend in need. I thanked him and thought how pleased Joe would be that I had solved our problem.

Joe, however, ranted about the water heater. Apparently, he thought it came with some kind of bad juju. I did understand that he wanted me to take it back to Rob.

"Okay," I said, confused but seeing no choice. "I'll drop it off next week when I'm in Los Alamos."

"You'll take it back right now."

"It's almost nine o'clock," I objected. "I have to work tomorrow."

Joe's loud voice and furious face made me want to dive under the nearest piece of furniture. "I don't care of it's midnight! Get that piece of crap out of here!"

I covered Peaches, who was making anxious *rawwwk*s in his cage, then called Rob and headed back up The Hill. Rob looked at me with a raised eyebrow before storing the water heater back in his garage, hugged me, and sent me home to lie in the bed I'd made.

ON THE WING

I hesitated to make good on my promise to let Peaches' wing feathers grow out. What if we weren't staying? We'd end up in another apartment, and I'd have to renege on his flight privileges.

When things didn't blow up in six months, I decided to let Peaches' wing feathers grow out. The first time he flew from his cage in the back of the trailer up to the living room curtain rod in front, he *awk-awk-awk*ed while Joe and I cheered.

Peaches also registered his delight when Joe and I arrived home, greeting us with an escalating *Squa-a-ack, squa-a-ak!* as we turned into the park. He never reacted to another vehicle that way.

He did, however, develop a fascination with big yellow earthmovers. When he heard one rumbling down the road, he zoomed to the front window and watched like a little boy who wanted to be a D-9 Caterpillar operator when he grew up. I never understood the attraction, or why he disliked noisy eighteen-wheelers passing our truck but adored noisy earthmovers passing our house.

HEALTH CRISIS

Peaches seemed healthy, but his early bout with psittacosis had taught me to use paper towels on the bottom of his cage instead of newspaper. One early autumn morning, black, tar-like blood stood out against the white paper.

By the time we could get an appointment at the clinic, Peaches was listless, his appetite flagging. Dr. Ramsay suggested I leave him again. I rubbed his beak between my thumb and forefinger and said a cheery goodbye, assuring him, "She cured you once, and she'll cure you again."

All the way home, and for days afterwards, I feared that Peaches would never be well. As if to justify my worries, the infection resisted a series of medications, including the one that had worked before.

Peaches grew too weak to eat. It was hard to watch Dr. Ramsay force-feed him a predigested liquid through a metal tube shaped to fit his esophagus.

I arrived at the clinic one day to find Peaches too shaky to stand. He lay on the floor of an Isolette, head drooping. His breastbone protruded. Every breath was a struggle. I rocked him over my heart and sobbed, certain I would never see him alive again.

I drove home teary and puffy eyed to no squawked welcome. Joe filled the gap with another dose of the criticism he'd been dishing out: "I don't understand why you're not at the vet's every spare minute."

"I can't get off work early enough every day," I said, falling into that lifelong need to justify myself. "I don't want Peaches to use his energy responding to me. He needs it to heal." I faltered, knowing that the largest reason was my own weakness. "It's agonizing to watch him fail."

"You have to act the right way," Joe snapped, "no matter what you feel."

I believed Joe was expressing his care for Peaches, however harshly. It didn't occur to me that this might be part of a pattern. It *was* beginning to dawn on me that he might not want to deal with my emotions because he didn't want to face his own. The toxic combination of fear for Peaches, guilt at not being with him all the time, and intimidation kept me from calling Joe on his behavior.

* * *

Only two days later, Peaches heard me at the clinic's front desk and screeched a greeting. I dashed in and found him on his feet in a cage, eating solid food. His breast bone had disappeared beneath renewed flesh.

"If I didn't know his features and his voice so well," I told Dr. Ramsay, "I'd think you'd switched parrots."

"I ordered a new antibiotic for dogs. I was so desperate that I crushed up a pill, put it in water, and tried it on Peaches."

She wrapped him in a towel and showed me how to pry his beak open with the end of a plastic syringe and dribble the reddish fluid into his mouth. "Stroke his throat until it trickles down, or he'll shake it all over the place. Medicine on the walls is not as effective as medicine in the parrot."

I laughed and then gulped a breath. "Does this mean I can take him home?"

"I don't see why not. If the symptoms show up again, dose him right away. We're never letting this problem get ahead of us again."

* * *

Having medicine on hand turned out to be a boon. Peaches suffered two more psittacosis episodes, which I dosed at home. The side effect of either the illness or the antibiotic was that the tiny orange feathers around his white eye rings fell out, and only a few grew back. It seemed a small price to pay for his good health.

CRASH, BANG

Peaches was still healthy on a Saturday morning in late January, when the sun topped the Sangre de Cristo Mountains and hit our east-facing windows. Joe had left in the dark for his ski-instructor job. At nine, I was still nestling under my afghans.

It was a real luxury. I'd gone back to work for Dr. Krohn in Los Alamos, making the same commute in reverse that I'd hoped to avoid by moving in with Joe.

Peaches' squawks were easy to translate: *Morning has broken!*

I mumbled, "I hear you," though I didn't promise to do anything about it. Maybe I would stay in bed until noon.

He squawked again: *Get up, lazy bones.* His third squawk was more indignant—*Ahem, the parrot requires attention.*

I rolled out of bed, let him out long enough to share my breakfast, and set my snowboarding boots, brace, and waterproofs by the door. Once the snow melted, I'd have plenty of Saturdays to be a sack rat.

* * *

Macha and I were almost to Los Alamos when I slowed on the curved transition lane to State Road 4, in case there was ice in the shadow of the overpass. There wasn't. It was a cloudless day, visibility limited only by mountains and mesas.

Ahead, a two-tone gold Dodge pickup meandered around in the right lane. The two men in the cab were gesturing, perhaps about which way they should have gone at the intersection. The driver nearly stopped in the lane, then wandered onto the shoulder.

My Southern California freeway instincts went on red alert. Fearing he might pull back onto the road, I looked over my shoulder, signaled, and swung into the left lane.

The driver didn't signal, just lurched to U-turn around the end of the concrete divider. With no time to stop and no room to swerve behind him, I jammed down the gas pedal and veered into the empty oncoming lane.

Macha almost had enough power to get clear. The big truck slammed into her flank, just behind her right rear wheel well. She shied sideways, tires screeching. The shoulder harness slammed me against the seat. Air burst from my lungs, and a bruise spread over my breastbone. Mesas carouseled around us. In my head I heard, *I could die in this.*

I steered into the skid the way they'd taught us in drivers ed. That didn't keep the passenger-side wheels from going light. An instinctive prayer sprang to my lips: "Godsaveme, Godsaveme, Godsaveme!"

Macha rolled with such force that my left shoulder and the left side of my head slammed against the window. I thought she might go all the way over and settle on her wheels. Instead, she spun down the pavement. The din of shattering glass, grinding sheet metal, and collapsing frame steel went on and on. I left my body and found myself looking down at her six-ply mud-and-snow tires grabbing air.

Then I was back in her crushed-in cab, upside down. Bedlam gave way to a disconcerting silence. Opening my eyes, I struggled for breath against the belt and experienced a *wow* moment: *I can feel my body! I'm alive!* What couldn't I do, now that I'd been close to death and been spared?

A surprising calm claimed me as I took stock. My chin was jammed against my chest. The tops of my knees broadcast a demanding pain from banging against the bottom of the instrument panel. I could move my hands and feet and took that to mean my spinal cord wasn't severed.

The steering wheel had pinned my left hand against the pavement in the space left by the jettisoned windshield and collapsed roof. With my right hand, I yanked the wheel. Twenty-seven hundred pounds of compact pickup shifted and freed me, though not with the result I expected. Pain surged to my fingertips and up my arm to my shoulder. The crushed flesh swelled and bled. I groaned and cradled it against my chest. By some innate survival logic, my mind shifted from throbbing pain to gratitude that neither Joe nor Peaches was in the truck.

The sudden odor of gasoline and the sound of it running somewhere out of sight cut my relief short. Could a random spark ignite it? The engine had quit from lack of fuel, but the electrical system was still on. I fumbled with the key, too disoriented to know whether I succeeded in turning it off.

I couldn't get enough air to shout for help. Who would hear me, anyway? Ravens? Coyotes? I was so shocky that I imagined other drivers thinking no one could have survived such a crash and driving by. Letting someone know I was alive and in danger was worth any risk. I honked the horn, praying that it wouldn't spark the gas.

SHE'S ALIVE

The first person to arrive told me she was an emergency room nurse. She lay down and reached through the crushed-in driver-side window. I couldn't see her, but the touch of her hand on my shoulder shifted me from panic to reassurance. Her voice connected me to the normal world that had disappeared the instant the Dodge had struck Macha.

After questioning me about my injuries, she asked, "What's your name? Address? Phone number? Can you remember your Social Security number? Where do you work? Is there anyone I can call when I get to a phone?"

These questions were meant to assess my mental state and keep me alert and distracted. I was thinking clearly enough to give her the information, including the ski school's phone number and Dr. Krohn's.

The second arrival was a man in a tan jumpsuit, who knelt down and peered in the windshield space. "Are you all right?"

"Sure, considering I'm upside down and trapped, and there's gas everywhere. Did the other driver take off?"

He pressed his lips together, then said, "I'm the other driver."

"You goddamn son of a bitch!" I gasped for air against the shoulder harness. "What the fuck did you think you were doing?"

He blinked. So did I. I didn't talk that way.

"I never saw you," he said.

"Of course you never saw me! You were too busy arguing with the guy next to you! You were looking right and turning left!"

A miraculous moment of grace and sanity stopped my tirade: *If I had caused such an accident, I'd feel badly enough without somebody yelling at me.*

I began feeling claustrophobic but didn't want to move for fear of causing more injuries. Could I get out if my truck burst into flames? I might be able to wriggle through the passenger-side windshield space, but it would be chancy. If Macha rocked, I could be crushed. If she rolled down the bank at the side of the road while I was half-way out . . .

I stayed put but mentioned my fear of fire to the nurse. She laughed. "A couple of dozen cars have stopped. You're surrounded by people holding fire extinguishers."

A man I couldn't see called, "Fire ain't got a chance."

"One spark," a woman added, "and we'll smother it."

My breath caught. At an OSHA training for work, I'd learned

that any substance that would deprive flames of oxygen would do the same to people.

I hung against the belt and focused on slowing my shallow breathing. Time coiled and uncoiled like a snake. Perhaps twenty minutes after the crash, big diesel engines thrummed, and heavy tires crunched on gravel. The cavalry had arrived, and just in time. Despite thermal underwear and sweats, I was shivering in the shadowed interior of Macha's ruined bulk.

A firefighter in a tan uniform and yellow helmet peered in through the passenger window, grimacing as if he expected the gory worst.

"Hi," I said. "Could you please get me out of my truck?"

His eyes widened. He turned to people I couldn't see and shouted, "She's alive! She's all right!"

Firefighters took turns yanking at Macha's passenger door but couldn't open it. They tried to lever it with crowbars. Then they warned me to cover my face as they wedged the Jaws of Life between the door and the frame. The shriek of ripping metal and shatter of glass triggered the terror I'd felt as the cab collapsed.

The door creaked open, and a blue-uniformed medic got down on his knees and slid in a backboard. He asked the man next to him, whose black steel-toed shoes I could see, "How are we going to get her on it?"

The same adrenaline that had let me lift the steering wheel off my hand gave me the answer. "I'll pull up on the bottom of the seat, and you release my belt. If someone pushes through the driver-side window, and you pull on my sweatshirt, I ought to swing right around."

The medic straightened and talked with others I couldn't see. When he reappeared, he said, "Sounds like our best bet."

A hand found my left shoulder, and another man called, "Ready."

"Wanna do it on three?" I asked.

The medic I could see nodded.

In seconds, I was lying on the backboard, and the medics were pulling me into thin winter sunshine. It was like being born out of a crushed metal womb. Bystanders cheered. A medic fitted me with a whiplash collar, and others lifted and carried me toward an ambulance.

"Would you please turn," I asked, "so I can see my truck?"

"Uh," one man said, "that wouldn't be a good idea."

I could imagine how bad the damage was to my driving companion of so many miles. What I couldn't guess, as medics swung the ambulance doors shut behind me, was the extent of my own injuries.

WORLD'S BIGGEST ASPIRIN

We pulled into Los Alamos Medical Center under siren and flashing lights. Paramedics wheeled me to the emergency room.

After a preliminary exam, I asked for a phone. The nurse at the accident site had kept her promise and had contacted the ski school, so Joe was waiting for my call. I told him I was banged up but all right and that Macha had died saving me. I was in the best possible place in case anything went wrong, so Joe should finish his lessons and pick me up on his way home.

As I was hanging up, Frances, our office manager, arrived with homeopathic remedies for trauma that calmed my rapid heartbeat and tremors.

An orderly wheeled me to X-ray. My hand was a dreadful black-and-blue mess, the cuts swollen open and full of dirt and glass, but nothing was broken. Back in the ER, two nurses said the wounds should be cleaned but didn't want to hurt me. They walked me to a sink, ran warm water, and handed me a soft scrub brush.

I rinsed my mouth over and over but kept spitting out grit and glass dust. Dr. Zalma, the longtime ER physician, told me, "You can expect to cough up debris lodged in the mucous lining of your throat and lungs for a couple of weeks."

"That sounds very appealing."

We stared at each other. Then we burst out laughing.

I mentioned the bump behind my left ear, which had swollen to the size of half an extra-large egg, but the pain in my hand claimed most of my attention. I asked for the world's largest aspirin, something the size of a dinner plate. Dr. Zalma shot me up with a painkiller that dropped me into a relaxed haze. The hurt didn't go away, but it kept its distance while he splinted my hand.

The state policeman who'd directed traffic around the wreck arrived to take my statement. He told me he'd ticketed the other driver for making an illegal U-turn.

"That's all? What about reckless driving?" My voice spun up in volume and pitch. "What about almost killing me?"

"Illegal U-turn." His tone said there would be no argument. "And how do you like this? His father was the passenger, and he owns the truck. He's a retired Santa Fe policeman."

I stared at the statey's shoulder. The driver's ex-cop old man had probably made him feel like a flustered ten-year-old. No wonder he hadn't been paying attention.

"At least they were able to drive the truck home," the statey said.

"What about *my* truck?"

"Frame was too bent to tow. Dragged onto a wrecker and hauled to one of the garages here in town." He thumbed through his notepad and told me which one.

* * *

My comment about Macha dying to save my life was more true than I could have imagined. On our way home, Joe stopped at the garage. I was still vibrating with shock and with survivor's excitement and gratitude. I hadn't shed a tear, but the sight of Macha's mangled body made me double over and sob.

With unsteady hands, I helped Joe unload my belongings. My fire extinguisher had been behind the driver's seat the whole time— inches away and utterly beyond my reach.

FLASHBACKS

I greeted Peaches when we got home but didn't take him out of his cage. I sealed my smelly clothes in a garbage bag and set it outside. Then I rubber-banded a plastic grocery sack around my splint, stepped into the shower, and scrubbed from head to toe twice. The gasoline smell still lingered.

When I let Peaches out, he ran across my shoulders, looking for the problem. I showed him my splinted hand and let him nibble the gauze. He nuzzled his beak into my ear and made soft, anxious cries: *Are you all right, Mom? Really? Are you okay?*

I had my other ear to the phone. In the rebound stage of trauma—frightened at my close call and ecstatic to be alive—I felt driven to connect. I started each call with, "First of all, I'm all right." My parents and friends gasped, knowing it for the preamble it was.

Exhaustion finally caught up with me—the collapse stage—and I fell into bed, barely strong enough to pull up the covers. Joe propped a pillow under my splinted hand, which throbbed like a bass drum.

Sleep was not the healing gift I hoped for. Every time I dozed off, a flashback shocked me awake. I relived the accident in every sensory detail, from impact to rollover to the smell of gasoline.

Then my imagination became creative. I dreamed that the other truck elongated as it pulled out, so there was no place for me to go and nothing to do but T-bone it. Then the underpass turned into a giant's mouth, great teeth gnashing and crushing me to the sound of grinding sheet metal and shattering glass. I kept jerking awake, trembling and gasping for breath against an imaginary seatbelt.

No matter how violent my spasms, Peaches wouldn't leave me. He stood on my chest, riding the swell of my breath, until well after dark, when Joe took him back to his cage and came to bed himself.

* * *

Joe took pictures on Sunday morning of my swollen, discolored hand—the only visible damage—in case we needed them for evidence in court. Afterwards, I sat on the edge of the bed and wept.

Peaches winged to my shoulder and nibbled my earlobe.

"What are you crying about?" Joe snapped. "You survived."

I fell back into my old habit of explaining and justifying myself. "I've just been through this terrifying accident. I'm in a lot of pain. I've barely slept. I've lost my truck, and I'm scared to get back on the road." Cars had always been my wombs—safer, when I was a teenager, than my parents' alcoholic home.

I broke down again, not knowing that uncontrollable crying was a common effect of trauma. What I'd told Joe was true. There were deeper reasons, though, that I wouldn't understand for some time. I was grieving for the person I had been right up until my head hit Macha's window—for the woman I would never be again.

Despite Joe's aggravated tone, I reached for his hand, seeking strength and support.

He pulled away. "You always look for comfort instead of confronting your problems."

My jaw dropped. Somewhere I found the backbone to tell him, "That's not true. Besides, you're my partner. I'm asking for help."

"I have to go to work. Will you be all right?"

I wiped my cheeks and said, "Sure," thinking, *Peaches will be here.* He might not be able to dial 911, but his companionship would give me more solace than Joe's.

BANG, CRASH

Joe wasn't working on Monday, so he took me to Santa Fe to pick up an antibiotic for my infected hand, along with a pain medication that might help me sleep.

It seemed important to get in a car again. I kept from hyperventilating until we got to Walgreen's. A woman in a brown Ford sedan at the far end of the lot was backing toward us, accelerating as she turned to talk to her passenger. With vehicles parked to our right, others leaving the lot on our left, and more coming in behind us, we had no place to go. I felt a whole-body shock of *déjà vu* as Joe honked and jammed on the brakes.

As the other car slammed into us, my shoulder belt hit my already bruised sternum. My body crawled with terror, disbelief, and rage. Staying in the car for another second was impossible. I yanked off the seatbelt and leaped out on shaky legs. What was going on? Was I wearing a target? Never getting into a car again seemed realistic. So did walking the eight miles home.

The damage to the cars was minor. Joe and the other driver exchanged insurance information while I leaned against a parked car, breathing hard, every muscle quivering. His voice sounded calm and reasonable, and that surprised me. For the first time, I realized he wasn't at the effect of his emotions. He could turn his anger on and off.

Suddenly, the woman shouted that she was in the right. "You hit me! I'm going to sue you!" she screamed, trying to get as much public exposure for her lie as she could among the small crowd that had gathered.

The world tilted, and I gripped the parked car to keep from falling. Then, out of the blue and the grace of a generous universe came a slender, long-haired man in his thirties. He handed me a slip of paper on which he'd written his name and contact information. Underneath, he'd added, *Saw the accident in the Walgreen's parking lot* and the date.

"Call me if you need a witness," he said. "I saw the whole thing. She was at fault."

"Thank you," I whispered. "You're a godsend."

He looked at me closely. "Are you all right? You're white as snow."

NOW THAT YOU'RE FINE

Four days after the accident, I talked Joe into driving me up The Hill to Dr. Krohn's office, so I could go back to work. Getting into his car almost stopped my breath. I forced my shaking hands to buckle the seatbelt. I was hyper-vigilant on the highway, scanning the traffic for threats.

More compelling than my fear of another accident was the urge to get back to a normal life. I thought that being injured was like having the flu: In a few days, I'd be fine.

Beyond wanting to keep my job, I felt desperate to appear all right to myself and others. It was the sick-parrot ploy. I should have been tipped off by the fact that Peaches didn't buy it for a second. He still clung to me every waking moment I was home.

My co-workers were equally perceptive. They were glad to see me, but I could tell from their expressions that they were disturbed. I knew why. I'd looked in a mirror. The woman looking back appeared shattered. I'd spent my life making myself a smooth-surfaced stone to cover my many mental and emotional flaws. Like a dropped rock, I'd broken along those hidden fault lines.

It felt important to have work to distract me from the physical pain. I hurt all over and couldn't let a chiropractor touch me yet. The painkiller we'd driven to Walgreen's for helped a little but also made me spacey. I wasn't thinking well enough to realize that the pain that kept me from sleeping also prevented me from concentrating at work.

Flashbacks made it worse. They were still disrupting my sleep and were now happening while I was awake. I wanted to shake my head to clear the visions and the smell of gasoline but thought it had been shaken enough.

Then I discovered another problem. My eyes refused to track, drifting off every time I tried to focus. Moving my finger along under text or sliding a ruler down line by line helped me return to the right spot but didn't prevent the persistent wandering.

Worst was my short-term memory. I couldn't recall what I'd just read. I found myself standing in front of my desk, staring. I had a single task to do but couldn't remember what it was or who had asked me to do it.

People were bound to notice. Over the next couple of weeks, staff members took me aside almost every day and asked how I was doing. One spoke the truth that the others were avoiding: "You're not functioning as well as you're pretending to."

I was busted. I dried my tears and called for an appointment with Dr. Zalma.

Half an hour later, he was asking if I was experiencing dizziness, lightheadedness, balance problems, or lack of coordination. Was I disoriented, unsure of where I was or how much time had passed? Having trouble remembering conversations and things I read? Unable to do simple math? Irritable and prone to emotional swings and crying jags?

"All of the above." I described my drifting vision.

Embarrassed at having missed the seriousness of my head injury, he said he'd talk to Dr. Krohn and Frances later in the day. Meanwhile, I was to go home as soon as Joe could pick me up. I should rest for two weeks and give my concussed brain a chance to heal. Then we'd see.

* * *

In the hall outside the ER, I encountered an EMT crew in their blue uniforms. I tried to jolly myself out of rising panic by tilting my head one way and another.

One of them asked, "Ma'am, what are you doing?"

"I'm trying to see if you look familiar upside down."

"Oh, yeah, we're the ones who pulled you out of that blue truck. Hey, thanks for the letter you wrote to the fire chief. We got a lot of atta-boys."

I didn't tell him that the two-paragraph note had taken me days to compose, that I had had to look up the chief's address several times to get it right on the envelope.

"You know," another man said, "when we rolled up, we all agreed that nobody could be alive in that truck. We were jazzed."

"Yeah," said a third. "We didn't want to say so when you were shocky and we didn't know the extent of your injuries. But it's okay to tell you, now that you're fine."

FINE

Fine was the life preserver I clung to as Joe drove me home. I related Dr. Zalma's parting comment: Six months after an injury, a head-trauma patient was either functioning and feeling much better or was *another* eighteen months—maybe longer—from significant improvement. There was no way of knowing which category I fell into.

Joe pressed his lips together, gripped the wheel, and stared straight ahead. I tensed, wondering if he was working up to a tirade. When he said nothing, I imagined he was chewing on my uncertain prognosis and the prospect of my being a burden. Who could blame him? Those were my top worries, too.

At home, Peaches reminded me that I was never a burden to him. He perched on my collar and murmured encouragements.

I turned away from Joe's silent scowl and let the grateful tears spill.

* * *

During my two-week hiatus, I spent hours staring at movies on TV. I was lucky to remember their names afterwards.

I blocked my body with pillows so I couldn't roll over and dozed with Peaches on my chest or hip. As if to compensate for my short-term memory loss, my long-term memory shifted into overdrive, jolting me awake with hyper-vivid childhood memories.

It was a struggle to muster even a fraction of my former optimism. All I could see were worsening symptoms. Had the head injury altered my personality, perhaps permanently? I didn't confess this fear to Joe but went right to the worst-case scenario: If I didn't recover, Peaches and I might have to find someplace else to live at the time when I was least able to manage it, physically or financially.

* * *

After two weeks of bed rest, short walks, and intensive parrot therapy, I went back to work. Before, I couldn't remember what I was supposed to do. Now, I couldn't remember how to do it. Simple arithmetic drove me to the calculator. Everyday computer functions were beyond me. I snapped at the staff members who showed me nothing but concern.

One evening, after the last patient left, Dr. Krohn asked me to step into her office. When Frances told me to close the door, I knew what was coming. They told me they had stood by me as long as they could. Now they had to let me go.

In the cubbyhole I shared with the copier and fax machine, I dabbed away tears as I gathered my hand lotion, water cup, and pictures of Peaches. The prospect of having no income frightened me almost as much as my deteriorating mental abilities. As I waited for Joe, I told myself I had to trust my need to heal.

* * *

I had to trust Peaches, too, and his instinct to keep me engaged. He spent hours nuzzling my ears and grooming my eyelashes. He chased my pen as I chronicled the accident's effects, and begged for food and water that he could have gotten for himself.

Peaches resisted being locked in his cage at night and when I went to the medical appointments—scheduled around Joe's work days, so he could drive me—that now took up the bulk of my days. Aside from Peaches and Joe, my main social contacts were the chiropractor, physical therapist, and lymph drainage technician.

Physically, I made a slow, uneven recovery and continued to be in pain. That didn't surprise the hand specialist at the physical therapist's office, who told me about a roll-test movie she'd seen in school. Even though the dummy had been belted in, it had undergone complex twists and wrenching stops.

The dummy didn't have the added burden of mental decline. I had episodes of aphasia, where I couldn't tell what language people were speaking. My ends of conversations were weird, too. I often couldn't think of a word—usually a noun—and unconsciously replaced it with something else.

When I couldn't remember *Tucson*, for example, I said *Phoenix*. That wasn't bad; they were both large cities in the same state. When I couldn't remember *spoon*, however, I might say something unrelated—*shoe* or *bicycle*. I could point at something I wanted, mime a description, or say, "Please hand me the, you know, has a handle, round on the end, you eat with it," but only if I realized the right word was eluding me.

I was at the mercy of what I started calling drain bammage in an attempt to glean a little humor. I wanted to cry every time I couldn't remember a conversation or something I'd just struggled to read. Who was I if I couldn't recall what had happened five minutes ago? How could I live a useful life and make a living?

I could live with Peaches, nonjudgmental as he was, but how could I manage among human beings? When Joe drove me to the supermarket or the health-food store, I often encountered people I knew. I would stare, certain I'd met them before, though I had no idea who they were.

Luck was with me. Many were patients from the environmental illness side of Dr. Krohn's practice. They had experienced similar symptoms from toxic exposures. Despite their own severe health problems, they showed me unfailing compassion.

Like me, most of the patients who had serious cognitive deficits showed no visible damage. Their friends, relatives, and employers sometimes accused them of being crazy or faking. I'd wondered myself. Not anymore.

* * *

The head injury did something I would never have imagined: It made me more left-handed. I was thrilled. When I was little, my parents had taken silverware and crayons out of my left hand and forced me to use my right. They were well intentioned, wanting to avoid the bumped elbows at table, the smeared writing, the difficulty of using scissors.

They didn't know that forcing a left-hander to switch could trigger dyslexia. The form I had involved switching numbers. A few times before the accident, I had let myself get stressed and fatigued enough for letters to trade places and turn upside down, making words meaningless.

Now, without thinking about it, I picked up a dropped pen, ate, and reached for Peaches with my left hand. I was reclaiming a basic neurological part of myself. The accident was offering me one benefit against the physical and emotional pain I was beginning to think would never end.

MORE LOSS

Taking comfort from Peaches was like leaning on a great, solid wall of strength. He was small, but he was sure of who he was. Domestication hadn't changed that. I, on the other hand, kept losing things essential to my identity.

I was especially grateful for Peaches' care on Father's Day, less than five months after the accident, when Dad called. In a voice weary and frail, he told me that Mother had died in the hospital that morning from kidney failure.

My heart and lungs felt adrift in my chest. Mother had been in and out of hospitals so often I had almost stopped worrying. She had survived a rare enzyme deficiency, sudden blood pressure spikes, and a cardiac aneurysm. Decades of active alcoholism had aggravated her adult-onset diabetes. The circulation in her feet was so poor that her doctors had considered amputation. She had spent the last few years on an oxygen concentrator for emphysema. Perhaps the reduced oxygen to her brain had caused or worsened her dementia. Yet every New Year's Day, she was still with us.

I wanted to go to California, but long drives and airplane rides were beyond me. In my mental state, I'd have been useless, anyway. My brother Vance, who was closer to our parents emotionally if not physically, flew from Houston to help arrange Mother's cremation. We'd been estranged for years, part of the alcoholic family syndrome.

Mother had specified no funeral or memorial service. I interpreted that as her final way of controlling her family: *Don't get together and say bad things about me.* I wasn't in a position to do anything about it and was going to have to grieve on my own.

Well, not quite. I had a lot of green, feathered support. When

Joe couldn't see any good in my relationship with my mother and criticized my sadness, Peaches would stand on my shoulder and sip my salty tears. He would play with my pen while I journaled to vent my grief, and would snuggle under my chin when I lay down to ease my aching back.

BACK ON THE HORSE

At least I was driving again. A couple of months after the accident, I had acknowledged that life without a car was impractical. My insurance company gave me a small partial settlement, and I started looking for another vehicle.

A stick-shift Chevy Blazer showed up in the classified ads, and Joe drove me to Española to try it out. It was a good size and handled well, but the heavy clutch spring overwhelmed my weak knee.

Then an automatic appeared in the paper. The owner was kind enough to drive it to the trailer park. As the handsome vehicle pulled in, I told Peaches, "If that truck drives as good as he looks"—I winced at my bad grammar—"I'm going to buy him for us."

He did, and I did.

The following day, as Joe drove me to Motor Vehicles to pick up and register the Blazer, he expressed his concern about its weight and gas mileage. "Are you sure this is the vehicle you want?"

Without taking my eyes off the traffic, I said, "No. I want a Sherman tank with a laser cannon, so I can vaporize anyone who threatens me on the road."

"Right on!"

On my way home, I enjoyed the truck's solid feel and the luxury of power windows. I named him GW Blaze, short for gray and white Blazer.

Nervous though I was behind the wheel, I started driving myself to medical appointments, first with Joe in the truck and then alone. Joe had been wonderful, shopping for me and taking me to appointments, but I was still too vulnerable to cope with his backseat driving and hair-trigger rage at other motorists.

* * *

I had my own angry confrontation at De Vargas Mall in Santa Fe with an able-bodied driver who had parked in the striped area between two handicapped spaces. I pulled up behind him and called from GW's window, "Excuse me, sir, people need that space to get in and out of their cars, especially if they have to maneuver a wheelchair."

He leaned out his window, glared at me, and snarled, "Go to hell."

"Go there yourself, you asshole. Get your fucking car off the zebra."

I was startled at my uncharacteristic tone and language but parked GW a few spaces away and walked back with a note pad and pen.

"What the hell are you doing?" he asked.

"I'm writing down your fucking license plate number, you jerk. I'm going into the mall to call the police to give you a ticket and haul your lame-ass vehicle to impound."

He threw his car into reverse and lurched out, tires squealing. All the way to the end of the parking lot, he shouted obscenities out his window.

I didn't go into the mall right away but sat in GW until I calmed down, wondering, *What was* that *all about?*

I'd yelled at the driver who'd hit me, too. Years before, I'd witnessed a motorcycle accident where the driver hadn't been wearing a helmet and had banged his head on the pavement. Bruised and bloodied, he'd stood in the middle of the two-lane highway, kicked his bike, and cursed.

Joe found this pattern curious. The following day, he did some research at the community college library and found that uncharacteristic anger was a common symptom of head injury.

* * *

I had to question whether I should be driving at all in my

damaged state. In addition to the recurring rage, my eyes wandered from the road the way they did from printed words. At street speed, that might not take me very far. At highway speed, it might take me a quarter mile.

Then there was the dissociation. Every time I saw a vehicle approaching from a side road or idling on the shoulder, I went into a heart-palpitating, hyperventilating panic attack. I would disconnect from my body and watch the road from above GW's roof until the real or imagined threat passed.

I'd never paid conscious attention to the automatic sorting of stimuli until I was driving home from a neuropsychological assessment. The battery of tests had left me exhausted and apprehensive about my future.

Suddenly, I couldn't figure out what to pay attention to. Snow blowing off the top of an adobe wall? A car backing out of a driveway? What about the sparrow flying across the road? The UPS truck in the oncoming lane? Sunshine glimmering off bare aspen limbs? Overwhelmed, I gripped the wheel and concentrated on staying in my lane, unsure if even that was important.

When I finally got home, I staggered past Peaches' cage, collapsed into bed, and slept for fifteen hours.

HELP

The stimuli-sorting problem made it clear that I had to either quit driving or get help. The following morning, while Peaches scraped the last of the soft-boiled eggs off my dish, I called friends and doctors for referrals. I had a series of discouraging conversations with psychoanalysts (too analytical), psychologists (too drug-oriented), and psychotherapists (more interested in their pet modalities than in my situation).

I kept at it, though. The next day, I found Cheri, a degreed counselor with a similar spiritual background to mine—and a near-fatal auto accident in her past. During our first session, she told me, "The last thing I did was look down at the speedometer to see how fast I was going when I died."

Having come close to death in our vehicles forged an immediate bond. We started with the stimulus-sorting problem and moved quickly to the way I dissociated on the road, my adult self bailing out and leaving my terrified inner child behind the wheel.

On my way to a session one afternoon in July, an oncoming pickup crossed the open highway median right in front of a *Stay Off Median* sign. The driver skidded a U-turn, throwing up dirt, rocks, and wildflowers, then roared toward the northbound lanes. I slammed on my brakes. Even so, he almost clipped GW's front fender.

I couldn't stop hyperventilating. Every muscle vibrated. All that kept me from pulling off the road and indulging in a little recreational catatonia was the fear that I might never get myself moving again.

When I pulled up at Cheri's office forty minutes later, I was still trembling. "It's been six months since the accident," I told her, "and it's as if it just happened. I can't get any distance. I'm still having flashbacks. I can't sleep through the night."

"Drugs."

I shook my head. Cheri wasn't the first therapist to offer. My personal and family histories included too many addictions for me to want to risk another. I relented enough to take home some reading material about antidepressants.

It took a couple of weeks to get through the books because of my wandering eyes and memory problems. Peaches would stand on my finger as I moved it along beneath the lines. He cocked his head as though he found the information about neurotransmitters fascinating: *I didn't know serotonin re-uptake worked that way.*

I wrote down my insights and read them to Cheri at my next appointment.

"One: Taking my own life is the farthest thing from my mind these days. Nothing like a brush with death to make suicide look ridiculous.

"Two: I used to think the only time I was depressed was when I was suicidal. If what I've read is true, I'm hanging from the precipice of chronic biochemical depression all the time. It's never taken much to tip me into the downward spiral.

"Three: Anxiety and hyper-vigilance are so much a part of the way I learned to cope that I'm hardly aware of them.

"Four: I have the same predisposition to depression and anxiety as my mother. I shouldn't be surprised. I inherited her brown eyes and bad knees, so why not her faulty brain chemistry?"

Cheri nodded and asked, "Ready for drugs?"

Reluctantly, I said I would give an antidepressant a try.

* * *

My response to Prozac was right out of the textbooks. I didn't notice much change until the fourth day, when I wanted to crawl out of my skin. My heart raced. I had to control my breathing to keep from hyperventilating. I couldn't stop pacing. Peaches gave up trying to stay on my shoulder and kept an eye on me from the dining area curtain rod.

After that, I felt better every day. The flashbacks stopped. I slept through the night. The accident receded, and my therapy moved forward. I was still nervous on the road, but my inner adult stayed in control. My conversations became more lucid, even if aphasia sometimes made me say *branch* when I meant *computer*.

Peaches noticed the difference. He no longer hovered as if he were afraid of losing me. I would find him snoozing on a curtain rod or the top perch of his cage. We were both de-stressing and catching up on our rest.

* * *

Winter rolled around again, and Joe's mood improved when he started teaching skiing. All I could do was stand at the closet and sigh over my snowboard.

I still couldn't write poetry or fiction and needed something to fill the snowy days. I stumbled on my own form of healing, making holiday cards for friends with watercolor paints.

Working with shape and color revived some part of my brain that had been knocked unconscious during the accident. I became more alert to my surroundings. I might still say *tire* in place of *cottonwood,* but I was able to work simple math problems and focus my eyes better.

Peaches, of course, wanted to get in the middle of those interesting colors. He grumbled when I wouldn't let him sip the paints and walk across my handiwork. From his cage, he complained in *Aw, Mom* squawks until I hid the cards and let him out.

* * *

In January, a year after the accident, Dr. Zalma said he was glad for my improvements. Then he furrowed his brows and said I still had a long recovery ahead of me.

It was a good thing he didn't tell me how long.

A HOME OF OUR OWN

Fifteen months after the accident, spring was greening the trees, but there was no love in the air between Joe and me. He didn't say a word, just glared as we edged past each other in the narrow kitchen.

He was on his way to watch television. Even with Prozac, I couldn't tolerate the political news, the OJ Simpson murder trial, and the shoot-'em-up cop shows. I'd asked Joe to wire a jack into the TV's sound circuit. He plugged the headset into it now, shooting me a sour, put-upon scowl.

The physical closeness forced on us by our little home had been tolerable and even fun the first few years, when I was at my job five days a week and at the library many evenings for some quiet writing time. Since the accident, the constant proximity had been wearing on us.

As I sat down at my desk, Joe glanced up from the television, raised his voice to hear himself over the headset, and said, "The only time I'm happy is when I think of you moving out."

The first time he'd said this—around the first anniversary of the accident—I felt as if I'd been kicked in the solar plexus. It was painful enough that he didn't want to live with me, but how could I find another place? My checking account was dwindling, my savings were nearly gone, and I had no prospect of being able to work any time soon.

With impeccable timing, Peaches flew to my shoulder. I whispered that we might have to live in GW at the disused Santa Fe rail yard, at the corner of Down and Out. Plenty of people occupied "rooms" at the "Hotel Atchison, Topeka, and Santa Fe" year-round, though I couldn't imagine how they managed the winters.

And it might not be available for long. Plans were in the works to turn the area into an artist venue/tourist destination.

Imposing on friends was the last of my last resorts.

Peaches pressed his face into my ear and murmured, *Squertle-dee-wertle,* a comforting version of his louder call. I whistled back— anything to keep from making eye contact with Joe and setting off a tirade.

I pushed the papers around on my desk. One was Joe's note to return the insurance claim adjuster's phone call. I decided to put it off until the following day, when Joe would be teaching. If it was bad news, I could have a therapeutic cry before he came home.

* * *

When I picked up the note the next morning, some circuit in my banged-up brain reconnected. "Peaches! I have disability coverage on my auto insurance policy!"

Then I sobered. In more than a year, I hadn't once remembered this significant fact. The claims adjuster knew I'd lost my job because of the accident and hadn't said a word.

I phoned her. A few days later, a check for my lost wages to date arrived, with a note that monthly payments would continue to the policy limit.

Peaches gave them the official corner-shred of approval.

* * *

On my way to the mailboxes the following day, I stopped to chat with LouAnne, who lived kitty-corner across the road. She told me her own good news: She, her brother, and their parents were buying land and were going to install a brand new double wide. First, they had to sell the three mobile homes they owned in the park. Did I know anyone who might be interested?

LouAnne's was in the best condition and had the most attractive view. As we walked through the gate, a breeze stirred the bare Virginia creeper vines that grew up the metal awning's wrought iron supports. In full leaf, they would give the place a charming, vine-covered-cottage appearance.

The best thing, though, was the sunshine pouring into the living room through three south-facing windows. LouAnne had painted the dark brown paneling pale pink and turquoise. I grinned as I soaked up the New Mexico light and Santa Fe colors.

My sunny mood collapsed as I walked home, though. The lump-sum disability payment wasn't enough. I couldn't turn it down, though. A few minutes at a time over the next several days, I checked and rechecked the math. Once I knew that the monthly insurance payments would cover food, auto insurance, and space rent, I did one of those things I'd hoped never to have to do: I phoned my father and asked for help.

Two days later, his check arrived. LouAnne and I sealed the deal on a handshake. All I had to do was wait for her to move.

Having a place to go made it easy to be snarky, at least in my mind. I looked at Joe a dozen times a day and thought, *The only time I'm happy is when I think of Peaches and me moving to our own place.*

HOME OWNERSHIP

The day after LouAnne moved out, I lugged Peaches, in his cage, across the road and stood for several minutes in our empty living room. I could almost breathe the light coming in those big windows.

I checked for places where Peaches might get out, then let him loose in what amounted to his own personal sixty-foot flight cage. He winged from the kitchen in front to the larger bedroom in back, then lit on the pass-through and looked at me with a wide-eyed expression: *Wow, Mom! For me?*

"For us," I told him, thanking the Green Parrot Goddess.

* * *

The next day, Joe and a neighbor moved my belongings over. My outlook took such an upturn that it didn't even flinch when Joe, having trouble assembling the daybed that was to be my sofa, threw down his screwdriver and screamed, "It's you! It's always you!"

I went to the bedroom and made up my second-hand bed. Between the mattress and box spring I slid the frame of the home traction unit my chiropractor had prescribed.

Joe left without a word, slamming the front door hard enough to rattle the windows. I lit some sage and smudged the house inside and out, affirming safety, good health, and serenity for Peaches and me and everyone who visited, including Joe.

* * *

Peaches' and my first night in our new home didn't offer the peace I'd hoped for. About three o'clock, a thump on the roof startled me awake—one of the local outdoor cats, I supposed, jumping from an overhanging tree limb.

I was dropping back to sleep when the cat screamed and ran. Its retreat was cut short when something thudded into it, probably a great horned owl. I got up in the spring chill and followed the sound as it dragged the cat along the roof, finally finding a comfortable place to dine above the living room.

On my way back to bed, I turned on the desk lamp and lifted the cage cover to see whether Peaches was upset. He yawned, ground his beak, and was asleep again in seconds, unaware of the life-and-death struggle that had taken place above us.

* * *

Life and death had more in store of us the following day. LouAnne's parting shot had been, "Keep an eye on the propane heater. It doesn't like to stay lit in the wind."

I'd rolled my eyes. What did New Mexico have in the spring if not wind?

I relit the furnace half a dozen times while Peaches watched from the hall window curtain rod. Exasperated, I pushed back the cover from the small glass window on the front of the firebox. The flames were being blown out, all right. Wind was gusting down the vent pipe—and out a fist-sized hole in the back of the box. I stared at it. Even if the automatic shutoff was working—was it?—probably some amount of carbon monoxide had been seeping into our home.

I phoned my bank and found out that my check to LouAnne had cleared. My father said his had, too. That left me no leverage to renegotiate the purchase and come out with enough money to buy a new furnace.

No one wanted the liability of repairing an old heater. The prices of new mobile home furnaces made me wince. How was I going to keep us warm? I locked Peaches in his cage, bundled up, and walked to Joe's for some ideas.

Then I drove to Santa Fe. When I got home, I hung one plastic drop cloth over the living room-hall door, one over the dining room-kitchen door, and one over the pass-through, then set up three electric space heaters. The strategy was to keep the bedroom door closed, sleep under a pile of afghans, and heat the other three zones only as much as I needed to. It was like living in a plastic bag, but it would keep our heating bills down.

* * *

After his initial fear of the drop cloths passed, Peaches learned to time his flights to coincide with my lifting them for him. He would zoom from the back of the house into the living room and circle until I crossed to the dining area and pulled back the plastic. He perched on my shoulder while I cooked, and we'd play the same game in reverse, heading for the warm office/bird room.

GENDER QUESTION ANSWERED

Around the time the Virginia creeper leafed out and the drop cloths came down, Peaches did something I never expected. I was sitting at the dining table when he flew in from the kitchen. He pecked my fingernails, jerked his head, and regurgitated.

I was thinking that he looked like a male bird offering food to an intended mate when he grabbed the skin between my thumb and forefinger with his beak, hoisted himself onto my hand, and rubbed his vent on my fingers. After a few seconds, he rocked forward, the feathers on his upper back lifting. He relaxed, let out a sigh, and climbed off, leaving a drop of pale gold semen.

It was hard to say which surprised me more, the suddenness of the deed or that Peaches had confirmed his gender at last. My hand was a logical choice. I was his flock. My fingers groomed and fed him, as another bird would.

How would I deal with it if he did it again? There was a difference between a small parrot mating with my hand and, say, a dog humping my leg. I decided not to encourage him but to wait and see what happened.

BIRDLOCK

Living apart gave Joe and me a bit of our old relationship back. It was easier to enjoy each other, now that he didn't have to use headphones to watch TV, and I didn't have to put up with his clutter and his attitude.

The only thing we lost patience with was having to lock Peaches up every time we wanted to open my outside door, so we made a deal. I signed over my interest in his trailer, and he built me a birdlock. He surrounded the small front porch and stairs with wood and screen and installed a door at ground level. The rule was simple: Only one door was to be open at a time. If Peaches got out the front door, he would be contained.

The structure might have been exit-proof, but it wasn't entrance-proof. One morning, I found a befuddled ground squirrel standing on the porch. He stood back while I closed the front door and opened the birdlock door. Down he bounded, waving his bushy gray tail.

I came home from a doctor's appointment not long afterwards to find a brown towhee on the porch, looking as bewildered as the squirrel. He flew out with a puckish chirp and a flip of his tail, becoming the first in a regular parade of towhees. Or perhaps "they" were the same bird, over and over.

No matter how many times I inspected the birdlock, I couldn't figure out how the towhee(s) got in, not to mention a creature as large as a squirrel. I could only hope that Peaches never found his way out.

MONEY MATTERS

On a snowy February morning, just after the second anniversary of the accident, I hung up the phone, went into the bedroom, and hooked myself up to the traction unit. Peaches landed on my chest, nibbled my chin, and murmured sweet distractions.

His affection took some of the sting out of the day's telephone conversations. The first call was from my auto insurance claims adjuster, telling me I had reached the policy limit on my disability payments. The next was from the utility company, threatening to turn off my electricity if I didn't come up with the entire amount of my bill. They refused to accept partial payments.

I asked to talk with a supervisor, thinking that if I explained my situation, he might be willing to negotiate. He made it clear that the company wouldn't volunteer to help me. The sole circumstance under which they were required by law to keep the power on was if Social Security had deemed me disabled.

Social Security had turned down my initial disability request. I had filed the first appeal, but the bureaucratic wheels were grinding too slowly to help with my utility problem.

Before lying down, I had phoned state and county aid programs. I could have gotten assistance if I was working for minimum wage or had children. "Sorry," a sympathetic woman at one office had said, "but a parrot doesn't qualify."

I skritched Peaches' head, waited for the timer to ping at the end of my traction session, and thought how grateful I was for Joe. He was getting financial aid to take classes at the local community college. I didn't want to accept money from him anymore than I wanted food stamps or the food bank's handouts, but I took all of those.

When the timer went off, I urged Peaches back to my shoulder and returned to the phone. Begging was another thing I'd hoped to avoid, but I called all the organizations in Santa Fe that offered financial assistance.

*　*　*

The next day, I sat in the Salvation Army waiting room with a lot of other people in need. Judging from their conversations, most were long-term down-and-out. Some had children. I couldn't imagine how they managed.

Before going in, I had faced GW's rear-view mirror and given myself a pep talk: *I didn't* ask *for these injuries. I* am *going to lead a useful life again. I* am *doing my part to heal.*

My part had included a visit to an Albuquerque back specialist. The four-hour round trip had been agonizing but fruitful. He determined that I was suffering from osteitis, an inflammation of the bones in my lower back. It would clear up of its own accord, but there was no telling how long it would take.

None of this helped me turn off the self-berating thoughts as I sat in the Salvation Army parking lot: *I'm an adult. I'm supposed to support myself and the animal I'm responsible for by myself.*

I wanted to kiss the feet of the needs assessor who pledged help with my utility bill. A few days later, I had the same reaction at the Saint Vincent de Paul Society.

By the time I got to the Eagles, asking for help was becoming a spiritual practice. Humiliation was losing its grip, and humility was taking over. I made up a new mantra to overwrite self-condemnation: *This is my path. Let me do what's in front of me.*

Out of gratitude, I promised that when the insurance companies settled, I would repay these groups double, so they could help others. This provided me with a mission that made me feel better about myself and my future. I made the commitment to Peaches aloud. He sealed it by nibbling my lips.

JOB HUNTING

Despite my lame brain, chronic pain, and persistent fatigue, I called about jobs in the Santa Fe paper and filled out applications until my eyes wouldn't focus. After each job-hunting foray, I came home and slept until the following morning.

Most of the interviews went all right until people asked what I'd been doing for the last couple of years. No one wanted to hear about auto accidents and brain trauma. One medical clinic where I interviewed used the computerized billing system I had taught at Dr. Krohn's. I had known that program inside and out but couldn't dredge its name out of memory. The office manager showed me to the door.

* * *

The following day, I was sitting at the living room table, holding a piece of balsa wood for Peaches to chew. Outside, a howling March wind whipped the elm branches as I tried to console myself with the idea that I couldn't lose. If I could do a job, I was healed enough to support myself. If I couldn't, Social Security would have to consider my appeal. I was at a low ebb, I said to Peaches, if those were my alternatives.

The dreams I had harbored of writing poetry and fiction again were evaporating. Grief sent me into tears at least once a week, though I was careful to keep my emotions to myself, my therapist, and my parrot. The last thing I wanted to hear was Joe's assertion that I had walked away from the accident and had nothing to be upset about.

To distract myself, I decided to paint the one wall in the house I didn't like. I brought in a dusty old paintbrush and a can of white paint someone had left in the shed.

Peaches followed the screwdriver around the lid, "helping" me pry it off. That was cute. His attempt to sip the paint was not. Against his protests, I locked him in his cage, then came back to the living room and pulled the daybed aside in a series of slow moves to keep from aggravating my back.

The smell of fresh paint filled the room as I worked the brush up and down the wall. In the couple of days it would take to apply six or eight coats over the eye-stinging, high-saturation yellow, I would probably hurt worse. I couldn't say I didn't care, only that I was tired of twisting my life around my limitations.

I woke the next day to Peaches' morning calls and my conditioned expectation of back pain. I took a deep breath and realized that my back hurt less. I finished painting the wall and scooted the daybed into place.

The following morning, I hurt even less. I hated to stand up and cheer too soon, so I called the back specialist and asked whether this was a temporary respite or whether I might be recovering from the osteitis.

"I have this living room that needs painting," he told me, a smile in his voice. "Can't tell you the future, but experience suggests we should be optimistic."

He was right. My pain level continued to drop, and my optimism soared. I slept better, thought better, and started to believe I could work again, perhaps even write.

* * *

Nothing came of my job hunting in Santa Fe. Joe knew the acting director of a local nonprofit organization and mentioned my plight to him. He said they were looking for a bookkeeper.

I didn't know QuickBooks but sat with the departing bookkeeper for half a day and picked up the basics. I drove home tired but elated. Whether I got the job or not, I knew I could still learn.

The director hired me to work three days a week. Though I was feeling better, the commute and the challenge of the new job wore me out. I slept through my lunch hours, an alarm clock perched on GW's dashboard. My days off were a series of naps with Peaches. But I managed. My life and my checking account were on the mend.

Out of sympathy and for the irony of it, I donated a few dollars each month to a power company fund that helped people in financial distress pay their electric bills.

SQUARE ONE

I did the homework for my auto insurance case as I was able, keeping a diary of the accident's impact on my life and an accounting of mileage to medical appointments.

I wasn't ready to sue anyone but took an attorney's advice to spend an hour in the county recorder's office, listing property belonging to the Dodge's owner and driver. The threat of having to sell the properties could get them to pressure their insurance carriers into a decent settlement. The lawyer had told me to be tough, but I couldn't imagine taking someone's home.

Nevertheless, I drove GW into Santa Fe to see what the addresses on the list represented. Cruising down a narrow *barrio* street, I found a well-kept house that had probably been in the family for generations.

The two-tone gold Dodge pickup that had hit me was parked in the driveway, facing out. Passing it made my breath stutter and my heart race. I white-knuckled the steering wheel, using every bit of control I had not to speed away.

I turned the corner and looked at the commercial building on my list. There was no place to stop on that side of the street, so I U-turned, parked at the curb, and shut off GW's engine.

While I was consulting my list and my map, motion and the clatter of a diesel engine made me turn. The gold pickup was accelerating toward me. A gray-haired man was at the wheel, looking right at me.

My heart seized. Sour fear sweat popped out all over my body. I was a sitting duck with my engine off. I screamed and threw up my hands, still holding the map, and waited for the slam and rip of metal, the shatter of glass.

The driver turned right. He was gone before I could catch my breath.

My elation was almost as great as when Macha had stopped

spinning down the highway on her crushed-in roof. Once again, adrenaline produced clarity: The truck's owner wasn't aiming at me. He couldn't have recognized me. He'd never seen my face at the accident. I was driving a different vehicle now. To him, I was just some woman parked at the curb, reading a map.

Despite this rational self-talk, two years of therapy, and the support of an antidepressant, I slumped and gasped for air. I was still shaking when I swung GW around and headed out of town.

Before I collapsed on the daybed, I let Peaches out of his cage. He did what he'd done the day of the accident: stayed on my chest as I fell into a sleep full of accident reruns. I startled awake again and again with the overwhelming feeling that I had been knocked back to square one. Peaches stayed right with me.

MAGGIE

With Peaches' care, I regained the ground I'd lost in the Dodge truck trauma. A few weeks later—on the Saturday of Memorial Day weekend—I was standing in the office/bird room door, trying to calm my companion as he clung to the inside of his cage and *rawk-rawk-rawk*ed.

"It'll be worth your wait," I said. "I'm coming home with a surprise."

The insurance companies hadn't settled yet, so I couldn't afford to repay the charitable organizations that had helped with our electric bill. I had squirreled away enough from my part-time job, however, to buy Peaches a feathered companion.

On my way to Santa Fe, I reconsidered my decision. What would Peaches want? Given a choice, I believed he would be happier—eventually—with another parrot in his life.

Would I lose Peaches' affection? To some degree, but it had never seemed fair for such a social creature to be an only bird. He'd spent a lot of time alone in the last eight years and had become something of a curmudgeon. I hoped to shake up his attitude in a good way.

But the shake-up might not be good. Nothing Dr. Ramsay had said about the risks of getting a second bird was lost on me. Neither was my stressful experience with Chamisa the budgie. I harbored no fantasy that Peaches and another parrot would act out the avian equivalent of falling into each other's arms. If they bonded, it would take time. On balance, I believed it was worth the risk.

* * *

Darlene greeted me at the entrance to Feathered Friends. The exotic bird-lover's paradise resounded with a cacophony of macaw, cockatoo, Amazon, and smaller parrot calls.

As I paused inside the bird room, a baby Myers parrot—a conure-sized African bird—toddled across the floor and nibbled the ends off my shoelaces. The thin white plastic must have looked and felt like keratin feather sheaths. The little guy lowered his head, asking for grooming. I gave him a scritch before scooping him up and placing him on a tree-branch stand. He was so adorable that I questioned the decision I'd made during previous visits.

I'd narrowed my selection to a pair of green-cheeked conures, hand-raised siblings who were now eleven weeks old. There they were, clambering around inside their cage, grooming each other and cocking their heads at people and other birds.

The babies were a darker green than Peaches, with brownish-gray on the tops of their heads, a bright green patch on each cheek, and white eye rings. Their neck feathers were tipped with grayish-yellow, giving them a scaly appearance. The birds had dark red bellies, and their tail feathers, which were just growing out, were the same shade.

Why had I set my mind on a parrot of a different species from Peaches? One reason was that I didn't want to be in the baby bird business. I stood a fifty-fifty chance of bringing home a female. Parrots of different species might not share the same sexual rituals. They might pair but not mate. If they mated, their genes might not match.

There was also the advantage to knowing at a glance who was

who. I could yell, "Hey, (parrot's name), quit chewing the (book, dresser, spider plant, electric cord)!"

I let the babies nibble my fingers while I spoke and whistled and kissed. Then I stepped behind a branch stand and watched them. Both were affectionate and feisty. One, though, cocked its head and seemed to think about everything going on in the bird room. I could see that she (?) would provide plenty of stimulation for Peaches. When Darlene asked if I'd selected a name, I thought of Maggie, the precocious daughter of family friends.

I had none of the wild-caught-parrot angst I'd felt over Peaches. Maggie had hatched in Arizona, according to the breeder band on her leg, and hadn't been exposed to diseases in quarantine.

While I wrote a check, the assistant separated Maggie from her sibling and put her in the travel cage I'd brought. The remaining baby lurched back and forth on his perch and screeched. I assured him that he would go to a good home where people would love him and where he might meet other birds. Darlene was careful in selecting potential bird owners and had repeat customers, so my promise was likely to be fulfilled.

Darlene knew that Peaches flew free in my house, so I didn't expect Maggie to leave the shop with clipped wings. The assistant, however, didn't know. At least he left Maggie's primaries intact and her secondaries cut back just enough to keep her from flying level.

INTRODUCTIONS

At home, I set the travel cage on the dining table and let Peaches out. Maggie didn't like being alone in a strange place and called in an urgent, high-pitched voice. Peaches zoomed into the dining room, eyes wide and flashing, and landed in front of the travel cage. He held his wings out from his sides, ruffled his feathers, and pecked at her between the bars. I was relieved when Maggie pecked right back. I didn't know what I would do if she cowered.

I needed reinforcements for the next step, so I put Peaches back in his cage and walked across the road to get Joe. For the parrots' out-of-cage introduction, we chose my bed, covered with a cotton comforter.

Over the next twenty minutes, Peaches alternately ignored Maggie, prodded her with his beak, and charged and pecked her. Joe and I put our hands between them to show Peaches that he couldn't hurt the baby and to assure Maggie that we would protect her.

We conducted these refereed visits at least once a day, several times on weekends. Maggie was a quick study. She realized that when Peaches turned away, she could dart in, yank his tail feathers, and count on us to defend her. We leveled the playing field by letting Peaches charge her when she misbehaved, as a parent or other flock member would have done in the wild.

When I went to work, I left Peaches and Maggie in their full-sized cages at opposite ends of my desk so they could get used to each other. It went slower than I expected. They either screeched or ignored each other.

Joe kept asking if they would ever make friends. I wished I knew.

ACCEPTANCE

Not long before Maggie's arrival, I read a magazine article about parrots' vision. Color and pattern, it said, were central to their recognition of members of their own species. This came back to me a few weeks after Maggie arrived, when she sidled up to Peaches on the living room table, and he pecked at her yet again.

Peaches' enmity stemmed in part from this young upstart invading his home. That was predictable, but was it the only problem? Peaches knew what his kind looked like, both from his younger days in a flock and from his encounters with mirrors. Maybe it was hard wired. Maggie didn't fit his picture.

How *did* the birds perceive each other? They saw into the ultraviolet portion of the spectrum. Their feather patterns might look different to them than they did to me.

The most obvious difference I could see was Peaches' orange

patch. I'd saved some of his tiny forehead feathers from previous molts. Joe stopped by and watched while I used a pair of tweezers to dip the feathers in flour paste and stick them on Maggie's head.

The job was far from perfect, but I never got a chance to see Peaches' reaction. Maggie rubbed the paste and feathers off against the corner of a book.

"That worked well," Joe said.

"Not to worry. I have an ace in the hole."

Or so I thought. On my way home from work the next evening, I stopped at a drug store and bought an orange lipstick. Applying it was harder than pasting on the feathers. Maggie struggled, smearing it all over her head and my hand.

I wrapped her in a towel, exposed the area above her beak, and reapplied the lipstick. It lay there in dark, greasy globs.

"Perhaps it's for the best," I told Joe as I wiped the goo off Maggie's forehead. "If Peaches groomed her and ate the lipstick, it would probably make him sick. He'll have to accept her the way she is."

But what if Peaches didn't accept Maggie? He was acting like an older sibling, jealous of a new baby. To compensate, I gave him time alone out of his cage every day, fed him sunflower seeds and apple chunks, scritched his head, and let him sit alone among the plants on the living room table, where he liked to watch the wild birds.

I let Maggie out with him, too, when I could keep an eye on them. Peaches would groom her, then peck her and fly off to be alone. The curtain rods became his MFZs—Maggie-Free Zones.

Was Peaches failing to accept Maggie because she couldn't fly? She was the weakest member of the flock. Perhaps his instinct was to drive her away so she wouldn't attract predators.

Not that Maggie didn't know what her wings were for. She would tremble them and crouch down as if to leap into the air. Then she would either stop or flutter to the floor. After each failed attempt, Peaches pecked her.

As Maggie's wing and tail feathers grew out, she practiced

flapping. She would lean forward to take off, then pull back. I thought she needed some training to build her confidence and began tossing her short distances to the day bed. She flung out her wings and flapped to break her fall.

She was an impatient and distractible learner, though. She would crouch to launch, then preen a back feather with her beak, stand on one foot, and scratch her head with the other, all at once. It took her quite a few tumbles from furniture and my shoulders to develop the patience to do one thing at a time.

Then one afternoon, Maggie flew from the dining room floor up to the day bed. She tumbled forward onto her chest and beak when she landed, back arched, tail straight up. Peaches didn't care how clumsy she was. He flew to her and used his closed beak to nudge her into the air. Down the hall to the bedroom they flew, Peaches shouting his delight. Maggie flapped for all she was worth to keep up.

I clapped and cheered and sighed with relief. My decision to get a second bird had been validated. And a smart bird, at that.

It hadn't occurred to me yet that a parrot could be too smart for her own good.

TOO CLEVER BY HALF

The first morning Maggie was loose at breakfast time—this was before she could fly—she ventured along my arm, climbed onto the rim of my bowl, and peered in. Then she hopped into my scrambled eggs and marched to the middle, where she stood eating.

Peaches was in the kitchen, munching on a pine nut, so the task of discipline fell to me. "Maggie, in this house, it's customary for parrots to perch on the edge of the bowl and not walk through the food."

Twelve-week-old Maggie looked up with what appeared to be perfect comprehension: *Oh, I'm glad you told me.* She turned around, hiked back to the rim, and ate from her proper place.

I stared. As far as I knew, I hadn't made a gesture that might have cued her. "Smart parrot, Maggie. Who are you, anyway?"

She glanced up as if she understood the question but had been taught never to speak with her beak full. After that, she always perched on the rims of dishes and plates.

* * *

Around that time, I ran across an English saying that turned out to describe Maggie all too well: too clever by half.

One morning, I was sponging off the bathroom counter while Maggie prowled around on the floor. She cocked her head and peered into the narrow space on each side of the washing machine. When she flew to my shoulder, I figured she was bored. That would have been typical of her attention span: intense but brief.

The dark spaces continued to fascinate her, though, as I realized when she winged to the control panel on the back of the washer and peered down. She looked charming—until she hopped onto the cold-water hose and shinnied to the lowest point in its curve. Then she jumped.

I spun around. *Deep, slow breaths,* I told myself as I scrambled for a hand mirror and a flashlight. I shined the light behind the washer, but the cabinet above it was so low that I couldn't angle the mirror to see to the floor.

I had to make like Maggie—stand back and think. I pulled a bath towel from the cabinet and dangled it down in the corner. "Come on, Maggie," I urged. "Beak over claw over claw, the way you climb up the curtains and my bathrobe."

All that hung on the towel when I pulled it up was a dust bunny as big as my fist, spotted with mouse droppings. I would have to pull out the washing machine but hesitated. Were there openings in the back that Maggie could climb into? Could the scooting metal crush her? On the other hand, what choice did I have?

It took several minutes to jockey the washer forward. I used a plastic footstool to climb on top and shone the flashlight down behind.

Maggie was gone. There were no openings in the back of the washing machine. Could she have crawled under it? I called. The only responses were from Peaches on the hall curtain rod.

Then I spotted a crescent-shaped hole in the wall, next to the drain pipe. It didn't look big enough for even a small parrot to squeeze through, but it was my only lead.

I muscled the washer back into place and went around to the office/bird room closet on the other side of the wall. Peaches squawked directions as I piled out gift wrap, rejected bird toys, craft supplies, and other miscellany. I pried off the quarter-inch-thick plywood panel above the built-in drawers, smiling at the irony of trying to save a parrot with a tool called a cat's paw.

Maggie didn't respond to my calls. Did this space lead outside? Had Maggie gotten loose and flown away?

Now I was scared. I locked Peaches in his cage. Back on my knees—an appropriate position for prayer—I leaned into the closet and manipulated the mirror and flashlight until I could see inside the wall.

Red tail feathers reflected in the mirror from a foot an a half below the ceiling. I found the long bird ladder, which I maneuvered up to where Maggie sat on the defunct heater's propane line.

"Maggie, up," I said.

She knew the command, but no amount of encouragement would make her budge.

It was time to back off and think again. I paced the hall, imagining how scared Maggie must be. All right, maybe Maggie liked it, but she couldn't stay there forever. I asked the Green Parrot Goddess for help.

I was just considering pulling out the worthless heater when I noticed the quarter-inch plywood panel above it. I grabbed the cat's paw and pried it off.

There on the gas line, rock still and silent, stood Maggie. She didn't fly to freedom when the wall opened up, just blinked at the sudden light. As soon as I said, "Maggie, up," she climbed onto my finger. I brought her out and scritched her head. She made muttonchops, fluffing her green cheek feathers with pleasure.

Once I had her locked in her cage, I said, "Don't do that again. You scared the daylights out of me."

The little picture of innocence blinked: *Moi?*

I re-installed the pried-off panels, restocked the closet, and pulled the washer out again, scooting it toward the bathtub so I could squeeze behind and sweep up the dust bunnies and mouse droppings. I packed the gap around the pipe with steel wool and covered it with duct tape. Joe later cut a clever wooden patch that fit around the pipe and sealed the hole for good.

TOUGH PARROT

This was the first of several mishaps, each more serious than the last. To keep myself mindful, I hung a cluster of her red tail feathers from a mirror bracket above the bathroom sinks—after I accidentally pulled them out.

I was sitting down to put on my shoes when Maggie dove off the shower curtain rod, landing on the toilet lid just as I reached it. I leaped up. She screamed—a good sign—and made a wobbly flight out the door, minus her tail-feather rudder.

Having her tail feathers pulled out made Maggie cautious for a few months. Then one afternoon, when I was about to settle into a living room chair, she launched from the table and was underneath me in a fraction of a second.

"No!" I cried as I leaped up, expecting to see her flattened like a piece of cardboard.

The yielding chair cushion had prevented that, but it hadn't left her undamaged. She lay on her belly, head turned to one side, unconscious and breathing in shallow gasps.

I lifted her cautiously, afraid to do more damage. Her eyes opened, then rolled up.

"Come back, Maggie!"

Maggie exhaled and didn't draw another breath. Her tiny heart fluttered against my palm—and stopped.

I didn't expect CPR to work, but it was all I could think of. I turned her on her back and with one finger gave her chest small, sharp compressions while I blew tiny puffs into her open beak.

After the longest minute of my life, Maggie started breathing on her own, though she was still unconscious. I slid her into a travel cage, herded Peaches into his cage on the desk, and called Dr. Ramsay's office. We zoomed north as fast as I dared to drive.

Maggie was on her feet within half a dozen miles but still looked dazed. Her head and wings drooped, and she staggered for balance with every bump and lane change.

* * *

When Dr. Ramsay opened the cage door, Maggie surprised us by darting past her hand and flying around and around the exam room until she wore herself out. An assistant caught Maggie in a towel as she fluttered down from the ceiling.

Back in her cage after an injection for shock, Maggie ruffled her feathers into place and looked normal in a couple of minutes.

I covered my face, wept with relief, and asked, "Why does she fly under me?"

Dr. Ramsay put her arms around me. "I wish I knew. We can't always count on our animals to be careful."

I gushed my thanks for her help.

She looked at Maggie and observed, "Tough parrot."

WORK AND PLAY

Maggie was not only tough, she was affectionate and playful. Thanks to the Green Parrot Goddess—and Dr. Ramsay, of course— she lived to repeat her most endearing behavior: somersaulting in my lap and lying on her back to have her tummy tickled. She would throw back her head and kick her feet like an ecstatic baby.

Peaches' initial reaction to Tickle Maggie's Tummy was to flash his eyes, squawk, and nip my hand. I didn't scold but insisted that I wasn't hurting the baby. Peaches became calmer, though he often landed nearby to make sure she was all right.

One day, he did a remarkable thing. Maggie and I finished the tickling game, and she flew off to clamber among the spider plants and watch the wild birds. Peaches flew right in and took her place on my lap. He somersaulted forward and lay there, utterly vulnerable, with his belly and throat exposed.

I stared with amazement, finally remembering to tickle his tummy. He strained to maintain his position, then scrambled to his feet and stared at me, eyes wide. I was so awed that it took me a moment to find words. "Fine green Peaches parrot! You are an amazing bird."

* * *

Amazing, and with all his wild instincts intact. In January—the beginning of the conure mating season—Peaches ripped into the side of a cardboard box filled with bubble wrap and foam packing sheets. He worked with daily diligence, hollowing out a space large enough to turn around in.

Then he stopped. Peach-fronted conures sometimes dug nests in termite mounds. Once they were satisfied with the hole, they abandoned it until the termites sealed the inner surface.

As usual, I had more questions than answers. "Are you doing this for Maggie? Have you done it before, in the wild? Did you give it up because you think that termites will seal it, or because you don't have a mate? Is she too young? Or is Maggie a *he* instead of a *she*?"

Peaches squawked: *Enough with the Twenty Questions!*

I was sure Peaches knew whether Maggie was male or female. Could he be taught to disclose another bird's gender? It would be a whole new development in avian sexing. Maybe I could quit my day job.

Peaches returned often to a ready-made cavity—the cabinet under the bathroom sinks. He would land on top of a door and squeeze under the front of the overhanging counter. Maggie learned to follow him. They spent hours there, chewing up items in the cheap-toy category: toilet paper rolls and pieces of cardboard.

Sometimes, they made squeaking sounds. Were they mating? That wouldn't necessarily make Maggie a girl. If no females were available, two males might engage in mating behavior.

Should I sneak into the bathroom, I wondered, fling open the cabinet door, and catch them at whatever they were doing, to satisfy my curiosity? I valued my own privacy too much to invade theirs.

* * *

Maggie was almost two years old when *she* answered the gender question, climbing onto my hand and moving from side to side. *He* left a golden drop of semen, just as Peaches had. Maggie was a boy.

WILD BIRDS

The year Maggie joined Peaches and me, I started scattering millet and black-oil sunflower seeds under the awning that shaded the front of the house. I bought suet, thistle, and peanut butter feeders to hang from the Siberian elms in back.

Attracting unusual birds was part of the plan, and some showed up: a Harris sparrow with an apostrophe-shaped ear mark; a rose-breasted grosbeak with a pink bib; and a verdin, its yellow face standing out in a flock of duller bushtits. More important was giving Peaches and Maggie some company. They hung on the curtains by the hour, chattering with their wild relatives.

On Maggie's first New Year's Day, a roadrunner flew over the back fence. The state bird was uncommon here, so I was thrilled. I'd heard they liked dog kibble, so I set out a pie tin full from the bag I kept for strays.

What I didn't know was that roadrunners hunted small birds, especially when snakes and lizards were hibernating. The parrots knew, though. One look at the big bird with its jaunty crest and flipping tail sent them screaming out of the living room. I took the hint and stopped putting out dog food.

The parrot panic reaction happened a lot. In a typical scenario, Peaches, Maggie, and I were lunching at the living room table when a sharp-shinned hawk dropped into an elm. It grabbed at several small birds and missed. The parrots screeched and winged for the back of the house.

The hawk settled on a branch four feet from the glass. Peaches flew back into the living room, got an eyeful, and headed back to the bedroom.

Maggie surprised me by landing on my shoulder. He shifted from one foot to the other and made rusty-hinge creaks. Then he squawked with more confidence. Pretty soon, he was shrieking at the hawk: *You can't hurt me, you big bully! I've got my body guard!*

Another time, a sharp-shin scattered the wild birds and took off after a scrub jay that had been hanging on the peanut butter feeder. With the hawk's beak inches from its tail, the jay raced out of sight. The parrots rooted for it in anxious voices.

One summer morning, I went out to water the back-yard irises and stopped to watch the wild birds race off as a young Cooper's hawk sailed toward them. The raptor wasn't hunting, just looking for a place to perch. It wasn't aiming for a tree branch, though. It was sailing toward the top of my head. It let down its feet and back-flapped to land.

I threw my arms up and yelled, "Hey!" The bird stumbled in mid-air and veered away, craning its head around to see what disaster it had avoided.

What if I had let the hawk land on my head? No, I thought, those talons could do some damage. Besides, Peaches and Maggie, screeching on the other side of the kitchen window, might have had heart attacks.

* * *

Our closest encounter occurred while I was writing at the computer one afternoon with Peaches perched on my head and Maggie on my shoulder. Peaches let out a gargly *rrrr*. I glanced out the window and didn't see anything, but I wasn't fooled. The raptor might have flown out of sight beyond the newly leafed-out elms.

Peaches' warning calls became more strident. Maggie craned his head, spotted the threat, and joined in. I followed his gaze. I'd often wondered why we didn't see ospreys—fish-catching hawks—since the nearby ponds were stocked for fishing. Maybe we just weren't on the osprey flyway.

That day, we were. The bird was flying straight toward the window. As it glided over the arroyo, Peaches' and Maggie's warnings escalated. It crossed our fence line, and the parrots collided on the wing, scrambling out the door, down the hall, and into the bedroom, where the curtains were closed. Maybe they thought that if they couldn't see the osprey, it didn't exist—or that if the osprey couldn't see them, *they* didn't exist.

Suddenly, I wasn't sure the bird would veer off. At the last instant, I threw my arms over my face, expecting the shatter of glass. After all, the osprey hadn't evolved to understand a solid substance through which it could see prey but not catch it.

I glanced up in time to see the osprey cut a hard U-turn, its wingtip inches from the window. Then I realized that the bright sky and relative dark interior might have turned the window into a mirror. Maybe the osprey couldn't see the parrots at all but thought it was challenging a territorial rival.

TAKING IT TO LAW

Not long after our osprey encounter, I got a phone call from the company that insured the Dodge pickup's driver. A man delivered what he said was their final and non-negotiable settlement offer for property damage, personal injury, medical expenses, lost income, and pain and suffering: eighteen-hundred dollars.

Stunned, I asked him to repeat the figure.

"My emergency room visit cost more than that," I said.

"Take it or leave it."

I took a page from Maggie's book. "You can't bully me with that weak offer. The next call you get will be from my lawyer." I slammed the phone down hard enough to startle Peaches off the dining room curtain rod and Maggie, wet from a bath, out of the spider plants.

* * *

Not that I had a lawyer. I thought I might hire the one who had suggested I check out the property of the Dodge's owner and driver.

Surely I owed him a chance to pitch his approach. Joe, however, was watching a lot of television and harangued me into calling a lawyer who advertised for personal injury cases.

On the wall behind the lawyer's desk hung an antique shotgun that he said he would use on the insurance companies. Joe loved it. He couldn't get me to sign up fast enough. I knew I'd have no peace if I didn't.

To the lawyer's credit, the suit produced a reasonable settlement offer from the other driver's insurance company in less than a week. The guy who had offered me eighteen hundred dollars phoned to offer the policy limit.

My lawyer was handling the matter, I told him, and gave him the phone number. He sighed and said the accident was the insured's most recent in a series. I might have felt sorry for the insurance company, if I hadn't imagined the premiums they were extracting. The driver probably couldn't buy a policy anywhere else.

The lawyer's secretary mailed me the acceptance form, along with one from the truck owner's insurer. I signed them and sent them back, thinking my worries were over.

* * *

I had settled with my own insurance company before seeking legal help. The lawyer had agreed that he was not entitled to a percentage of that money.

That didn't stop him from trying to withhold it at settlement time. When he told me he had a right to it, I gripped the phone as though it were his throat.

Joe didn't apologize for pressuring me into signing with the greedy lawyer. Instead, he rubbed his hands together and grinned at the chance to play good cop/bad cop.

My part involved phoning the lawyer's business partner, who ran the firm's office in another town. In sincere and humble tones, I said, "I'm sure this is a misunderstanding. The last thing I want is to turn it over to the bar association."

Meanwhile, Joe paid my lawyer an unannounced visit, slathering on his best Mafioso-style accent and body language and suggesting threats without actually making them. He enjoyed it so much that he could hardly stop talking about it.

The following morning, my lawyer called, insisting that I had misunderstood, that he hadn't intended to deprive me of the money. My medical claims were being paid as we spoke. My portion of the settlement would hit my account in a couple of days.

I made him tell me how much it was. It matched my calculation to the penny.

SHAKING THE MOTHS OUT OF MY WALLET

The first thing I did with my pain-and-suffering money was hit the clothing sales. Buoyed by retail therapy, I made the rounds of the organizations that had helped with my electric bill. The surprise of the people who accepted the checks was as gratifying as the opportunity to keep my commitment.

GW's automatic transmission had been slipping for a couple of weeks. I'd promised him that if he held out until the case closed, I'd have it fixed. He took me at my word. Three days after the settlement, we climbed the Main Hill Road to Los Alamos, going five miles an hour, with a train of frustrated motorists behind us. We drove straight, if not rapidly, to the nearest mechanic.

The real fun was buying a larger cage for Maggie, who had been living in Feathers' old cage. The new one was bright fuchsia and had pink plastic food and water cups. Maggie scrambled over the perches, chirping and squawking as if it were the best present ever. I left the old cage out for several days, but he never went back.

Apparently, real men—at least in the parrot world—loved pink.

HEAD OF THE LINE

My life was blessedly uneventful for the next six months. Then, on a Friday night in January, when I was engrossed a novel, the telephone startled me. My brother was calling from a Southern California hospital. Our father had died of congestive heart failure.

I took a slow breath to quiet the vibration in my chest and to give myself a chance to think. "I'm coming out to California," I said. *Home* wouldn't have been accurate. Home was where my parrots were.

"I'm executor of the estate, and I'm already here. I can handle everything."

In three years, I had recovered from the accident enough to claim what was mine, including the closure that would come from being in the house where I had grown to adulthood. "I'm coming out."

"Suit yourself. I'll pick you up at LAX."

"I'll take the train. Maybe Elida can meet me." After the accident, I'd promised not to do anything unnecessarily anxiety-provoking, such as getting on an airplane.

I phoned my boss to arrange the week off, then Amtrak, then Elida, who agreed pick me up at the Fullerton station, southeast of Los Angeles. Then I sniffled my way across the road.

To his credit, Joe didn't sound irritated when he said, "It's hard to understand why you're crying over someone who damaged you."

"That's so black and white. My parents also did me a lot of good."

"Why are you going all the way to California for him?"

"I'm not going for him. I'm going for myself."

In Joe's jumbled monolog about his parents' passings and the evils of hospitals and surgeons, he said the two things I wanted to hear: He would take time off from work to drive me to the train station, and he would care for Peaches and Maggie.

Walking home by flashlight, I shivered, and not just because of the winter chill. I'd survived an auto accident and recovered as much as I was likely to from brain trauma, and here I was, the elder child in the family, having moved to the head of the line.

FOR WHOM THE BELL TOLLS

Elida welcomed me back to California with a long hug on the

Fullerton station platform. It was a cool morning, ripe with the smell of impending rain.

Over a coffee-shop breakfast, she commented on how stressed I looked. Then she recited a rhyme:

Ask not for whom the bell tolls,
don't get yourself in a stew.
If you can hear the clanging bell,
relax, it's not for you.

After a semi-sleepless night in a train seat, pushing away the snoring drunk who kept falling onto my shoulder, this irreverent ditty made me burst out laughing.

* * *

My parents' house was full of surprises. A cabinet yielded a cascade of family snapshots and photo portraits, many of which Vance and I had never seen. After I found our paternal grandmother's original birth certificate, dated 1895, in a file drawer stuffed with Medicare explanations of benefits, we realized we would have to look at every piece of paper. That was how we found income tax returns going back to 1941, when Dad made two thousand dollars as a bookkeeper. They were probably paying forty dollars a month to rent their two-bedroom house.

In Mother's closet, I came across a double-wedding-ring quilt. It wasn't the kind of thing Dad's family would have made or kept. It had to have been handed down by Mother's Amish and pioneer ancestors—*my* ancestors. Smoothing the folds was like touching the loving hands that had made those fine, even stitches.

Then there was the small river-rounded stone on which a careful hand had painted tiny flowers bracketing the word *Shit*. Perhaps Mother's younger sister Dawn had sent it. It made me smile to think of my troubled mother laughing over it.

* * *

The night after Vance's wife Marilyn arrived to help, the three of us sorted through Mother and Dad's most personal belongings, their jewelry. Tears spilled all around when I gave Mother's diamond wedding and engagement rings to Vance and Marilyn. Their children might want to have the stones reset for their spouses when they married.

When I asked where Dad's wedding band was, my brother shook his head. The policeman who had broken into the house and found Dad had said he was wearing the ring. When Vance got to the hospital, it was gone.

Dad's corporate service pins reminded me of the nights he had worked late and the weekends he'd hunched over spreadsheets and ledgers on a card table. Whatever personal problems he'd had, I was grateful for his dedication to supporting his family.

* * *

On our last day in the house, Vance came across Dad's cancelled check that had helped me purchase my mobile home, and asked what the payback arrangement was. I explained that I'd kept asking Dad when he wanted me to repay him. He'd always told me not to worry about it.

Privately, I thought that writing off my debt was Dad's small compensation for the assets being divided heavily in Vance's favor. The reasons were no mystery. Vance was the male child and had lived the kind of life our parents approved of. He had also kept contact with Mother and Dad during their alcoholic decay. I knew few of the details but gathered that he had refereed their drunken antagonisms. Perhaps he'd pressured them to stay together when they were considering a rasher course.

Irritated as I was by what seemed a lack of acknowledgement and fairness, I knew Vance had probably earned everything they were giving him. I couldn't have done what he had.

TOXED

By the time Elida and Rod drove me to the Fullerton train station, I was emotionally wrung out and physically ill. Mother had had a thing for mothballs; we had thrown them out by the gross. The curtains, upholstery, and bedding reeked of tobacco smoke. The back wall of Mother's closet was covered with black mold.

The train rocked me to sleep most of the way home. I was grateful for Joe's welcoming embrace and the bracing New Mexico air. For years, I had worried that I might be called upon to take care of Mother and Dad. I didn't think the parrots could survive the atmosphere in their house. I didn't think I could, either.

KNEE SURGERY

The following Saturday, I spent an hour on my knees by the bathtub, kneading years of dust and tobacco smoke out of the double-wedding-ring quilt, which I thought too fragile to launder in the washing machine. I hung it over the shower curtain rod and was limping down the hall to make lunch when my weak left knee collapsed. Peaches and Maggie squawked and flew off my shoulders as I sprawled on the floor.

I clambered to my feet, glad I was accumulating vacation and sick time and was making the rounds of orthopedic surgeons. The cartilage was gone. I was walking—hobbling with a cane, actually— bone on bone. For exercise, I'd ridden hundreds of miles on my stationary bike, going nowhere.

* * *

On the morning of my knee replacement surgery, Joe dropped me off at Los Alamos Medical Center on his way to a two-day ski instructors' exam in Colorado. That was fine. He was antsy around hospitals and medical procedures. Phyllis, a writer friend and former nurse, was there to see me off to the operating room.

The spinal block felt like a warm hand pressing on my back, so comforting that I relaxed into it. I listened to Rob Marley on the operating room speakers and swapped jokes with the surgical team while they measured, cut, sawed, measured, drilled, glued, measured, hammered, stitched, and stapled. In the recovery room, they X-rayed and congratulated themselves. Phyllis and I high-fived.

Half way through my five-day stay, my friend, Jennifer, brought her Dalmatian puppy Ariel up in the elevator. The Medical Center was the kind of small-town place where no one stopped her.

Afterwards, I told one of the nurses how their visit had buoyed my spirits. She told me about the elderly man who had been brought in in a coma. Tests showed no physiological reason. It looked as though he had given up on life.

His family brought in his cockatiel and put the bird on his chest, where she nibbled his chin. Tears came to the man's eyes. He took a deep breath and came back. A few days later, he went home.

Tears ran down my cheeks. I imagined that my love for Peaches and Maggie could bring me back from death's precipice. My longing to get home to them made me a very motivated physical therapy patient.

* * *

Despite having undergone an invasive and traumatic surgery, I was in less pain when an orderly wheeled me out of the hospital than when I had limped in.

Joe gave me a cursory hug, but I was too excited to notice the coolness in his manner. I filled him in on the surgery and physical therapy as he drove us home.

Instead of telling me how glad he was that everything had gone well, he dropped the verbal bomb he'd been saving. He demanded to know how Rob Marley's music had influenced me to make him fail his ski exam.

This was the most twisted accusation I'd heard him make. Inarticulate with shock, I responded to the tight fury in his voice by sitting rigid, pressing my lips together, and barely breathing. Neither of us said another word the rest of the drive.

Peaches and Maggie squawked excited greetings as I clambered up the front steps, using the railing and a walker. Their voices and the sunlight streaming through the living room windows opened my heart. Life in my little refuge made sense.

* * *

The parrots enjoyed two and a half weeks loose in the house, caged only when Joe drove me to physical therapy appointments. A couple of friends asked if that meant we had made up. I told them that making up wasn't Joe's style. We just went on as though the hurtful episode hadn't happened.

The birds and I napped and watched TV together while a passive mobility machine extended and flexed my knee to keep the muscles from stiffening. They didn't care that post-surgical blood thinner turned me black and blue everyplace I bumped into something. They were just glad to have me home.

I did stretching and strengthening exercises while the parrots sat on the day bed and squawked what I imagined was *Five more reps, four, three.* My personal fitness trainers chirped nothing but encouragement.

I wasn't taking pain medication, even to sleep. And what sleep! I no longer woke several times a night, struggling to find a knee position that would allow me to doze off.

One day, I walked down the hall and realized I'd left the walker in the bedroom. I could get in and out of the car by myself a few days later and started driving myself to PT and back to work.

* * *

When I told my surgeon I couldn't wait to rip up the slopes on my snowboard, he pitched a fit. I just grinned a pain-free grin.

The first snowflakes, however, brought an unexpected realization: I had too much to lose. Before, if I'd trashed my knee, I would have shrugged and had joint replacement on the emergency plan. If I did it now, they'd have to drill deeper into the bones. I'd be having the surgery that the doctors hoped to put off until I was in my sixties or older.

I sold my board, boots, and waterproofs at the ski swap but kept arguing with myself. Was I copping out or being sensible? What was so great about being sensible, anyway?

Joe assured me I'd made the right decision. The friends who had thought all along that I was acting like a teenager were relieved.

There was no use asking Peaches and Maggie. Anything that increased my time at home with them was an unqualified hit.

WILLIE

About a year after my knee surgery, when the spring wind was shoving the tree branches around outside our windows, Jill called from Los Alamos. The doctors had found out what was causing her younger teenage daughter's respiratory symptoms. The culprits included pollens and molds.

I commiserated. There was no getting away from the sheet of yellow ponderosa pine pollen covering Ashley Pond in June. Then there were the fall grass pollens. Really, I reacted most of the year.

"Megan," Jill said, "is allergic to the birds."

My breath caught. The family had already had a pair of budgies when Megan fell in love with a dusky-headed conure in a pet shop. Willie was a lovely young bird with a gray head, bluish-gray eyes, and white eye rings. His feet were so large and fleshy that I had nicknamed him Willie Bigfoot.

I glanced at Peaches and Maggie, who were chewing on the wicker paper-napkin holder. How would I feel if I had to give them up? Dr. Krohn and Frances had suggested it several times as a way of reducing my total allergy load. With all the pollinating plants and the mold kicked up by weeks of summer monsoons, bird dander seemed like the least of my concerns—which was a euphemistic way of saying, *Not in this lifetime.*

Jill, however, was taking no chances with her daughter. She had found a home for the budgies. Now she needed one for Willie.

I hadn't considered bringing a third parrot into our home, so I didn't let the conversation go there. I told Jill I didn't know many bird people in the area, but I'd call around.

* * *

I couldn't get Willie out of my mind, even after praying to the Green Parrot Goddess to find him a home somewhere else. I remembered how he and the budgies had snuggled and groomed through the mesh in their large divided cage. One of his favorite games was flying up and down the staircase. He loved to hide on the top shelf of any closet he found open, while Jill, Megan, and Annie called and searched for him.

Willie spoke a different language from Peaches' and Maggie's, full of sibilants, nasals, and gutturals. It sounded almost like an exotic human tongue. He understood at least a little English. I had once placed my finger in front of him and said, "Willie, up." He'd climbed right on.

When I called to tell Jill I'd had no luck finding a home for Willie, she asked if I would take him for two weeks while she went to California for a professional training.

Skeptically, I said yes. "If he works out, he can stay. If not . . . "

Sometimes, I had to say the wrong thing to realize what the right thing was. What if I'd taken that attitude about Peaches and Maggie and sent them away before we'd worked out our adjustment problems?

I phoned Jill back and told her Willie could live with us. Anxious, but trusting that at least Maggie would understand what I said, I told him and Peaches that our flock was about to increase.

* * *

Willie was standing in a cage, surrounded by toys, when I arrived at Jill's the following evening after work. Jill had packed a bag of his favorite foods. Megan had gone to a friend's.

In the car, I told Willie that he was coming to live with me, that he would have two other free-flying companions. He wasn't leaving because Megan didn't love him but because of a health situation that couldn't be helped.

Willie cocked his head and mumbled in his exotic tongue. He chirped a few notes, then settled down until we crossed the Rio Grande bridge, where we picked up an oldies station. Raised in a musical household, he squawked and sidled back and forth on his perch.

At home, Willie crouched in his cage on the dining table and looked around. Peaches and Maggie flew in. There was some pecking through the bars but nothing worse.

After dinner, Peaches and Maggie settled down to sleep on top of the medicine cabinet, while I set Willie's cage between theirs on my desk. I covered it with a towel, then peeked underneath. Willie was wriggling under the washcloth Jill had left on the cage floor.

At least he had a familiar place to sleep before he dove into life with his new family.

TIFF DU JOUR

Willie's arrival united Peaches and Maggie as nothing else had. From the first morning I let them loose together, they treated Willie as the common enemy. When he landed near one of them and lowered his head for grooming, they pecked and chased him away. Even though Willie was a little larger, he backed off, disadvantaged in a home already claimed by other birds.

The two-against-one tiffs that occurred on my shoulders made it clear that Peaches and Maggie didn't want to divide my attention any further. There were no longer enough hands to go around. Someone was bound to feel slighted.

Fortunately, Peaches and Maggie spent hours under the bathroom sinks and napping on the medicine cabinet, giving Willie time to snuggle inside my shirt. I would peek in and find him asleep with his head on my chest.

This was more a work-around than a cure, and it didn't always work. One morning, Maggie left Peaches in the bathroom and flew to the living room, where Willie and I were playing with a pen. Maggie hurled himself at Willie, starting an all-out screaming, feather-pulling fight.

I grabbed Willie with a towel. Maggie bit one of my fingers. Peaches flew in to cheer him on from the curtain rod.

Maggie grabbed my other hand and held on. When I tossed him into the air, he let go, then flew after me. I ducked to protect Willie as I hustled down the hall and closed the bedroom door behind us.

I left Willie on the chair and went back to the living room, sucking blood from the bites. Peaches and Maggie were zooming around, screeching. Dodging them, I went into the kitchen and came out with the broom, one of those hated objects in the same category as balloons and brimmed hats. All I had to do was show it to them. They retreated to their cages, where I left them to think over what they'd done.

When I opened the bedroom door, Willie shot down the front of my shirt. I made some chamomile tea and sat down at the living room table, petting him through the fabric and picking up yanked-out feathers. Once again, I wondered if we were going to live out the scenario that Dr. Ramsay had portrayed, with cages at opposite ends of the house and alternate times loose.

Mutual avoidance wasn't my first choice, but perhaps it was the best we could do.

CERRO GRANDE

Willie wasn't the only complication in our lives. I was passing Ashley Pond in Los Alamos after work when I heard distinctive bird cries. Two dozen willets--long-legged shorebirds—circled overhead. Their reddish-brown summer feathers flashed in the lowering sun.

I parked, phoned my bird-lover friend, Jean, and crossed Central Avenue. The willets settled on the other side of the pond. My field guide confirmed they were migrating north.

Neither Jean nor I had ever seen willets at the park. Wouldn't it make sense, I asked, for them to stop at the reservoir, away from traffic and people?

Jean said they probably didn't like the smoke. A controlled burn on Bandelier National Monument land had gotten out of hand. Jean and I could see it if we pushed our wind-whipped hair out of our faces. Under normal circumstances, unusual birds excited me, but the out-of-place willets and the fire glowing against the darkening mountains were ominous.

* * *

Willie's and the parakeets' departures a couple of months earlier were fortuitous. Jill and her daughters didn't have to cram the big cage into the car when Los Alamos was evacuated. After taking refuge with friends in Tesuque, they watched TV coverage of their home burning to the ground.

Only news and emergency personnel were allowed on The Hill. Usually, I'd have relished time off. Instead, I watched through binoculars as the blaze ran up canyons and burned homes and Lab buildings. Smoke turned green, purple, and yellow, depending on what chemicals the flames encountered.

Payday arrived, and I couldn't reach the nonprofit's new director. None of the people I could reach knew where he was. I made an executive decision and called the local Federal Express facility to see if I could pick up our payroll service's package.

Throughout the weekend, co-workers came to collect their checks, bringing spouses and children. Displaced friends arrived, too. Our home became a refuge by being in the broadcast shadow of the mountains and without cable—a relief for those overwhelmed by 24/7 fire coverage.

Healthy snacks and soothing music were on the agenda. So was parrot therapy. After some initial shyness, the birds landed on people's heads, groomed their hair, nibbled their ears, and walked up and down their arms. No one complained about the occasional dollop of bird poop on their clothing.

Our visitors sidetracked the birds' usual animosities. Willie performed his two tricks. He landed on my hammer dulcimer and plucked at the strings with his beak, screeching and whistling to accompany his modal masterpiece.

When he was finished, he sneezed. Someone said, "Bless you," and he sneezed again to get the same response. He went on like this for minutes at a time, providing a charming distraction for people who didn't know whether they still had homes.

SIGNS OF LIFE

The wind finally drove the Cerro Grande fire onto the forested slopes beyond Los Alamos. Firefighters and tanker planes beat it down to smoldering tree roots that wouldn't be extinguished until the monsoons began two months later.

In aerial newspaper photos, the burned neighborhoods look bombed. It was a sobering irony, given the town's atomic history.

When the general public was allowed in, I drove GW up The Hill early in the morning to prepare for the office's reopening the following day. I was stunned, as I crested the mesa, by how dead and black my beloved mountains looked.

I held my breath as I approached the major intersection of Trinity and Diamond. Suddenly, dozens of turkey vultures glided down Los Alamos Canyon. I couldn't imagine how, but their roost trees had been spared. More than ever, these birds that ate the dead were harbingers of life.

This shot of optimism buoyed me as I drove through the destruction. Portions of the Western Area and North Community—about ten percent of the housing in town—had been reduced to foundations and greasy ash. Plumbing pipes had melted or been vaporized. Cars with their paint fried off stood glued to the pavement by melted tires.

Disoriented songbirds hopped from one scorched tree to another, calling for mates and unfledged young. A man and woman in their thirties sat on the tailgate of their pickup, arms around each other, staring at the empty space where their house had stood.

Then I came across a miracle: an old green house with eaves perfect for catching cinders. The yard was full of dry pine needles, and trees grew close to the wood-clad walls and over the wood-shingled roof. Not a tree stood unburned as far as I could see, and not another house stood at all, but the green one hadn't been singed.

Two weeks later, I attended a fire-safety talk and asked the brave men who had served on the fire line about it.

"We know that house," one of them said.

The others just shook their heads.

THE MONTANA CURE

Peaches' and Maggie's continued antagonism toward Willie

seemed as inexplicable as the green house. Six months after Willie arrived, Joe commented on it after watching me leap out of my chair and shake three screaming, biting parrots out of my shirt. They flew to separate curtain rods and preened their ruffled feathers between agitated squawks: He *started it! No*, he *did!*

I wondered aloud what I'd been thinking in private: Would it help if I got away for a while? Without the object of their territorial tussles, the parrots might sort things out. Elida and Rod had invited me to their retirement home west of Missoula, Montana, and I decided to take them up on it.

* * *

Thirty-six hours on a Greyhound taught me a lot, starting with how small a box on wheels could feel when four small children threw screaming tantrums at once.

The rest of the time, the bus was a rolling state of grace. The changing scenery refreshed me. I meditated and spent hours absorbing Joseph Campbell's *The Power of Myth tapes*, my favorite music, and the *Poets in Person* series.

Elida and Rod picked me up in Missoula. The smells of wild grass, pines, and berry bushes sharpened as we drove up Ninemile Valley. Elida had computer-designed the house they planned to build, but at that point, they were living in the original four-hundred-square-foot cabin and sleeping in the loft. Their travel trailer would be my refuge.

Elida showed off the creek (*crick*, Rod insisted) that tumbled among tall pines. Birds serenaded us—merganser ducks, big pileated woodpeckers, Clark's nutcrackers, chickadees, flickers, and nuthatches.

That evening, white-tailed does and fawns browsed through the yard. A black bear had killed and eaten a doe a few yards from the cabin. Bones lay scattered in the trampled grass, one shoulder blade poking up like a white flag.

We watched Rod's video of a grizzly, studied its paw prints circling the travel trailer. My shiver was as delicious as the one that tingled my spine when the Ninemile wolf pack began its howling chorus.

* * *

A couple of days into my visit, Joe's excited voice came over the phone. Willie had landed on the back of a dining room chair and sidled up to Peaches. They had groomed each other while Maggie stood on the table and watched without aggression.

"Three cheers for the Montana cure!" I said. We hung up, and I thanked the Green Parrot Goddess with all my heart.

* * *

I came home to a flock dynamic built on acceptance and bonding. The parrots had sealed a truce that grew into a lasting if not perfect peace. There were still brief skirmishes, but it wasn't unusual for me to be reading at the living room table with Peaches perched on my head and Maggie and Willie each claiming a shoulder. The birds were seeing each other in a better light.

EYES OF THE BEHOLDER

The last time Dr. Ramsay had seen Peaches, Maggie, and Willie, she had complimented me on their good condition. Their bright colors and shiny feathers meant I was doing the right things with their diet.

Almost a year after my autumn visit to Montana, her words came back to haunt me. The birds' feathers were taking on a dingy, yellowish-brown tinge. Were they passing some illness around or suffering from a nutritional imbalance? I read my conure care books and pet bird magazines and searched the Internet but couldn't figure it out. They were eating well and were energetic, curious, and full of play. I put off taking them to Dr. Ramsay but kept an eye on them.

Something else disturbing was happening: The Northern New Mexico air was the color of the smog that had driven me out of Southern California. Los Alamos was starting to look like Los Angeles.

On a day off, I sat at the living room table with my road atlas.

"Where do you think we ought to move?" I asked the birds. "Chama's nice. What about Pagosa Springs? Maybe Durango?"

Peaches chased my finger, making the map harder to decipher than it already was. I couldn't read the small-print town names with the drugstore magnifying glasses I'd used for years. Computers were giving me so much trouble that I had bought stronger glasses.

Driving home one night, as I waited to make a left turn, oncoming headlights splattered the world with glaring white. I sat with my foot on the brake while my heart thudded and my breath came in gulps. The effect passe, but my anxiety didn't.

The ophthalmologists' group that took my insurance didn't have an open appointment for a month. There was nothing to do but pack for my second bus trip to Elida and Rod's and tell Joe to call me if the birds showed signs of illness. I left Dr. Ramsay's phone number on a bright pink three-by-five card next to the phone.

9/11

Elida and Rod had had their house built with a door into the cabin, where I slept. In the dim morning light of September 11, 2001, Rod woke me and described the unimaginable: Hijacked commercial jets had rammed the World Trade Center; one of the towers had collapsed.

I snapped awake and dressed, praying for the dead, the injured, and those who had lost loved ones. As we watched the second tower fall and saw film of the Pentagon crash and the downed jet in Pennsylvania, I knew I would have to do the hard spiritual practice of praying for whoever was behind the attacks.

I was grateful that we were safe but worried about how close Joe, the parrots, and many friends were to Los Alamos National Laboratory. What if the Lab was on the hit list? Joe's voice and the birds' squawks over the phone reassured me only a little.

When the TV networks started repeating the same news, Elida and I walked down to the gazebo by the creek and had a nice, long meditation. What a relief to wash away the morning's insanity and suffering in waves of breath, breeze, and birdsong.

* * *

Three days later, Joe picked me up at the Santa Fe bus station and drove me home. Peaches, Maggie, and Willie looked worse than when I'd left, and I said so. Joe insisted he didn't see any change.

Are you blind? I thought but knew the problem wasn't his. Elida and Rod had looked jaundiced when we said goodbye in Missoula. On the trip south, streetlights had blurred like moonlight behind clouds. Traffic signals had created cottony halos, and headlights had burst into whiteouts.

SENSES

Two days after I arrived home, the ophthalmologist shone her penlight into one of my dilated eyes, then the other. Each time, the room flared to featureless white. She couched her diagnosis in terms a lay person could understand: "Eew, big, ugly cataracts."

At my age? Both my parents had had cataracts, but not until they were in their seventies. I sat in the waiting room while the dilating drops wore off so I could drive home, repeating, *Okay, I'm fifty-five years old, and I have cataracts.*

Then I remembered to be relieved. I'd feared something more serious—macular degeneration, glaucoma, tumors on my optic nerves or visual cortex, or some disease with a long Latin name that I wouldn't be able to pronounce because I couldn't read it.

Driving at night was out. For reasons no one knew, the cataracts were growing at an accelerated rate. People at work were startled when they caught glimpses of them. The eerie flashes in the bathroom mirror unnerved me every day.

I thought of the dogs and cats I'd seen with milky, opaque lenses. There were no sight-saving surgeries for them. What about parrots? An Internet search, assisted by a magnifying glass, revealed that they could develop cataracts, too. Causes ranged from vitamin deficiencies to lightning strikes to radiation.

* * *

The earliest surgical opening was two months after my diagnosis.

Less than half-way to the date, I stranded myself in Santa Fe on a brilliant autumn morning, unable to read street signs or determine how far ahead the next car was.

I managed to get GW to the Chevy dealership for some scheduled repair work. The service manager had a driver take me to the ophthalmologist's office, where a technician made laser measurements of my eyes for artificial lenses. I took a cab home, called my supervisor, and told her I couldn't drive to work, much less do my work.

During my hiatus, I played my guitar, phoned friends, and listened to movies I had seen before and could visualize from the music and dialog. I went outside only before dawn and at dusk. Sunlight, even filtered through elm limbs, blinded me; I kept the curtains closed.

As I sat in the shadows with the parrots, I wondered what senses humans had given up on the evolutionary path to color vision and depth perception. Semi-blindness gave me some hints. My hearing and field sense—the awareness of objects around me—became acute. I heard my footsteps echoing off the walls and furniture. Objects emanated palpable energy fields, pressing pictures into my skin.

The parrots might not have understood the change, but they knew I was different. They became very solicitous, spending hours perched on me or nearby and giving me extra grooming and birdie sweet talk. I moved slowly, and they stayed out of my way until I sat down. Then they love-mobbed me.

I harbored a curiosity I didn't tell a soul about: What might it be like to let myself descend into complete blindness and then, through the miracle of surgery, be reborn into light and color? It sounded like quite a trip.

* * *

The ten-minute surgery was trippy enough. The surgeon inserted a vibrating tube through a tiny incision in my anesthetized right eye, broke up my cataracted lens, and sucked out the debris. This stimulated my optic nerve and replaced the scattered white light from the overhead fixture with a dancing color show. When the soft plastic lens unfurled, and I could *see*.

Marian, the friend who drove me home, listened while I raved about the colors of the sky—BLUE!—the trees—GOLD!—and the Virginia creeper that was turning RED!

After she left, I caught sight of myself in the tin-framed mirror in the office/bird room and sucked in a breath. The many small facial lines I hadn't been able to see were visible now. Others had seen me age by degrees. To me, years had been added to my face overnight.

I sat down at my desk and covered my left eye. With my right, I studied the parrots. Their feathers were bright and vibrant, their eyes clear and lively.

Two days later, I went back to work, arranging my time so that I didn't have to drive at night until after the second surgery. I thrilled at the sight of the Sangre de Cristo Mountains, the Jemez, the Rio Grande. And, of course, my feathered companions.

The one with hair on his chest—that was getting to be a different matter.

FUSS AND FEATHERS

Joe looked older, too, and he was more colorful. He sat in my living room a week after my second cataract surgery, face flushed RED!, making agitated gestures as he railed about an instructor's minor violation of a college rule.

This was his fourth or fifth retelling, each angrier than the last. I had been sitting on the daybed, propped up against one cushion, my work-weary feet on another, when he started. Though his anger was aimed at someone else, it hammered me into a slouch.

I could barely keep my eyes open. Then I couldn't.

When I came to, Joe was still rattling on. He hadn't noticed my absence, which might have been seconds or minutes. He leaned forward to propel a question into my face: "Don't you think that's wrong?"

"The rule seems reasonable." I sounded bleary from my brief

nap.

"Was I out of line?"

"I'm sure you were appropriate," I hedged, knowing he had made a noisy scene.

"That's really what happened. You know I'm incapable of lying."

He took my silence as an invitation to start in again.

"I spent most of my day in front of the copier," I pleaded, "and running up and down the stairs. I'm beat. Maybe we could talk about this tomorrow."

Joe clamped his mouth shut, jumped up, and charged out the door. It was easier to breathe, now that he wasn't taking up all the air. I pulled an afghan over me, grateful for winter's early dark. I wouldn't owe the birds time out of their cages until morning.

My mind wouldn't let me sleep. I hadn't moved far enough from Joe. He rarely said two civil sentences in a row. I felt both sad and glad that he wasn't coming around much. I had hoped that college would focus his energies on challenging subjects. Instead, it exposed him to more people who did things he didn't like.

It wasn't just school. Recently, he'd insisted I wasn't angry enough about an acquaintance's racism. He had topped off that monolog by claiming that 9/11 was the fault of people like me, cowards who hadn't fought to take back the planes.

Then there was his assertion that he couldn't lie. He'd told a whopper recently at a neighborhood potluck: "So this guy hits Cappy's truck, and it rolls over three times, and she's unconscious when the paramedics roll up."

I'd confronted him as we walked home.

"You were in shock," he said. "You don't know what happened."

My eyebrows shot up. "And you do because you were there?"

Joe went on the offensive, making one of those demands calculated to shift attention from himself by striking at the heart of my insecurities: "Why should we stay together? What do you do for me?"

In the past, I'd refused to answer on the grounds that the question was too manipulative. This time, I had a comeback: "I put up with you."

Joe's fist snapped out. He pulled his punch right in front of my nose, sending a puff of air across my cheeks. "That's not enough."

It's more than you deserve, I'd thought, but didn't want to sound mean spirited and aggravate him. Besides, I'd rationalized, I was imperfect, and he put up with me.

I let the memory go now, not wanting it to be the thought I fell asleep to. I focused on the good the following day might bring. I pictured Peaches standing on my finger, nibbling my closed eyelids. After he bathed, he would let me inhale the scent that I could register only up close, something like a damp, green forest. The parrots and I would share breakfast and doze in the light streaming through the living room windows.

LITTLE GREEN MAN FANTASY

All the good I hoped for blessed me the next day. Then, after Peaches and Willie had gone to sleep, Joe arrived, with no apparent purpose but to rage at me. It was impossible to follow his double-talk. As he shouted into my face, I became so frightened that I wanted to dissociate. The only thing that kept me in my body was the fear that he would get physical. I needed to be present enough to protect myself and the birds.

Joe bragged for the hundredth time that he operated best in chaos, and all at once I understood why. Confused and frightened people were easy to intimidate.

It worked on me. I sat frozen. Maggie was more courageous. He gripped the shoulder of my blouse and faced Joe, tense and alert. My feathered protector reminded me of the high-school sweetheart who would take a ready stance when my drunken father threatened me.

I sat at the dining table after Joe stormed out, head in my hands, trying to remember why I had thought this relationship was a good idea. It was unnerving to think that I might have taken comfort in the familiar angry-man scenario.

I didn't have time to follow the thought. As soon as Joe slammed the birdlock door, Maggie sidled across my shoulder, nestled against my neck, and murmured in my ear.

My heart leaped to life. The contrast between them was so strong that it triggered a fantasy. I grabbed a pen and paper and wrote down the outline:

A woman (a fictionalized version of me) in a deteriorating relationship (a fictionalized version of ours) buys a small green parrot for company. She reads poetry to him; he quotes back the most meaningful passages. They eat, wash dishes, and shower together. They sing and call to one another from opposite ends of the house. (Incorporate Peaches' and my "Morning Has Broken" duet.)

The man comes to the door one night and finds the woman wearing a low-cut evening dress and high heels, her hair piled elegantly with a jewel-studded clip. The lights are off, and candles burn on the dining table. (All right, electric candles. The burning kind are artifacts of the woman's past--too much risk of parrot flambé.)

The man is cruel to her, and the woman turns him away. As he leaves, he catches sight of her through the window, dancing to romantic music. She turns, and he sees the parrot standing on the scooped neck of her dress, head resting over her heart, wings caressing her as she strokes his green back and long red tail.

The lyrics they're dancing to mimic a 1930s song: And I seem to find the happiness I seek / when we're out together dancing beak to beak.

I put down my pen, leaned my head against Maggie's, and made grateful kissing noises. In a clearer frame of mind, I confronted the perversity of staying with Joe.

It took all my concentration to keep from drifting back into fantasy. I'd recovered some of my strength after the accident but still imagined friends showing up to move me out, with or without my consent, because I couldn't or wouldn't do it on my own.

PUSH AND SHOVE

Between increasingly frequent rages, Joe acted as though nothing ugly had happened. We had the occasional passionate time in bed, and he would insist I was the perfect woman for him. Then I wouldn't see him for days, until he had built up steam behind some new upset.

It was hard to contemplate giving up someone who wanted me, however sporadic the reinforcement. I was forced to think about it, though, when Peaches began picking his feathers in earnest.

Joe had started speaking angrily to the parrots—*at* them was more like it—and shaking his fist, insisting, "I'm bigger than you."

I would try to jolly him into a better mood. "They weigh four ounces. Everyone's bigger than they are."

Joe would glare at me.

Nothing that had ever worked for Peaches' feather picking worked now. I was wishing for parrot Prozac by the time a pet store employee suggested hemp seeds.

What would I get if I planted them, I asked, envisioning a pot of, well, pot. He said it wasn't that kind of hemp, that it would smoke like old rope.

I didn't ask how he knew, just bought a bag and mixed the seeds with Peaches' food. He sampled one now and then and ignored the rest. I crushed them and mashed them into fruit, but he wasn't fooled.

I changed his toys and rearranged his dishes, perches, and playthings. I gave him one-on-one attention every day, while Maggie and Willie complained from their cages. The combination worked, sort of. Peaches stopped picking, then started, again and again. He wouldn't pluck a single feather for weeks. Then gray down feathers would poke through.

My main solution was keeping the birds caged when Joe came around. He never physically injured them, anymore than he did me, but *physical* wasn't the only way to hurt a person—or a parrot.

* * *

Peaches was probably reacting to me, too. I was on edge and hurt by Joe's meanness. My ability to bounce back was as flat as an old tennis ball. A couple of times, I took my stress out on the birds, slapping their cage tops and yelling at them to be quiet.

This wasn't like me, wasn't who I wanted to be. Ashamed, I asked the parrots' forgiveness, prayed to the Green Parrot Goddess to make me a better bird mom, and made living amends by improving my behavior.

I also donated to The Wildlife Center, Dr. Ramsay's rehab organization, in the birds' names. There was nothing like money going out the door to sharpen my consciousness and my conscience.

Peaches, Maggie, and Willie were more forgiving than I had any right to expect.

OVER

As Christmas approached, I realized how worn down I was from living off balance. The message I thought I was giving Joe was that I would stick with him, no matter what. Maybe the message he got was that he could behave badly with no negative consequences. He could hurt me, and I would come back for more.

We ate Christmas Eve dinner with Jill, her girls, and some friends of theirs at a Santa Fe restaurant before taking the traditional Canyon Road walk. The night was clear, starry, and crisp. The roofs of the century-old buildings were outlined in *faralitos*—paper bags with an inch or two of sand inside to hold them open and upright, a candle nestled inside. These lighted the way for the Christ child to bring peace and goodwill. Bonfires danced shadows against the walls. Gallery owners offered hot cider, and people sang carols in misty exhales.

It was a perfect New Mexico holiday for everyone but Joe. The crowd triggered a frantic hyper-vigilance that made it impossible for him to relax and enjoy. I didn't understand why he was so wound up but realized I could offer him an out: "You could drive GW home, and Jill could drop me off later."

His face twisted. "And leave you here with nobody to protect you?"

"From . . . ?"

Joe scanned the crowd. Suddenly, he charged a scraggly-haired man in his fifties who sprawled in the shadows against an adobe wall, sipping whiskey from a bottle. Carolers struck up a rousing "Jingle Bells," so I couldn't hear what Joe yelled. He seemed to be playing "I'm bigger than you" with the person least able to cause trouble.

Joe kept himself reined in until near the end of the walk, when he ordered me to march straight into a group of people coming up a narrow street. When they and I stepped aside to make room for each other, he sneered, "That's why people like them think they can get away with it: People like you let them."

I whistled the *Twilight Zone* theme under my breath. The episode had my fear of angry men stamped all over it. Yet, instead of freezing or crying, I felt my mind clear. Joe would make a scene about anything because that was what he wanted to do. It wasn't about me.

Suddenly, there wasn't enough left at the end of my rope to tie a knot and hold on. As we reached the car, I mentally put words to what I felt: *This relationship is over.*

I felt not a flutter of reaction—none of the regret, remorse, grief, or denial I expected. Their absence said a lot.

For once, Joe didn't criticize my driving. He sat with his arms crossed, brows in glower mode, mouth pressed into a furious scowl. The rage emanating from his body felt as if it could melt the ice from the windows.

Instead of coming in to share my bed, as we'd planned, Joe slammed the car door and huffed off to his place.

"Merry Christmas," I called after him. I waited until his trailer door banged shut and said out loud, "This relationship is over."

I had no reaction. I'd cried all the tears I had for Joe.

CONFIRMATION

I sat with the idea of breaking up with Joe, just to make sure. A few days after Christmas, he invited me over to listen to some music he'd been working on.

I regretted going almost immediately. He had another furious outburst. I felt trapped in his narrow trailer and had trouble breathing. My body shut down. I barely had the energy to shuffle back to my house. But shuffle I did, without a word of goodbye and with Joe shouting after me, "If you leave now, you can never come back!"

Promise? I thought, surprised at my boldness and cheered by the realization that he might save me the strain of breaking up by doing it himself.

* * *

I was all right until I woke up the following morning, lying on my back on the day bed in the living room. Peaches, Maggie, and Willie were squawking for attention on the other side of the wall.

I kept trying to get up, but my body wouldn't respond. I thought to call for help but discovered I couldn't speak. My breath came in short, panicked gulps as I stared at the ceiling, certain that the previous day's stress had triggered a stroke. My mind still worked, though, expressing my panic: *I might be paralyzed for life. What will happen to me? What will become of my beloved parrots?*

To my relief, a more reasonable possibility occurred: I might be experiencing hysterical paralysis, a protective catatonia that prevented me from crossing the road to Joe's place or answering the door and letting him into mine.

Whatever the cause of the paralysis, a calm clarity suffused me. Over the next couple of hours, I was able to draw some voluntary deep breaths, then move my hands and feet. Around noon, I pushed myself out of bed.

Speech still eluded me. I shuffled to the dining table, tried writing, and discovered I could only print, my letters as large and labored as a second grader's. At least I was able to get down on paper what had happened. That might be useful if I needed medical—or mental—help.

By dusk, I could speak. I phoned Jill and then Nischa, a longtime friend from California, and told them what had happened. I promised to break up with Joe. Accountable to friends, I was less likely to chicken out.

Finally, I let the parrots out of their cages. They flew through the house, then settled on me, preening my face and hair and murmuring their concern. It seemed clear that they had known, throughout the long day, that I was in distress.

I made the same promise to them that I had to Nischa and Jill, adding, "You deserve better."

* * *

I took the emotional numbness that followed for the calm that resulted from making the right decision, and that might have been part of it. Wherever it came from, it evaporated the next afternoon as I sat on Joe's porch, trembling as I struggled to say that I couldn't tolerate his hurtful behavior.

I was still shaking when I went to bed. Joe had ended the conversation by saying, "Should I describe how I would break your neck?"

AFTERMATH

I thought that would be the end of it, so it was a shock to learn that Joe didn't think we'd broken up. He believed we had entered a negotiating phase. He showed up to press his claim almost every time I came out my front door or arrived in the car. He alternately criticized and wooed me in monologs that left no space for me to wedge a word in.

One day, for the first time, he told me he loved me. Another, he insisted I was beautiful, making sure I knew how that flew in the face of his deceased mother's view of beauty, the basic tenets of which were *skinny* and *stylish,* two words no one ever used to describe me.

I let my actions speak for me. While Joe leaned against his car and watched, I installed a new front door lock. He could get in, but he would have to up the ante by breaking down the door or shattering a window. I'd told the park manager and my neighbors what was going on, and they had promised to keep an eye on my place.

At three o'clock one morning, I got up for a drink of fruit juice and turned on the hall light. Within seconds, the phone rang. I picked it up, thinking it might be a friend in distress. Of course, it was Joe with his repeated demand—"We have to talk"—as though *he* hadn't been.

I hung up. The phone didn't stop ringing until I turned out the light.

After that, I ate dinner, read, and made phone calls in the office/bird room. The company was wonderful, and the closed door prevented light from showing on any of the curtains facing the road.

* * *

Surely, I thought, Joe would give up. He kept accosting me, though, until a Sunday night in February. He stood outside my gate and shouted, "Maybe I should tear down the birdlock so you can haul your house somewhere else."

I saw every blink of the electric clock that night. In the morning, I called my supervisor at home and told her I would be late to work because I had something to do that couldn't wait. I would tell her the details later.

My first impulse was to drive toward work, in case Joe was watching. Bravely or foolishly, I took my courage in both hands and steered GW toward the county courthouse. I kept checking my rearview mirror, expecting to see his car careening after me.

* * *

At the courthouse, I went up to the domestic law section clerk and asked for an application for a restraining order.

The nineteen-year-old popped her gum, looked me over, and asked, "Is he beating you up?"

"Not physically."

"Then you can't get a restraining order." She slapped her hand down on a stack of forms.

I sagged inside, then realized I was dealing with a person whose only power in her job came from her ability to say no. Making myself stand straighter, I said, "Please give me the paperwork, anyway."

She popped her gum. "You might as well forget it."

I gave her a hard look. Anxious and sleep-deprived, I may have appeared a little crazy. She shrugged and handed over the forms.

As I sat on a bench to fill them out, I kept glancing up, expecting to see Joe raging toward me. How long I'd allowed myself to live in fear! Whether the court approved my application or not, the paperwork confirmed my intention to start taking care of myself and my birds.

I was bringing the forms back to the clerk when a middle-aged woman stepped out of an inner hall. She glanced at my paperwork, offered her hand, and introduced herself as Dolores, victim's advocate. I had no idea there were such people. It would be over the top to say that the skies had parted and an angel had appeared, but that was how it felt.

Dolores helped me file the papers and arranged to have a temporary restraining order served. Then she took me into an empty hearing room and described, from her own experience, the confusion, intimidation, and fear I was going through.

"How long have you been with him?" she asked.

I flushed with shame. "Almost ten years." I gave her a thumbnail sketch of how hard the accident had made it to get out.

"Well, better late than never. I'll be at the hearing with you. You shouldn't have to go through that alone."

No one should, I thought, but I'd taken it for granted that I would have to. That was how beaten down and isolated I'd let myself become.

When I left, nearly in tears from relief, Dolores was talking to the nineteen-year-old clerk. "The State of New Mexico considers psychological abuse to be every bit as serious as physical abuse. Don't you *ever . . .*"

That was what I wanted the restraining order to say to Joe: *Don't you ever.*

SERVED

The next few days were a long held breath while I waited for the Sheriff's Department to serve Joe with the temporary restraining order.

It was a good time to stay away from home. Between work and the accounting class I was taking, I was driving to Los Alamos five days a week. I worked late and heated up dinner in the break-room microwave.

On Tuesday, I attended a support group for people recovering from the effects of loved ones' alcoholism. Not only had I been raised by alcoholics, but Joe fit the description of a dry drunk: someone who didn't drink but behaved as though he did.

Wednesday, it was writers' group and dinner at Chin Shan Inn. The kind family that ran the restaurant let us stay while they washed the dishes and vacuumed the floor, after which we carried our conversations to the parking lot. The owners turned off the lights and went home, leaving protective incense smoldering by the front door. I pulled the smoke deep into my lungs.

I kept a low profile at home, lights out as I wheeled GW into his parking space, only night lights on in the house as I gave the parrots special food treats and lots of attention.

Then I checked my answering machine. I was getting calls at work from panicked friends who weren't able to leave messages. The machine took twenty calls. Joe filled it every day with angry demands.

My phone often rang as I opened the door. Previously, I'd been afraid to anger Joe by not picking up. Now, talking to him might give him ammunition against the restraining order. Judging from his messages, he hadn't been served.

On Friday, there was only one message from Joe, growled through clenched teeth: "So *this* is why you've been avoiding me. *This* is why you won't answer your phone."

I wanted to sigh with relief, but fear jammed the air in my chest. Would he retaliate against me, my vehicle, my house, my parrots? My imagination lit up with possibilities. After some relaxing breaths, I made myself turn on all the lights I needed. Whatever happened, I was through slinking around in my own home.

ESCAPE VELOCITY

I had freed myself. The trick now was to keep accelerating toward a healthier life.

Joe made it easy for me to want nothing to do with him. Every day, I found some fresh bunch of trash that he had dumped in my front yard in the middle of the night or while I was at work: old window shades; enough scrap lumber to build a deck; the plastic storage drawers he had said he wanted, thanked me for, and never used.

I noticed that he didn't bring back the clothes and the ergonomic desk chair I had given him for Christmas, in hopes that they would somehow improve his mood. This wasn't about returning gifts.

The stream of trash seemed endless. Where did he get it? Was he taking it out of the trailer park's dumpster? It seemed useless to call the Sheriff's Department. They would have to catch him in the act.

Loading the trash into GW and hauling it to the local refuse transfer station was a good way to work off my anger. With therapeutic delight, I yelled as I hurled things into the big metal bins.

I didn't haul so much as a scrap of paper to the transfer station without first taking pictures as evidence for the hearing, where I hoped to be granted a permanent restraining order. I locked the photos in my safe deposit box, along with tapes of Joe's threatening phone messages.

* * *

The court notified me of the hearing date, then rescheduled at the last moment because the hearing officer's elderly mother was having an emergency appendectomy. I was disappointed but kept to my routine. I worked, wrote, went to writers' group, and spent as much time as I could with the parrots.

The birds responded by hanging out on me, grooming me,

whispering in my ears, and sleeping on me when I napped. It was amazing how safe I felt, guarded by three four-ounce parrots. I did, however, follow friends' advice and kept an overnight bag and a change of clothes in my car, in case I had to grab the birds and run.

Except for dumping trash in my yard, Joe stayed away. Any time I came out my door, though—to scatter bird seed, water the Virginia creeper, or get something out of my car—he came out and stood with his arms crossed and glowered.

I must have been recovering. It wasn't easy for him to trigger my old fear anymore.

UNEXPECTED LOVE

While I waited for the rescheduled hearing, I got a call from my longtime friend, Rob, who had just returned to Los Alamos from California. Over dinner at a local restaurant, he related his extended visit with his mother, siblings, and daughters.

I told him about ending my relationship with Joe. In the seventeen years Rob and I had known and been attracted to each other, this was the first time we had both been unattached. We were free to fall into each other's arms, and fall we did.

In the embrace that began this new phase, I breathed deeply of the scents that so defined him: sawdust, automotive grease, cigarette smoke, WD-40, and the Ivory soap he used to wash his hands and lubricate stuck drawers. It was a heady combination.

Rob rolled out of bed the next morning and did half a dozen one-handed pushups—not bad for a man in his early sixties. I'd seen him do this before, though not naked.

* * *

Later, Rob took a stroll in front of the house, sipping coffee. I was cutting vegetables for the birds' breakfast when a streak of motion caught my eye. I spun to the window to discover Joe, crimson faced, charging down the road.

Rob backed up three steps. Joe must have seen something in the move, because he stopped. I heard them yelling but couldn't make out what they said. Joe stomped back to his place.

Later, over coffee-shop sausage and pancakes, Rob told me, "Never back away from an attacker unless you're getting ready to hurt him."

I raised an eyebrow. That must have been what Joe had sensed—not retreat but preparation.

"You know he's a coward, don't you?" Rob said.

I stopped with a forkful of cantaloupe halfway to my mouth, my insides still vibrating from their confrontation. "When I was a little girl, my mother told me that if I stood up to a bully, his fear would make him back down. She never told me what to do about the bully whose fear made him lash out."

"He's all bluster. He's playing on your anxieties."

It was good to hear a man's perspective, though I didn't quite believe it yet.

"He didn't used to be this way, not all the time." The excuse soured in my mouth, and I said so.

Rob didn't criticize. "If a person doesn't get help, his problems get worse."

The same applied to my problems. If I hadn't shaken loose of Joe, his effects on my parrots and me would still have been worsening. They might yet. Joe made himself seem unpredictable enough that he might harm the birds or use the threat of doing so.

Rob assured me I had nothing to worry about. "He doesn't have the courage."

"Smart man." I sat straighter, then leaned across the table, suddenly energized. "Do you know what I'd do to someone who hurt my birds?"

"Yeah," he said with that adorable Robert Redford grin. "I'll bet Joe does, too."

ORDER IN THE COURT

I had a lot to think about in the following weeks. Previously, I'd needed time alone between relationships to get my feet back under my heart. This was different. During my years with Joe, I'd had plenty of solitude and grief.

Having more years behind me than ahead made me either brave or foolish enough to go for a life with Rob. I barely thought about how discouraged I had been at the end of my relationships with Perry and Joe, how I'd figured I should give up on men and become an old maid with fifty parrots. My natural optimism soared. One of my dearest male friends seemed the perfect partner.

* * *

One of the many things I appreciated about Rob was what a stand-up guy he was. Like my angel Dolores, the victims' advocate, he didn't think I should have to face the hearing alone. He drove me to the courthouse and sat behind me with Dolores. Their support was a grace that allowed me to feel strong and calm.

Friends had suggested I let Joe take all the rope he needed to hang himself. It proved good advice. As the hearing officer entered, he blurted out a demand that she eject Rob.

The hearing officer leaned across her desk and looked Joe hard in the eye. "This is a public proceeding. Strangers off the street can attend. I'm not ejecting anyone."

I had one of those cloud-parting realizations: She had dealt with dozens of guys like Joe, and *she wasn't afraid.* Her confidence gave me a shot of courage as she laid out the ground rules: Each of us would have an opportunity to tell our side and to respond to each other's allegations; no one was allowed to interrupt.

I worked down the list I had written, emphasizing that I had told Joe I didn't want to see him anymore and that he had failed to respect my wishes. I described his threats and showed the trash photos.

Then I started the tape of Joe's angry phone calls. About half way through, the hearing officer motioned me to turn it off. Leaning forward again, she told Joe, "If you're a good boy from now on, I won't make it my personal goal to see you go to prison for telephone harassment. All right, let's hear your side."

Joe rambled without notes, sneering his way through a description of our breakup. He protested that he had told me he loved me, then paused and looked at the hearing officer, as if he expected her to forgive his bad behavior.

The hearing officer kept a neutral face. I tried to do the same, despite being amazed all over again that Joe had dismissed my insistence on breaking up. He didn't mention his trash and threats.

"All right," the hearing officer said, "I've heard enough."

My breath caught. What if I hadn't presented my case clearly enough? What would I do if she ruled in Joe's favor? What would Joe do?

The hearing officer said, "I declare that acts of domestic abuse have occurred, and I grant a permanent restraining order." She read the terms. Basically, we were to leave each other alone.

Joe stormed out. I sagged into Rob's and Dolores's arm. We gave Joe time to get to his car and leave while we discussed the court-mandated counseling that he and I were to participate in—separately, of course.

"The idea," Dolores said, "is that we don't want to see you back here again."

She glanced at Rob and smiled as if approving of my better choice. Then she guided us toward what looked like a closet but turned out to be the secret back stairs. She hugged me again and wished me the best.

I figured I had just that in Rob.

OLD FRIENDS

I was so certain of a future with Rob that when an old friend got in touch and asked if I was single, I told him I was in the best relationship of my life.

The contact began with a phone call from Dianne in California, asking if she could give my e-mail address to Dennis. He had been her partner when we'd all lived in Long Beach more than fifteen years before.

I remembered Dennis well. He had dancing blue eyes, a moustache, and thick, wavy hair going prematurely gray. The three of us had talked and laughed about everything from cars to cats, parrots to politics, relationships to religion. He and Dianne were lucky to have found each other. I hoped I would one day meet someone as attractive as he was.

A few months after meeting Dennis, I had moved to New Mexico. He and Dianne had explored intentional communities, housing cooperatives, and eco-villages that might offer simple living, shared goals, and like-minded companionship. The one in the central-Arizona mountains that Dennis decided to join was far from the medical help Dianne needed. For that and other reasons, they had broken up.

Under pressure from community leaders, Dennis had severed ties with friends. Dianne had kept track of him through his mother, with whom he'd continued to have some contact. That was how she learned that he had married a woman in the community.

Now, Dianne said, Dennis described the community as a quasi-spiritual mind-control cult whose leaders were adept at snaring people and their money. Every aspect of members' lives were regulated, from where they lived to the kind of work they did. People who didn't like it were subjected to psychological punishment or expulsion.

Dianne believed that Dennis craved this kind of external direction. I thought there was more to it. Dennis wanted to be part of something greater than himself, but he also had a free-spirited side that must have chafed. He knew how the leaders would work on his mind if he complained. Instead, he packed some clothes and, with $2.86 in his pocket and a quarter tank of gas in his car, got out.

He worked in Mesa as an appliance repairman and tried to convince his wife to leave the cult. After they divorced, he bought forty raw acres in southeastern Arizona that he hoped to build on. He was living in his mother's and step-father's Long Beach house while he settled their estates.

After listening to Dianne's tale, I had some reservations about how the cult might have messed up Dennis's mind. Dianne thought he was all right, so I decided to see if he was still that funny, adventurous, intelligent person.

* * *

A few days later, while Willie pried the N and B off the computer keyboard, I read a message that sounded just like the friendly Dennis I remembered. After catching me up on his life, he asked if I was single.

I retrieved the purloined keys and wrote to Dennis about my relationship with Rob. Dennis's return e-mail sounded disappointed, but it seemed we could stay in touch. Neither of us had so many friends that we couldn't use one more.

VIOLATION

I never believed I could hold up the restraining order as a shield. Even within the letter of it, Joe had leeway to taunt me. When I entered or left my house, he swaggered out, leaned against his car, and glared. He did the same to Rob and other friends.

Glaring was one thing; ignoring the order was another. I arrived home from work one evening to find Joe prowling around inside my fenced yard. He looked up when he heard my car and walked back to his trailer.

I went inside, checked on the parrots, and did as the hearing officer had directed: I called the Sheriff's Department.

According to the deputy who came out, Joe claimed he was entitled to buy my mobile home and to inspect the premises. The hearing officer had specified that we could communicate in writing about a possible sale, but Joe had no legal right to my home or to be on my lot. He knew the place well enough. He'd waited until I was due home, as if to show that I couldn't keep him out. It was more harassment.

The deputy took a copy of the restraining order across the road to reiterate its terms to Joe. I sat at my desk and tried to improve my mood by whistling to the parrots but ended up wondering how many times Joe had violated those terms when I wasn't there to witness it.

What was I going to do? Since the hearing officer had declared that abuse had occurred, friends and co-workers had asked if I was going to file criminal charges. I had said no, that as long as he left me alone, all I wanted was out.

The sad thing now was how long I'd imagined living in that charming mobile home in that lovely park for the rest of my life. As Peaches, Maggie, and Willie whistled and squawked from their cages, I wiped away tears for that dead dream.

Then my mood brightened. My next direction was obvious. I was working in Los Alamos, and Rob lived there, so it seemed sensible to move back up The Hill.

I turned to the closet and pulled out the half-dozen packing boxes I'd folded and saved, and the box of packing material that Peaches had dug into and abandoned. I started where I was, with the decorative items on my desk, hoping to do what Joe had suggested: have my home towed somewhere better.

DOUBTS

A couple of weeks later, snow still blanketed the mountains and lingered on the north side of the house. The first spring winds were kicking up, and though leaf buds were a month or more away, my liberated imagination told me it was a new season.

Packed boxes were stacked to the bottoms of the living room windows. Our house smelled of the newspapers friends had saved for me. Peaches, Maggie, and Willie were flying around, inspecting stacks of dishes, framed pictures, and anything else fragile that had to be packed before I could have our mobile home moved.

Once in a while, one of the birds would light on a box and chew a Styrofoam peanut or two, scattering bits across the floor. I let them make all the mess they wanted.

Where was I getting this energy and generous mood? Out from under the constant stress of hurt and fear, I felt as if I'd awakened from a decade-long sleep.

True, there were leftovers from the accident. When I got too tired or stressed, I lapsed into aphasia and might say, "lawn mower" when I meant "refrigerator." My creativity was slow to rebound. On the whole, however, I was feeling physically and emotionally stronger than I had in years.

In need of a break, I washed the newsprint off my hands and sat down at the dining table with a cup of Lemon Zinger tea. Maggie hooked his beak over the rim and hoisted himself up for a sip. When I set the tea bag on the saucer, he shredded the paper and squeezed tea from the leavings.

My smile didn't reach my eyes or my heart. I was fine when I was working at my job, packing, or spending time with Rob, when I couldn't think beyond what I was doing. Rob had mentioned dancing a few times over the years, but I hadn't taken him seriously until he spun me around a dance floor to a live band's version of "Bonaparte's Retreat." A lot of my time with him had that whirlwind quality.

Dancing was only one thing I loved about Rob. He was unfailingly generous. I had mentioned my frustration with the electric heater in the bathroom, where Peaches and Maggie slept. On the same setting, it might be seventy-four degrees or fifty-four. Rob wired up an electronic thermostat. I could set the temperature range to a tenth of a degree.

That memory didn't distract me from the bomb Rob had dropped one day while we were having lunch at his place. He thought we should go back to being Platonic friends. My rice and beans had lumped in my throat.

Why the sudden reversal? He felt overwhelmed. He was picking up remodeling jobs to cover expenses while he refurbished the old Los Alamos building he was living in. His mother's health was failing, and he felt desperate to move back to California.

He hadn't mentioned my going with him. Blood roared in my ears. I had committed to Rob, but he hadn't committed to me.

I hoped that with time, he would. In my mind, that required that we remain lovers. I wanted to put off the possibility of heartbreak, so I'd hidden my trembling hands in my lap and told Rob I hadn't waited seventeen years to give up this love now.

The possibility of heartbreak didn't go away, of course. We continued as lovers, suggesting that he agreed with me, but only because he didn't bring up the issue again. Not talking about it meant that we were resolving nothing.

I sipped my Lemon Zinger and thought, *What choices do I have?* I wasn't going to subject myself to Joe any longer than I had to. No matter what was going on with Rob, I had a job in Los Alamos. That was the stabilizing factor I kept circling back to.

NEW DIGS

My next disappointment was finding out that neither of the mobile home parks in Los Alamos had an open space. Not that it mattered. Both had the same restriction: No trailers could be moved in that were more than five years old. Though our thirty-five-year-old mobile was in good shape, it was considered ancient and undesirable.

I cruised the park on South Mesa, looking for "For Sale" signs on mobiles that were grandfathered in. According to the residents I spoke with, an out-of-state corporation had bought the park and was trying to pry the older homes out by hitting owners with bogus safety issues. Those older homes were the only ones I could afford. Besides, they had character that the manufacturers of the look-alike modern mobiles hadn't even thought of.

The park on North Mesa was friendlier to existing homes. I found a fourteen-by-seventy-two-foot single wide that had been there for a decade. The south-facing windows and large bathtub sold me right away. The walk-in closet off the master bathroom left the bedroom walls free for furniture, including my writing desk.

I went home and started packing all the things I hadn't packed when I'd thought we were going to move the trailer.

JOB SWAP

There was one tiny glitch in the parrots' and my move back to Los Alamos.

The day before I was to close on our new mobile home, I drove up The Hill to work, singing along with a Dan Fogelberg tape. I was still humming "The Leader of the Band" as I climbed the stairs, swung my purse underneath my desk, and hung up my jacket.

"Good morning," I said to my supervisor.

She waved but didn't look up from her spreadsheet. That was odd. We always started the day with a brief chat.

"How are you doing?" I asked.

She leaned over the columns of numbers and wouldn't meet my eyes. Something was up, and I wasn't going to find out about it from her. I turned on my computer and started processing the payables.

The organization had recently hired a personnel specialist so the director wouldn't have to deal with employee issues. Mr. Personnel showed up about ten, pulled up a chair, and cleared his throat. "I have a letter to read to you."

I glanced at my supervisor. She was studying the ceiling above his head.

The letter stated that my job no longer existed. The director wanted a "real bookkeeper," someone with a degree. They'd already hired her.

I had never mastered the emotionless mask that might have allowed me to endure this shock calmly. Adrenaline made my muscles shake, and my feelings ping-ponged off the walls. I couldn't hold back tears. My face burned with shame.

I liked most of my coworkers and missed them already—until it dawned on me that not one of them had had the courage to tell me or even drop a hint. My face flushed again, this time with fury.

Then with embarrassment. I'd gotten complacent. A couple of years before, I had tried in vain to get the director to address some employment-law issues that made the organization vulnerable. Two people had quit over unrealistic expectations, poor supervision, and outright harassment, and were looking into legal action. More were contemplating it.

Pressured by Joe, who loved to spin other people into fights, I had written a letter to the president of the board and dropped a copy on the director's desk. He hadn't dared to fire the whistle-blower at the time, but I knew it was on his agenda. He'd found a way to let me go that would be hard to fight.

A couple of deep breaths allowed me to discover that while I was stunned, I was also pleased. I had no idea how I would put kibble and corn in the birds' food dishes, yet I felt as free as when I'd broken up with Joe. I was being forced to shed another element of my life that had made my doctor prescribe a blood-pressure medication.

I suppressed a smile, wanting Mr. Personnel to stop droning through the details of severance and insurance. I wanted him to leave so I could jump on my desk and dance. Maybe I would, anyway, despite the caveat I'd heard at professional seminars against burning bridges.

* * *

The speed with which things happened after that struck me as a good sign. On my way to the restaurant where Rob and I planned to meet for lunch, I stopped at the grocery store. I was coming out with a cart full of packing boxes when a local businessman I knew hailed me. Fifteen minutes later, we shook hands on my first assignments as a self-employed businesswoman.

By the time Rob joined me for lunch, it was hard to remember that I'd grieved being let go just an hour earlier.

"I'm going to grab whatever opportunities come along," I told him over my spinach-and-cheese enchilada. "I may have to get a regular job eventually, but for now, I'm going to look for independent work."

"Good for you. What about the mobile home?"

"I'm going to buy it, move, and trust that things will work out." I looked around. "Who said that? Where am I finding the courage?

159

Am I being foolhardy?"

Rob laughed. "As usual, you underestimate yourself."

"I hope you're right."

FRESH START

A few days later, on a bright and breezy spring afternoon, Peaches, Maggie, and Willie were the last to leave our wonderful old place, their cages wedged among plastic bags full of towels and bedding in the camper shell on Rob's pickup.

I set up the cages on the shelf at the front of the master bathtub. The following morning, I let the birds out to explore while I cooked hard-boiled eggs, rice, and beans. Familiar smells made our new place feel more like home.

From the parrot perspective, the house's most interesting feature was the wall between the master bedroom and bathroom. It went up only as far as the outside walls. Above that was open space to the peaked ceiling. The top of the wall was flat, and the birds lined up on it to watch me unpack. That night, Maggie claimed it as his sleeping spot, wedging himself head first into the roof angle with his long red tail sticking out.

The birds also discovered the clerestory window above the master bathroom mirror, where they watched jays and sparrows fly by, carrying grass and twigs. Paper wasps were constructing their globe-shaped nest under the eaves. The kitchen café curtain rod was the perfect place to chat up the house finches on the feeder Rob had installed.

Later, Peaches led the flock into the front bedroom that would be my office. I followed to see how they liked the desk someone had left by the recycling bins. Maggie and Willie were just landing on it when Peaches spotted an eagle soaring far out over the valley and screeched the alarm. They jostled in an every-bird-for-himself dash to the back of the house and didn't return until the following day.

Raptors notwithstanding, the parrots' general stress level was already going down. When I called, "Birds in boxes," they flew into the bathroom to be caged. No more hands-and-knees searches for truant parrots; no more showing them the broom.

When I mentioned this to Beverly on the phone, she pointed out that I was the "unindicted co-conspirator." Joe had behaved badly, but I had stayed with him. I knew I had a lot to make up for.

Maybe my birds and I would benefit from not being able to bring our old home up The Hill. We wouldn't be assaulted at every turn by painful memories. We were starting fresh.

CLOSURE

The move had left our old mobile home—and my savings account—empty. I'd had the utilities shut off but was still paying the space rental. Yet the asking price I mailed to Joe was deliberately high. If he wanted the house he had made untenable to me, the cost was going make him itch.

Even before receiving Joe's predictable rejection, I taped "For Sale" signs in the windows and on the mailboxes facing the road, and ran ads in the local newspapers. I held weekend open houses while I searched for the one thing that hadn't shown up during the move: Maggie's all-time favorite toy, the MedicAlert bracelet I had ordered after I was diagnosed with asthma. He could open the complex clasp in five seconds flat. Its last known whereabouts: Maggie's beak.

Apparently, he had dropped the bracelet into a blacker hole than the one into which socks disappeared from the washing machine. Socks sometimes reappeared, though not until I'd thrown away their mates. The bracelet was gone for good.

No one showed any interest in my old mobile home. Then, on a May evening, my ruminations about groveling to Joe with a lower offer were interrupted by a phone call.

"Hi, I'm calling from Idaho. I've been taking *The Santa Fe New Mexican* because I want to move there, and I saw your ad."

Sara and I liked each other right away. A few weeks later, when we met at the trailer park to exchange her cashier's check for my keys, we embraced as if we'd known each other for years.

Joe, if he was home, didn't come out to glower. I told Sara that he and I had had a long relationship that had ended badly.

She gave me the strong woman's answer: She was capable of making up her own mind about her new neighbors. I didn't have to say another word. It was a great relief.

As I drove home to Los Alamos, I looked forward to a more tranquil existence for myself and my parrots. They deserved it, and I was beginning to believe I did, too.

BUSINESS MOM

During my encounter with the businessman at the grocery store, he had told me, "I need a mommy for my business." That gave me the idea to bill myself as Business Mom. I took out ads in the *Yellow Pages* and the *Los Alamos Monitor*. Beverly printed business cards for me, which I posted on public bulletin boards.

Pretty soon, I had all the work I could handle—two architects, a tour company, a county councilwoman, a man who'd had a stroke, and Willie's mama Jill, who was working as a neuropsychologist and writing her Ph.D. thesis.

It was practically impossible to turn around without spotting opportunities. I took an income tax course and prepared returns at a local office, became a freelance temporary employee, and was billed as a separate line item—assistant—on one of Rob's concrete jobs. That tickled me more than any of the office work I did.

I could do some of my work at home, giving the birds extra out-of-cage time. I couldn't beat the commute—from the bedroom in the back of the house to my office in front, in my bathrobe and slippers. The traffic consisted of airborne parrots.

I did have to drive downtown, but not every day, and it was five easy miles. I planned my forays to avoid the lunch-hour rush that some people complained about. Those of us who had spent chunks of our lives fulminating in big-city freeway bottlenecks laughed at the notion.

HUEVOS PAJARITOS

Early on a Monday morning in April, when I was scheduled to work at a law office, I shuffled into the bathroom to discover Willie lying on the floor of his cage. His wings drooped. His feathers were fluffed up and ragged looking, and his usually bright blue-gray eyes looked dull.

This was how I'd found Feathers before his death. I yanked the cage door open. An unusual heat radiated from Willie's body. No question: He was running a fever.

As I scooped *him* up, an inch-long, pale coral egg rolled out from underneath *her.*

I stared as I set the little expectant mother back on the cage floor. She pushed the egg underneath her with her beak, fluffed herself up, and settled down to incubate.

Dr. Ramsay had told me that hen parrots sometimes laid eggs when they reached sexual maturity, whether or not they had mates. Willie had a mate, I realized: Peaches. They darted into the closet every time I opened the door and nestled on a stack of sweaters on the shelf.

A couple of days earlier, when I was leaving for a shopping foray in Santa Fe, they'd both stood in Willie's cage, leaning forward and staring at me: *Get it, Mom? Get it?* I'd been tempted to leave them together but decided against it. If they squabbled, neither could escape, and one or both might be hurt.

Willie's "fever" made sense now. I'd spent the summer after my divorce on my friend Shaffia's farm in Oregon. Her bantam hen was a devoted sitter. We slipped the eggs the rock hens abandoned under her. She'd felt feverish, just as Willie did.

All I could think about, as I showered, was Willie's egg. No doubt there would be more. How many? Would they be fertile? Could a peach front and a dusky head produce viable offspring?

If so, the only way I could prevent clutch after clutch of hybrid youngsters would be to separate the parents. I hated the idea until I realized that the numbers of babies could become staggering. "Nice green shag carpet," I imagined friends saying when they came to visit, "but it's, uh, *moving.*"

Despite that, the possibility of baby parrots was irresistible. Should I buy a nest box? The disruption of moving her egg might make her stop sitting. Suddenly, that worried me.

I phoned Rob, who was visiting in California. "Wouldn't it be great to watch the babies hatch, watch their parents feed them, watch them grow up and learn to fly?"

"Cool. Maybe you could keep one as a companion for Maggie."

When I let Peaches out of his cage, he scrambled into Willie's, groomed her, then ate from her dish and regurgitated, so she wouldn't have to leave the precious egg. This was just what a male in the wild would do.

As he snuggled down beside her, I said, "Mom finally got it."

INCUBATION TIME

That evening, while Maggie ate quinoa pasta and black beans with me, I skimmed my collection of parrot books. There wasn't a single sentence on preventing a parrot from laying. I assumed that was because you couldn't. Willie would keep laying to replace any eggs I removed. At least if I let her sit on a clutch, she would stop laying when she'd accumulated five or six.

One author suggested supplementing the hen's diet with calcium to replace the mineral taken from bones to produce eggshells. Here was something I could do. Following the instructions, I preheated the oven to four hundred degrees, rinsed the chicken eggshells I'd been saving for the compost bin, and cooked them on a baking tray.

Three-quarters of an hour later, I set them out to cool. The rolling pin I used to crush them drove Maggie crazy. He perched on the edge of the tray and attacked the end of the nearer handle every time it went by.

I made a little pile of the coarse powder in a jar lid that I set in front of Willie. The way she gobbled it suggested she was already feeling the calcium depletion.

Peaches fed Willie everything else she ate. I left his cage open, in case he had second thoughts or needed some quiet time to himself. He never went back to it. Previously, he'd slept in his food dish. Now, he nestled shoulder-to-shoulder with Willie, protecting her and the egg.

Maggie's behavior changed, too. He stood guard over the expectant couple, either on top of the medicine cabinet or on the three-quarter wall between the bedroom and bathroom. He took his meals with me and resumed his vigil as if it were a duty of honor. Perhaps it was. Maybe that was what unmated green-cheeked conure males did to ensure the flock's survival.

Willie laid every night or two until she had six eggs. It was all she could do to keep them underneath her. She would pull a wayward egg back with her beak, fluff, and settle over the clutch until the next one got away.

She and Peaches piped, putting their beaks close to the eggs and calling in high-pitched tones. The message was: *You belong to us. You are part of our flock.* I crooned and whistled, unsure whether the chicks could hear me through the mass of Willie's body. I hoped they would recognize my voice, too, after they hatched.

EGGSY COME, EGGSY GO

But the chicks didn't hatch. Four weeks after Willie laid the first, I knew I had to candle them. How could I get them away from the protective parents and their feathered guard?

I took a cue from my Oregon farm friend, who clipped her chickens' wings by lantern light at night, when the birds were drowsy. I got an unexpected break. In the low illumination of the nightlight, I discovered that Maggie had gone to sleep in his cage. I closed and covered it, so he couldn't observe my larceny.

Peaches alternately flapped around and stood in front of his mate, eyes flashing, beak open. I caught him in a towel and put him in one of the small travel cages. Willie was easy to capture, sitting on her eggs and too broody to give me more than a few half-hearted bites. I put her in another travel cage next to Peaches' and covered them both.

The eggs were warm as I carried them into the walk-in closet and pulled the door shut. As I held a flashlight up to the first egg, I sighed with a mixture of relief and disappointment. No tiny heart beat, no blood circulated, no dark eyes showed. The yolk that would have fed a chick lay flat against the shell. I set aside the infertile egg and candled the rest.

"No babies for Peaches and Willie this time," I whispered as I put the birds back with their eggs and covered their cage. If they remembered the raid, I hoped they would think of it as an odd dream and not hold it against me.

I went back to my conure books. Had Peaches and Willie paired but not mated? Were their DNAs incompatible? Perhaps one was infertile, or both. Could Peaches' psittacosis or the medications he'd taken have affected his reproductive system? I found no answers.

Over the phone, I told Rob, "I'm at a loss. Willie will sit on those eggs until they rot. If I take them away, she'll lay more. Is it going to be like this every spring?"

"Hmm," Rob said. "Can a parrot be spayed or neutered like a dog or cat?"

BIRDIE BIRTH CONTROL

The following morning, I did what I should have done when Willie's first egg appeared: I called the veterinary clinic.

"Birds," Dr. Ramsay said, "aren't 'fixed,' but females can be injected with Depo-Provera. The hormone stops them from producing eggs."

"For how long?"

"Depends on the bird. You may need two or three shots to get through the season."

I sighed. "Sign us up."

* * *

On the day of our appointment, I locked Maggie in his cage

before catching Peaches. He was formidable in daylight. He bit the towel furiously and got through twice. I locked him in his cage and bandaged my fingers, something I hadn't had to do in years.

Willie was easy to get into a travel cage. I left her on the dining table while I went back to the bird room, covered Peaches and Maggie, took the eggs out of Willie's cage, and placed them in a plastic container. They were so beautiful—so much a part of this parrot I loved—that I couldn't throw them away. I stowed them in the refrigerator.

At the clinic, Dr. Ramsay palpated Willie's vent and determined that no more eggs were coming. She drew the merest drop of Depo-Provera from a vial and slid the needle into Willie's breast.

What would happen when Willie discovered that her eggs were gone? It turned out better than I imagined. She looked around her cage several times, not frantically but with determination. With her beak, she picked up her washcloth and the paper towels covering the bottom of her cage and peered underneath. Peaches joined in.

When their search proved futile, they climbed onto their lowest perch, cuddled together, and sighed. That was pretty much where they stayed for the next three days, eating and drinking just enough to get by. Maggie watched over them, and they all hunched in communal mourning.

* * *

I continued to give Willie eggshell powder to replace her lost calcium. A sedentary month had weakened her muscles, and flying came hard at first. I locked all the birds out of their cages when I was home, forcing them to fly to the kitchen for food and water. The short flight left Willie panting.

Her Depo-Provera shot lasted from April until July. She laid five eggs. Peaches fed her, and Maggie resumed his duties as guard parrot. I let her sit for three weeks, then repeated the late-night candling. The eggs were infertile.

Willie and I took another drive to Dr. Ramsay's. When we returned, I let Peaches out. He flew to his mate, in her travel cage on the dining table. I closed the bedroom door, covered Maggie's cage, and scooped up the eggs.

Peaches and Willie went through the same search but gave up more quickly this time. Their grieving lasted two days. Maggie continued to watch over them.

NEST SEARCH

I sighed almost as much as the parrots, partly for Peaches and Willie and their infertile eggs and partly for Maggie, who was still the odd bird out. He cast longing looks at his big brother. He and Peaches rarely groomed each other anymore. Willie was too possessive.

When Peaches did take a boys' hour out, he and Maggie would perch on their favorite living room curtain rod and run each other's feathers through their beaks. Maggie would lean against Peaches and close his eyes.

Maggie spent a lot of time on my shoulder, nestling into my hair and grooming my lips and ears. He liked to help me type, stomping over the keyboard or chasing my fingers and gently nipping them. He created interesting phrases in the middle of business reports: *Third quarter profits zdtgg bnjkoii76 hhtgf.*

One day, I picked up a pen and tapped him on the shoulders. "I hereby dub you my administrative assistant, with all the rights, privileges, and responsibilities thereof."

Maggie grabbed the pen and tried to twist it out of my grasp. For the first time in weeks, his eyes were bright and full of play.

Having a job wasn't enough, though. Maggie began a systematic—for a parrot—search through the house, much of it on foot. He explored the storage closet in my office and dug holes in a couple of packing material boxes. His instincts told him that if he had a nest, he could have a mate. Maybe he was attempting to lure Peaches' mate. Or maybe he thought I'd bring home another female parrot the way I'd brought Willie.

Maggie gave up on the supply closet. He rejected the dark areas behind my work desk and the filing cabinets that Rob had bought to celebrate my self-employment. The only secluded spot in the guest bathroom was behind the toilet—too public and much too noisy. Maggie rejected potential sites in the living room, too: under the chairs and the day bed and behind the oak entertainment center Rob and I had built.

I drew the line at the built-in bookshelves. Maggie's attempts to redesign dust jackets and paperback covers with his beak made it clear that he saw books not as entertainment and enlightenment but as nesting material.

He tried to explore behind the stove. By the grace of God and good engineering, it fit too snugly between the cabinets and against the wall in back for even a small parrot to squeeze in. The laundry room door stayed closed. When Maggie pecked at it, I told him his memory was too short, that he didn't want to mess around behind any more washing machines. He disagreed, hammering at the annoying door in a rapid-fire volley.

The master bathroom and walk-in closet belonged to Peaches and Willie, which left Maggie the bedroom. He explored under the bed and dresser, then behind my writing desk. Until then, the birds had ignored that space, and I hadn't closed it off after the move.

"You're a picky parrot," I told him one Sunday afternoon as I folded clean underwear and tucked it into a dresser drawer. "A realtor's nightmare."

Maggie cocked his head, but it wasn't what I'd said that caught his interest. He flew from the desk, landed in the drawer, and clambered around on the soft footing. He wouldn't come out, and I saw no reason to press him. I let Peaches and Willie into the closet while I hung up clothes.

At sundown, the birds put themselves to bed. Later, by the ambient light from the next-door porch fixture, I made sure Maggie was on the three-quarter wall, closed the dresser drawer, and went to sleep.

In the morning, I opened the drawer and found my underwear

covered with shreds of wood from the dresser's interior frame. Maggie flew down from his sleeping place and hopped right in.

"Maggie!" I snapped. There was no use telling him, *Look what you've done!* He already knew, and he was delighted. I tossed him into the air, grabbed my underwear, and shoved the drawer shut.

Maggie flew back to the dresser and stomped across the top, squawking in his aggravated-baby voice: *Rraaa, rraaa, rraaa.* When I went into the bathroom, he chewed the decorative molding around the top drawer.

This was the first of Maggie's vindictive attacks on the dresser. While I did bookkeeping for clients in my office, ate, or cleaned house, I had to lock him in front with me. Not that I didn't understand his instinct to nest and his frustration at being denied. I sympathized, but furniture destruction was carrying it too far.

BONDS

It came as no surprise that Peaches' and Willie's pairing changed my relationships with them. I was glad they were living somewhat normal avian lives, focused on each other. At the same time, I reminisced about intimate moments we had shared—napping, watching TV, eating from the same plate.

Willie tolerated occasional petting but no longer sought it out. When I offered Peaches a head scritch, she hustled between us. Sometimes, she nipped me. Was she intent on protecting him, or did she believe I was trying to steal her mate?

Peaches didn't forget me, though. Every few days, he would seek me out, snuggling under my hair or grooming the skin around my eyes. When Willie called, he ignored her until her squawks reached high annoyance: *AAAaaa, AAAaaa, AAAaaa.* Then he would wing back and be the dutiful mate.

Peaches still took night flights, though less frequently. I would get up, flashlight in hand, pick him up out of the bathtub, and place him back with his mate. Willie would give him a sleepy-eyed grooming before they fell asleep, shoulder to shoulder.

I would go back to bed, smiling at their affection, not knowing that I would soon have reason to envy it.

THANKSGIVING

It was the Sunday morning of Thanksgiving weekend, nine months after the parrots and I had moved back to Los Alamos and two months after Willie had laid her last clutch of the breeding season. Frost framed the north-facing windows. I lay in bed late, trying to go back to sleep, not wanting to face the day.

When I finally got up, Peaches and Willie flew into the closet. Maggie and I shared breakfast. Actually, Maggie ate eggs from the rim of the bowl like the little gentleman he was, while I pushed my portion around with my spoon.

Not that I didn't need food. I'd hardly eaten in days. My stomach was in too much turmoil. Every time I dried my eyes, a fresh wave of tears surged down my cheeks. My mind roiled through the all-too-familiar cycle of grief, self-pity, and inadequacy.

Weeks before, Rob had stopped inviting me to stay after our evenings together. I had forced myself not to panic. He was still refurbishing his building, and he couldn't get his mother's declining health off his mind. It was time for me to be a friend and let him work things out, but with every passing day, I felt more anxious and hurt.

On Thanksgiving Day, I'd been at Rob's, looking through my drawer in his dresser for a pair of green pants to wear to the part-time law-office job I'd taken.

"What's up?" Rob had asked as I tucked the pants into a plastic grocery bag.

I hadn't intended to pull out my long-sleeved T-shirt, but I slid that into the bag, too. He watched without comment.

"Well, you know," I said, not meeting his lovely blue eyes, "If I'm, uh, not sleeping here, then the clothes I've left are . . . well, they're unusable."

Into the bag went underwear, socks, and pantyhose. I couldn't stop. My chest was vibrating, and my eyes ached with held-back tears. "It's just that, if I'm not going to be dressing here in the mornings, you know, I should have these things at home where I can wear them."

"Okay," Rob said. "You can leave them here, though."

I glanced at him, suddenly irritated. *Right, keep your options open without committing.*

From the way he rubbed his chin, I could tell he wanted to say more, but I couldn't contain my emotions. I swept the drawer clean—sweater, gloves, hat, and scarf.

Hot tears poured out, and I insisted in a wobbly voice, "These can all come back."

Something solidified in my chest, and I knew I'd reached the hill on which I had to make a stand. "But only if I do. If we're not going to be lovers . . . "

There, I'd said it.

Rob sat tight-lipped while I tried to stuff everything into the grocery bag. I gave up, yanked on the hat and gloves and wound the scarf around my neck. Suddenly discovering myself dressed to go out, I took a step toward the door.

Rob stopped me with a tale about him and his ex-wife, in which he'd told her what he apparently wanted to tell me now: There was a chance "the fire might be rekindled."

I was so surprised that I stopped crying and stared. He and his ex had never gotten back together. This was supposed to encourage me?

Now, sitting at my own dining table, I felt broken, defeated, diminished. "If not my dear friend," I asked Maggie, "then who can I have a lifelong relationship with?"

Maggie cocked his head. I gazed into his dark eyes and added, "Besides you and Peaches and Willie, I mean. You know, someone with hair on his chest. A mammal."

I had wanted this mammal for a long time. Instead of being frustrated with Rob, I tried to figure out what I'd done wrong.

Hadn't I shown him how open I was sexually, how willing I was to be his helpmate, how quietly I could work beside him in his workshop or pouring concrete? Hadn't I always stopped by the Pojoaque Dairy Queen on my way home from Santa Fe and bought him his favorite pineapple milkshake?

As I stored the leftover breakfast, I remembered an acquaintance telling me, "I needed every drink I took to get to AA and get sober." I had wondered whether I needed every failed romance to get to a sane and happy one. Now, I doubted that was even possible.

Beverly's phone call broke my glum ruminations. "Just making sure you're not going down the rabbit hole—or, if you are, to throw you a lifeline."

"Lifeline," I said.

At least I had the good sense to be grateful for caring friends— and the little green parrot nibbling my earlobe.

THE LIST

Rob and I still worked on each other's homes together, played chess, and shot pool. Occasionally, I could talk him into taking a drive in the mountains. He was so tired that he often slept through the trip. Still, it felt better to be around him than not to be.

I believed that if I were a true friend, I had to want the best for him, even if it didn't include me. Sometimes, I could make that ideal work. Mostly, my heart ached. Obsessive thoughts about my romantic future—if any—didn't help, but they were hard to turn off.

Arranged marriages had never appealed to me, but as I sulked through my workdays and took refuge with Peaches, Maggie, and Willie, I wondered if I'd have better luck with a match set up by friends. I couldn't imagine facing the dating scene, the nightmare of personal ads, and the strain of getting to know someone new.

Dennis might have been a logical choice. We e-mailed occasionally. He was living in southeastern Arizona, where his vocational education degree allowed him to get substitute teaching jobs. I didn't tell him I was available. I needed time to recover.

As I did, I watched the parrots for stress reactions to my turmoil. Their worry showed up in more frequent shoulder visits, grooming, and murmuring in my ears that comforted us all and tapered off as I settled into the long haul of healing.

* * *

Several women friends tried to convince me that this loss was, indeed, what I needed to move on to someone better. A couple of them urged me to list everything I wanted in a partner.

I protested that list-making was unlikely to help me make better choices. It felt more like rubbing salt into yet another failed-relationship wound. Even salt could be healing, they insisted.

I rolled my eyes at their faith, though it was beginning to dawn on my befuddled mind that finding the right partner wasn't the only issue. I needed to be the right partner. Was acknowledging what I wanted enough? Would it make me a woman who could attract, finally, the man I would spend the rest of my years with?

For distraction—and because I felt I had to try something new—I slogged through the simplest preferences first—*non-smoker, non-alcoholic, likes my birds*, and *capable and handy*—until I could address deeper desires. *He loves me the way I am, warts and all* was a big one, along with *he wants to be with me, we have a couple presence*, and *he becomes one of my best friends*.

Right away, I recognized something disturbing: I was good at building supportive and lasting relationships with friends, male and female, and with parrots. With lovers, everything blew up sooner or later.

What was my part in the pattern? It probably included my willingness to put up with hurtful behavior because I was afraid of loss. The list encouraged me to take a stand for what I wanted, to recognize that those desires and needs weren't frivolous. They came from who I was. I deserved a real and satisfying partnership.

Despite my lingering suspicion that the list was nothing more than self-flagellation, I kept ending the revised versions with a mantra Beverly had suggested: "Rob or better," and one Nischa had given me: "All this abundance and more."

I made a "don't-want" list, too, that included *If you see a man at the end of his marriage or one who double-talks, run like hell!* It brightened my sometimes sulky attitude toward the exercise, which was right up there with my reaction to *Eat your Brussels sprouts; they're good for you.*

DREAM

During these heart-mending weeks, I had a curious dream. It took place in a garden full of the scents of flowers and vegetables. I rarely dreamed smells. Odder still were the light-surrounded man and woman who told me, "Love has been set aside for you."

"What?"

In unison, they repeated, "Love has been set aside for you."

I woke up with a start. Maggie murmured from his three-quarter wall, ground his beak, and went back to sleep. I dozed off, too, discounting the dream as mere wish fulfillment.

But it was more than that. It exposed what I deeply longed for. Normally, I'd have found that painful. Yet I couldn't deny the serenity and certainty that grew in me afterwards. I was still in emotional pain, feeling unloved and unlovable, missing Rob beside me in bed, yet I was gaining a surprising calm. Even if all the dream did was give me temporary solace, it was a horse I was willing to ride.

Along with this sense of impending love came acceptance. I had thought that staying in the troubled relationship with Joe and then taking up with Rob was stupid. Wanting another love relationship seemed insane, but maybe it wasn't. While I needed to make better choices in men—whatever that involved—I also needed to value my perseverance.

Maybe the list was reinforcing the idea that I might be worthy of lasting love. It was certainly creeping into my awareness.

AVAILABLE

The early-spring crocus pushed up through the snow. About the time Willie got her first Depo-Provera shot of the season, it became clear that "rekindling the fire" with Rob was as dead as a politician's pre-election promise.

I talked the situation over with the parrots—and with some human friends—took my courage in both hands, and e-mailed Dennis that I was available. I imagined he had given up on me, but he wrote back that this was the message he'd been hoping to find on his computer screen every day.

Our correspondence moved quickly into a possible future together. The same things were important to us: honesty, trust, mutual support, and daily affection. We wanted to come in out of the cold. At fifty-seven, we both wanted the relationship for the rest of our lives.

We had similar tastes in music and wanted to live in the country. We'd both enjoyed the California clothing-optional scene. And we were willing—so long as our basic needs were met—to let a lot of less important issues be negotiable.

These were necessary, but we both knew they weren't enough. We acknowledged that we had been attracted in California, but that was seventeen years earlier. What would we be like together now, given the painful and disappointing relationships we'd gone through?

Dennis was optimistic. Given my history, I had to wonder whether I was starting another dead-end romance and opening myself up for more grief.

RESPITE

Months would have to pass before Dennis and I would find out whether we had a future together. Meanwhile, my third September vacation with Elida and Rod in Montana rolled around. I was grateful for a break from work, heartache, and uncertainty.

My days of leaving the parrots at home while I traveled were over, and not just because I didn't have a partner to look after them. They would have gotten good care and plenty of stimulation at Dr. Ramsay's clinic, or I could have hired someone to come in, feed them, clean their cages, and give them some company. I just thought they would be happier on the road with me. I knew I'd be happier. They were the constants in my life. I couldn't leave them behind, thinking I'd abandoned them to strangers.

Compared to the three sixty-pound dogs Thor and I had traveled with, three four-ounce parrots were a snap. I seatbelted their full-sized cages into GW's back seat. At campgrounds, I put the seat down, and we slept in back, so I could share covers and body heat if it got chilly. Wild parrots tolerated severe weather, but my birds weren't acclimated.

I needn't have worried. In Utah, I woke at first light to a frosty tracery on GW's windows. I grabbed my flashlight and lifted Peaches' and Willie's cover. They were snuggling together on the cage floor, their tails sticking out from underneath the washcloth. It was the only time I'd seen Peaches get under it.

What about Maggie, alone on a perch in his cage? There he stood, wrapped in his own down-feather blanket, not a shiver to be seen. He flinched from the light as if to say, *Please, Mom, just five more minutes.*

I was happy to snuggle under the covers myself, thinking, *Isn't that what vacations are for?*

It was just the trip I needed. Piney mountains, the expanse of the Great Salt Lake, and miles of wheat fields provided a restful transition. White-faced ibises probed roadside marshes, and lakes where we took rest breaks floated gulls, geese, and pelicans.

* * *

Nature was soothing, but the greatest balm was long talks with Elida.

"I think Rob's a fool to let you go," she said over tea, my first morning there. "And Dennis is a fool if he doesn't sweep you up."

"He's coming to visit in October." My stomach fluttered.

"Does Rob know?"

"Yup."

"And?"

"And, so far, nothing."

"Better to know now. If you moved to California with him, and things got rocky there . . . "

"One of his friends said that if I did move with Rob, I ought to keep my car pointed toward New Mexico."

"What does that tell you?"

I stared into my tea and listened to the parrots screech at the wild turkeys foraging in the front yard. "He knows how obsessive Rob can be. I just thought that with me, because we've been friends for so long . . ."

Elida reached across the table and patted my hand. She knew how to heal what ailed me, starting with simple comfort.

Walks along country roads and shopping trips to Missoula's Front Street rubbed the rough edges off my psyche. Rides on the hand-carved Missoula Carousel revived my delight. By the time Elida and Rod saw the birds and me off for the drive home, my frazzled internal circuitry had been soothed and smoothed. Whatever lay ahead, I felt better prepared to deal with it.

E-MAILING IT IN

Almost everything about my relationship with Dennis was different from past ones. I hoped that meant that this one would last.

For one thing, we were starting at the computer keyboard instead of in bed. We rarely phoned each other, recognizing the need to work through important issues without involving the senses that could derail our judgment. If everything worked out as we hoped, we'd have plenty of time for joys of the senses.

I discovered the wisdom of this approach a few days after the birds and I got home from Montana. A swamp cooler support had broken, damaging our roof. I called Dennis for advice. When he said hello, my mind calmed, while my body went into such wild vibrations I could hardly hold the phone.

Not that our e-mail correspondence was prudish or unemotional. In fact, it included some poetic and steamy sentiment.

Cappy: *I continue to fly on wings of anticipation for the day when you arrive.*

Dennis: *Flying with you will be a great adventure.*

Cappy: *Think of our warm hands exploring each other's bodies.*

Dennis: *A poet I am not, but if I were, I would write scenes imagined only by those in love with life, as I say we surely must be.*

Cappy: *Here's to love, the revealing and the consuming.*

Dennis: *I can't wait to rise to our occasion.*

No wonder, when I got home from working in town or from writers' group, the first things I did were let the parrots out of their cages and turn on my computer.

Dennis admitted, *If I get home, and I don't have an e-mail from you, I figure you're calling it off.*

Right, I wrote back. *I have to remind myself that you have a life. You might be out shopping or playing penny-ante poker with your friends.*

You mean your mind goes to the worst-case scenario, too?

Does it ever. Like you're bored with me, or you've found someone more geographically desirable.

My e-mails to Dennis contained certain typographical oddities. I decided to leave my administrative assistant's electronic footprints in my letters, giving credit where it was due: *32qwweddxc (Maggie).* I did this for fun and also to remind Dennis that he was going to have to pass parrot muster.

Naomi, a California friend now living in Phoenix, told me, "If the time is wrong, you can't push a relationship with a bulldozer. If it's right, you can't stop it with one."

That was how it felt between Dennis and me: inevitable. Yet I didn't trust it. "Inevitable" might be powered by nothing more than wishful thinking, and I knew that could lead me to the worst heartbreak yet. Who knew what kind of unexpected problems could arise from our actually being together?

FAREWELL

The leaves were turning gold when Rob and I hugged a teary farewell. He was worn out from months of manic work, disappointed that he hadn't gotten what he thought the building was worth, and too anxious to be on the road to wait for a better offer.

As he pulled away, he shouted out his truck window, "I hate my life!"

What was I supposed to make of his parting shot? I wanted to believe that he was unhappy because he was leaving me behind. I felt sad that he was running himself into the ground, but my reaction reflected more frustration than compassion.

Whose fault is that? I wanted to yell after him. *If you don't like it, change it.*

Fortunately, a poster I'd seen came to mind: *God, thank You for putting Your arm around my shoulder and Your hand over my mouth.* By some grace, I whispered a blessing for Rob.

HELLO AGAIN

At two o'clock the following morning, the parrots were asleep in their cages. I was standing outside my house, clenching and unclenching my hands and bouncing on my toes as I watched Dennis's headlights swing into the mobile home park.

He pulled into my lighted driveway, and I saw through the windshield of his venerable Honda, La Cucaracha Azúl, that his hair had gone mostly white. He'd acquired a scar across his nose in an encounter with a roll-up garage door. Otherwise, he looked much as I remembered him.

Dennis unfolded himself from the little car after a full day of substitute teaching and nine hours behind the wheel. He groaned, leaned against GW, and said, "I'm getting too old for this."

We laughed and threw our arms around each other. I buried my face against his chest, inhaling the scent of glycerin soap. A huge, involuntary sigh rose from my toes.

Our bodies knew. We climbed the stairs, went straight to the bedroom, and fell into bed, never letting go.

PARROT MUSTER

I had covered the birds' cages so they wouldn't wake us up at sunrise, which was not long after Dennis and I fell asleep. We got up at a leisurely ten o'clock, ready for the love-me-love-my-parrots test.

Dennis's only previous encounter with a parrot had occurred when he was a little boy, visiting the family next door. Someone handed him the big macaw, perched on a wooden dowel. Polly's weight was too great for Dennis to keep the dowel level. As it tilted, the bird grabbed his hand. Her massive hooked beak ripped into his little finger. The doctor who stitched it up gave him a shot of penicillin, a drug I thought of as liquid fire.

Dennis watched Peaches, Maggie, and Willie pile over the three-quarter wall and observed with typical dry humor, "Mess o' birdies."

I had to smile. "When they fly together, they seem like a dozen."

The birds treated Dennis as they would have any stranger, perching on the curtain rods to study him from a distance. He showered and made breakfast. They flew closer. When he didn't react, they landed on him.

That was when he discovered how useful food bribes were. Pretty soon, all three were nibbling toast from his lips.

"I don't know about this," he told me between bites. He was a little edgy, and who could blame him? He liked the birds' soft feathers, but their beaks were sharp, and there was the usual jostling and pecking.

Maggie nipped his ear, an attention-getting ploy: *Feed me.*

"Ow," Dennis said.

"Did he hurt you?"

"No, not really. I just expected it to hurt. What's he doing now?"

"Grooming your hair. Consider it an apology."

When Maggie pressed his beak into Dennis's ear and explored with his tongue, Dennis only asked what he was doing. It must have been a disconcerting intimacy, but Dennis sat through it with aplomb.

* * *

For the rest of Dennis's week-long visit, male bonding was a high priority. Dennis was an incorrigible tease, and in Maggie he found the perfect target. Dennis took to gently tapping and tugging those long red tail feathers. Maggie would flatten his head feathers and nip at him. Dennis anticipated this defense most of the time and pulled away before Maggie could bite his fingers.

Maggie sometimes anticipated him, and Dennis pulled back his hand with a yelp. After several nips, he asked, "That's why you didn't stop me, isn't it?"

"Maggie can take care of himself. Remember what I said in my e-mails about the quick and the bitten?"

That didn't discourage Dennis from tapping Maggie's tail again. And *that* didn't discourage Maggie from flying off his shoulder, circling the kitchen, and coming back for more.

NO AND YES

I had thought Rob was done with me until Dennis and I listened to the answering machine pick up several calls from him.

"You know you have to talk to him," Dennis said.

I nodded, thinking, *What am I trying to do, keep my options open?*

"He knows I'm here, right?"

"I told him you were coming."

I picked up the next call. Rob's agitated voice came across a thousand miles of phone lines. "I must've been out of my mind, leaving you there. I want you to move here. We can get married if you want."

The gut-punch I felt was powered by the disparity between my proposal fantasies and the real one. It made me suck in a breath, though. Life with Rob was a choice I could still make, even with Dennis standing ten feet away.

I could say yes, I thought, *but I'd have to keep GW pointed toward New Mexico.*

Still, I sagged at the idea of hurting Rob's feelings. He'd always been honest with me, and I owed him the same. "I love you dearly, but if I'm going to happily-ever-after, it'll be with Dennis."

My stomach wobbled only a little as I thought, *There, I've thrown my hat in Dennis's corner.*

* * *

Within days, Dennis and I knew we wanted to live together; we just hadn't decided where. I hoped to entice him with a variety of New Mexico delights. We drove the High Road to Taos among sun-colored cottonwoods and aspens, wandered the art galleries hand in hand, and toured the pueblo that dated from the 1200s.

We crossed the bridge over the eight-hundred-foot gorge the Rio Grande had carved into the basaltic plateau, walked back to the middle of the structure, and gazed into the abyss. On our way home, we were treated to a bald eagle fishing in the river.

We dedicated another day to indulgence. We fed each other artichoke hearts in parmesan sauce at the Zia Diner in Santa Fe and cuddled in the public hot tub among the pines at Ten Thousand Waves, under the brilliant sparkle of stars.

When I had to work, Dennis explored Los Alamos on his own. He spoke with a business counselor about the local service economy, with an appliance store owner about doing repair work, and with people at the school district.

In the evenings, we lay on the living room floor and pored over the photos he had brought—a tour of duty in Vietnam, his families from two marriages. I dug out pictures of my high school proms, marriage, dogs, and of course, the parrots. It was a great way to deepen our intimacy and our understanding and appreciation of each other.

Dennis also showed me pictures of his land, with its rock-strewn butte and broad view across the Sulphur Springs Valley into Mexico. We agreed that I would fly to Tucson the Wednesday night before Thanksgiving, and we would spend the holiday weekend exploring southeastern Arizona. Then we would choose where to settle—his desert grassland, my mountains, or somewhere else.

SWEET SORROW

The morning Dennis packed La Cucaracha Azúl for the trip home, I put my father's film camera on a tripod, set the timer, and hustled across the bedroom to stand in front of my sweetheart. When the pictures came back from the developer, I saw exactly what we were feeling. We were smiling for the camera and for each other while verging on tears.

I had set the camera to focus on Dennis, so I came out a little blurred. I didn't care. It was the image of him that would sustain me through the nine weeks until we would see each other again.

After Dennis left, the parrots went through several low days. Maggie stuck to my shoulder, but when I tried to play Tap Maggie's Tail, he either ignored me or squawked with annoyance and bit my fingers. It just wasn't the same as having Dennis to pal around with.

I knew how he felt.

START PACKING

More than at any time since I'd moved to New Mexico, I felt excited at the possibility of living in a new locale, and it was a good thing. A few days after Dennis got home, he phoned. Without saying hello, he launched into the reason for his call: "I've shoveled enough snow. I don't like the building restrictions in Los Alamos and the lack of usable space around it. I want to spread out."

I understood. Los Alamos was a tiny county, hemmed in by the Lab, Forest Service land, and Indian pueblos. Dennis lived in a wide-open, right-to-build county.

"I don't want to give up my teaching career in Arizona," he added. "Even if New Mexico accepted my substitute teaching certificate, I'd be starting over. Los Alamos seems like a tough place to break into. People know me here."

People know me *in Los Alamos,* I thought, but recalled how hard it had been to make friends and get my first job.

We were quiet on the line for a minute. Before we'd gotten together, I'd never considered living in a 4,000-foot-elevation, mesquite-and-creosote desert grassland. But I had thought about moving when I was with Rob. I'd already weighed staying in my beloved mountains and the community I'd become a part of against having a relationship intended last the rest of my life.

Besides, Santa Fe was expanding in every direction, and land prices were going nowhere but up. The pueblos were building casinos and enormous resort hotels. Recent highway "improvements" included overpasses as close as Pojoaque, half an hour away.

I took a deep breath and asked Dennis, "May I start packing?"

He inhaled sharply. "Are you sure?"

"Yes." My heart opened in a flood, and I knew it was the right choice.

We decided not to make it definite until I visited him at Thanksgiving and saw what I would be in for.

After we said goodbye, I did some online research. I bounced in my chair when I found out that Cochise County was one of the top ten bird-watching areas in the continental United States. I could bulk up my life list with everything from gray hawks to magnificent hummingbirds to elegant trogons. I might even see some Mexican species—thick-billed flycatchers, for instance, or melodious blackbirds.

I added binoculars and field guides to my packing list.

A DIFFERENT THANKSGIVING

On Thanksgiving morning, I woke up next to Dennis at Twin Buttes, the RV and mobile home park a couple of miles north of the Arizona-Sonora border. Dennis was living in the old house that had belonged to the park's original owner.

After cooking breakfast hip to hip in the compact kitchen, we strolled around the park. Flycatchers darted after insects we stirred up. Mesquite still held their leaves, and creosote made the valley look like a green sea.

This was basin-and-range country, alternately driven together and pulled apart by tectonic forces, leaving tilted buttes. Around the valley, mountains rose to more than seven thousand feet. The nine-thousand-foot Chiricahua peaks showed their snow-covered heads to the northeast.

We took a bumpy dirt-road drive to Dennis's land, where it angled up the shoulder of Taylor Butte. This seemed a good omen: My maiden name was Taylor.

We encountered another portent as we got out of his truck. A pair of marsh hawks sailed over, their wingtips inches apart. In my birding experience, I'd seen ten of the reddish-brown females for every gray-and-white male. This was the first time I'd seen a pair flying together.

Dennis's forty-acre parcel had a rugged beauty. The nearby Swisshelm and Pedregosa Mountains were low and sparse by comparison to the Jemez and Sangre de Cristos but were spectacular in their own right. Sitting on the boulder that marked the highest corner of his property, we watched sun and cloud shadows race across the landscape.

I thought I could enjoy the changing colors of the rock formations for years and knew I might have a chance. We talked about retiring there.

* * *

That afternoon, we shared a Thanksgiving potluck at the Twin Buttes rec trailer. The feast was put on by owners Roger and Bev, the permanent residents, and snowbirds from as far away as Minnesota and British Columbia. They were mostly an older, retired group who cared about Dennis and made me feel welcome.

Afterwards, Dennis and I sauntered back to the house arm in arm, and I mentioned how easy a ready-made community would make my move.

"You love New Mexico. You're willing to pull up stakes for me?"

"I don't pack my books unless I'm going to move, and there are boxes of them stacked in my living room."

He stopped. "You started packing? Really? You want to live here with me, warts and all?"

"Warts and all." I hugged his arm, thinking how different this was from the previous Thanksgiving, when I'd cleaned my clothes out of Rob's dresser and driven home in tears. "You, too? Warts and all?"

"Of course." He made it sound easy, as though I was too good to pass up.

* * *

On Friday and Saturday, Dennis introduced me to the local communities. Douglas was a border town with a good library. The former copper-mining town of Bisbee was full of art galleries. We crossed the Mule Mountains and the San Pedro River to the "real shopping town" of Sierra Vista. Dennis wanted me to know I could buy shoes and wheat-free pasta in the borderlands of Arizona.

Saturday evening, after we had snuggled in front of a rented movie, I worked up the nerve to show him my ideal-man list. I made sure he knew that I'd written it before we had talked about making a life together.

I didn't tell him that I had made one last-minute change before printing it. Dennis lived from paycheck to paycheck, as I did, so I'd deleted, "He can and wants to support me, so I can have more creative time." I didn't want to hurt his feelings with a desire he couldn't fulfill.

After reading the list to him, I said, "So the only difference between what I want and what I'm getting is that you're an omnivore."

"How important is that to you?"

"Not as important as I used to think, as long as I don't have to prepare meat for you. Dietary choices are such a personal issue."

"Cooking dead animals will be my department."

* * *

Despite having resolved this last issue, I felt a mounting agitation as we made the two-hour drive to the Tucson airport the following morning.

If Dennis noticed, he didn't mention it. He seemed enveloped in that same mix of farewell sorrow and excitement about the future that I was feeling.

On the flight to Albuquerque, I realized that as much as I'd wanted a relationship to be this easy, I wasn't used to it. It made me nervous.

I had a stern talk with myself about the expectations I'd developed. *Maybe I've gotten too used to crazy. Maybe this relationship is easy because it's the right one.*

CONGRATULATIONS AND CONCERNS

First thing Monday morning, I took my law firm supervisor aside and told her the empty copier paper boxes I had taken home were going to Arizona at the end of the year. I broke the news to my private clients during the week. Nobody wanted to let me go—a wonderful affirmation—but they were all pleased for me.

The friends who had gone through my breakups with Perry, Joe, and Rob were more cautious. Beverly's take on the move was, "Oh, my God, here you go again. If this relationship blows up, it's going to be difficult to move back. You'll be a long way from people who care about you."

I thought that if people met Dennis, they wouldn't worry. He flew in at the beginning of his two-week break in December, and we threw a party among stacks of packed boxes. He sat through inspections by friends, neighbors, and co-workers, who gave us their blessings.

Beverly was the sole holdout. While Dennis helped me prepare for the move, she and her husband Bob vacationed in Cochise County. They drove by Dennis's place on their way to Bisbee. Beverly described it as "third house past the rock." She was worried about the park's isolation, which Dennis and I relished. Nothing would reassure her but seeing how well we did together over time.

LOCKING THE DOOR

All three parrots had welcomed Dennis back with shoulder visits and grooming. Maggie was the most ecstatic to see him. If Dennis was in the house, Maggie was on him, snuggling under his chin and enjoying games of Tap Maggie's Tail.

While Dennis bought two-by-fours and plywood sheets, and enclosed the flatbed trailer we had bought—our first shared financial commitment—Maggie clung to one of my hands or the other as I packed. Peaches and Willie gave up their closeted intimacy to supervise from the top of each box. The three of them took turns decorating the floor with shredded packing paper and Styrofoam peanuts.

I was grateful to see that they were more curious than anxious. Apparently, previous moves hadn't traumatized them. As long as the flock was together, they were happy. The flock now included Dennis.

We hired a couple of high school football players to pack the trailer on the last day of the year. It was almost dark when Dennis and I loaded the birds, in their full-sized cages, into the back of GW Blaze, along with my computers and house plants. We made a final sweep through the house, checked that the for-sale sign was firmly taped inside the front window, and locked the door on my old life.

ON THE ROAD

Dennis had driven big rigs in Vietnam, and I was glad to have him take the wheel. Even so, we didn't get off to an auspicious start. Despite selling my big house plants and some of my furniture, and despite numerous give-away trips to thrift shops, our trailer was loaded to capacity. GW's small V-6 engine strained as we pulled away.

"Maybe I should have driven my truck up here instead of flying," Dennis said. "It's a lot to ask of GW, but at this point, we have no choice."

A block from the house, we had to pull over. A short circuit we couldn't find kept the trailer brakes from releasing after a stop.

Dennis disconnected them. We would have to rely solely on GW's stopping power.

Fifteen minutes later, we were creeping across Omega Bridge toward the Truck Route. The canyon looked like a black chasm between two lives.

"Goodbye, Los Alamos," I called out the open window. "Goodbye, Jemez Mountains."

Tears stung my eyes. Dennis took one hand off the wheel long enough to pat my knee. Peaches, Maggie, and Willie complained about the rush of cold air until I rolled up the window.

* * *

The drive was uneventful until we neared the bottom of La Bajada Hill on I-25 between Santa Fe and Albuquerque. A bump in the pavement started the trailer fishtailing. The weight pushed GW's back end sideways and threatened to jackknife us.

My nerves lit up with fear as the birds squawked at the increasing motion. I throttled down a scream to keep from distracting Dennis. Time accordioned out as I flashed back to hanging upside down in Macha's crushed cab. Then, I'd been grateful that my partner was on the mountain and my parrot was safe at home. Now, a full-family disaster seemed about to overtake us.

My revved-up internal clock made GW's swings seem never-ending, though it may have taken Dennis only fifteen or twenty seconds to get the car and trailer under control. The birds went back to sleep, but I shook with adrenaline. I could barely choke out, "Wow, you did a great job."

"Small corrections—that's what they taught us in Marine truck-driving school. Otherwise, the oscillations get bigger, and then . . . "

He didn't have to tell me what would happen then.

* * *

By the time we got off the road for the night in Socorro, 130 miles south of Los Alamos, my nerves had quit jangling. I didn't entirely relax until I'd settled the birds in our second-floor room at Motel 6 and taken a hot shower.

My calm didn't last long. Dennis and I sprawled on the bed to watch the New Year's countdown on TV, replayed in Mountain Standard Time. The instant the ball at Times Square hit 2004, the nearby residential neighborhood erupted in gunfire.

Dennis sat up and gave me a running commentary. "Thirty-eight. Forty-five. Shotgun. Automatic weapons." He identified a rapid burst: "AK-47 or AR-15."

"Should we get down on the floor?" I asked. "I'll grab the birds." They were mumbling behind their towels.

Dennis and I looked at each other, both thinking, as we later admitted, that it was a crap shoot either way. We barely breathed until the racket diminished to the occasional crack of a twenty-two, and Peaches, Maggie, and Willie went back to sleep.

My adrenaline dumped in a hurry this time. My last thoughts, before I fell asleep next to my sweetie, were that we'd survived seeing the old year out and our new lives in, and that the rest of the trip should be easy by comparison.

GET OUT AND PUSH

We weren't home safe yet. I-25 crossed a series of canyons. Climbing out of the widest and deepest, GW slowed down. And slowed down. And . . . slowed . . . down.

Dennis downshifted and switched on the emergency flashers. "Get out and push, will you?"

The parrots squawked, low and uneasy.

"You might have to push, too," I told them. I tried to breathe energy into the engine, chanting, "You can make it, you can make it."

GW could, and he did. We topped the slope going six miles an hour and slowing.

Dennis patted GW's dash and promised, "Get us home, and you'll never have to pull this trailer again."

* * *

By the time we turned off the highway at Twin Buttes, rain had come and gone, and the air was alive with the scent of creosote. We set the parrots on Dennis's desk, covered them for the night, and scrounged what dinner we could from the kitchen and cooler. Then we dropped into an exhausted and relieved sleep.

MS. ROSE ELLEN

Dennis and I made the most of our four-day honeymoon. Then it was back to everyday life. At six-thirty on Monday morning, one of the school districts called for a substitute teacher. Dennis shuffled toward the shower. I got up and cooked his breakfast.

Despite all the years I'd struggled out of bed and gone to one job or another, I rated early-morning phone calls as a hard adjustment. Sleeping next to Dennis was an easy one. Waiting for my turn in the house's only bathroom fell somewhere in between.

The parrots' adjustments included spending nights in their cages for the first time in years. They didn't seem to mind. They were in a strange place, and their cages felt like home. Knowing they were safe allowed me to sleep in peace.

When I mentioned this at the Twin Buttes happy hour the evening after we arrived, several people joked that I should make Dennis sleep in a cage. I told them that as Big Bird of the flock, he was entitled to "certain considerations." That drew some laughs and a few lascivious winks.

* * *

It wasn't just the calls of great horned owls and coyotes, and the unfamiliar house noises that might have panicked the birds and sent them fluttering to the floor or the bed. There were also the nocturnal prowlings of Ms. Rose Ellen on the other side of the bedroom door.

Rose Ellen was the sweet-faced brown tabby who had welcomed me during my Thanksgiving visit. Her people had abandoned her when they left the park.

"Then I moved in," Dennis had told me. "Every time I opened the door, she would dart in. The house isn't very big, but I could never find her. As soon as I sat down in the recliner to read, she would rub against my legs or sprawl on my chest and purr."

"So you decided she could come in," I'd said, "but only on days that ended in Y?"

He thought about that for a moment and made a face. Then he pulled Rose's tail, lifting her hind feet off the floor, and called her You Bad Kitty as though it was her name. Rose stalked away, then wriggled back for more.

"I called her Dog Food," Dennis said, "until one of the local animal lovers got offended and informed me her name was Rose."

By the end of the Thanksgiving weekend, we had added to her name. Now she was Ms. Rose Ellen Stripy Kitty Cat.

Dennis and I had assumed that when the parrots and I moved in, Rose would lose her house privileges. I'd apologized to her as she rolled in my lap, begging me to rub her tummy. I'd never had a cat and was finding out what delights I was missing, but my parrots had to come first.

* * *

So why was Rose still in the house? Because circumstances changed the day after we arrived. We were standing in front of the house in the winter sunshine, chatting with our landlord Roger, when Dennis mentioned that we would be looking for a mobile home. He pointed across the park. "Maybe we could put it in that empty space, and someday we can move it to our land."

Roger rubbed his chin and said he had just bought a two-bedroom singlewide in Casa Grande, which would be hauled to Twin Buttes in about six weeks. The intended tenant was wheelchair bound.

Dennis glanced at the six-inch step up to the house and the high-sitting mobile homes around us. "The ramp will have to double back on itself. It'll take up the whole yard."

Roger grinned, said Dennis was quick on the uptake, and asked if we would we be willing to trade a rented house for a rented mobile home. Or we could buy the mobile on payments. Breathless at the speed with which our desire for our own home was being fulfilled, we agreed to consider both options.

Given our new plans, it made sense to leave the hauling trailer packed and covered until the mobile home arrived. We carried the computers and plants into the house, along with the one bag of clothes I could reach, standing on the trailer's wheel well.

We relented on Rose's transition back to outdoor status until we decided whether or not we were moving. We restricted her to the front of the house. The bathroom, with doors to the bedroom and entryway, made a perfect birdlock.

It didn't take the parrots long to realize that while Rose could snuffle around the living room door, she couldn't get to them. They were content to fly loose in the bedroom during the day and customize the covers of Dennis's phone books and his car and truck manuals.

One night over dinner, Dennis said, "I don't mind leaving Rose if we move. I'm fond of her, but I'm not attached. I don't think she is, either."

I set down my fork. "I think you underestimate Rose's affection."

"She's a whore. She'll roll over for anyone who'll feed her and rub her belly. If the next tenant doesn't want her, Roger will put out food for her in the workshop."

That was where we left it for the moment.

ADJUSTMENTS

The parrots adapted faster than I did, unfettered as they were by human neuroses. My rush to learn the names of native plants and animals and to read up on the area's natural and human history stemmed partly from genuine interest and partly from the need to counter the unmoored feeling that sometimes ambushed me. I had given up New Mexico but hadn't been in Arizona long enough to feel at home.

I registered GW and the flat-bed trailer right away, replacing their yellow Zia sun-sign licenses with saguaro cactus plates. Then I put off applying for my driver's license for months. I expected the photo to be as unflattering as all the others I'd had in California and New Mexico. I wanted to put a better face—literally—on the document that proved I belonged in Arizona.

Unexpectedly, getting my Arizona driver's license helped me feel more at home. Two days before the old one expired, I drove to the Motor Vehicle Division in Bisbee. I beamed at my new license. The photo made me look young and slender, capturing my new-love glow perfectly.

I asked the clerk how much he wanted for that camera, figuring I could make a million with it.

* * *

One of my big concerns was locating good medical care—less for me than for the parrots. I called the Douglas and Bisbee clinics, looking in vain for a bird expert, then started in on the ones in Sierra Vista, an hour away.

We lucked out. Dr. David Bone had kept conures and had done his thesis on sexing them—determining their genders. It was clear from the way he examined Peaches, Maggie, and Willie that he knew what he was doing. He sent us home with a remedy for feather picking that did Peaches more good than anything else we'd tried.

* * *

With the parrots' medical care handled, I expanded my bird-watching beyond Twin Buttes. The first place I visited was the Southeastern Arizona Bird Observatory, then located in the oak-covered Mule Mountains outside of Bisbee. I sat in the observation room, larding my life list with first-ever sightings. Visitors and locals smiled at my enthusiasm. "Oh, my God, that violet-crowned hummingbird is a life bird. That bridled titmouse. And that Mexican jay. And . . . "

From other birders, I learned that I could find the big hummingbirds in the Huachuca Mountains near Sierra Vista. The blue-throats came to the Nature Conservancy preserve in Ramsey Canyon, along with turkeys, redstarts, and warblers. The magnificents frequented a nearby bed and breakfast.

I packed a lunch and visited the B&B. I was congratulating myself on spotting both male and female magnificent hummingbirds when I heard a strange call in the dry creek bed. It was hooty but un-owlish, more like a chuckling pig.

Birders sprinted to the bottom of the yard. We couldn't see the bird in the dense foliage, but several people identified it as an elegant trogon, a sub-tropical bird that looked like a cross between a pigeon and a parrot, with a longish, coppery tail. Unfortunately, seeing one would have to wait for another day.

IN THE HURT BOX

Life was pretty idyllic during the weeks Dennis and I waited for the mobile home to be delivered. We sat outside in the late afternoons, chatting about my bird sightings and his substitute teaching.

One day, he said, "I had to stop a girl from stabbing a smaller boy in the eye with a pencil."

I shook my head, watching Ms. Rose Ellen explore GW's hood. "I could never teach."

"You have a lot of patience with the birds and Rose," Dennis pointed out, as the cat hopped off the hood. "Maybe you would—"

Rose's scream ripped through the conversation. We ran over to find her dangling, her left hind leg wedged between GW's body and front bumper.

Dennis ducked one way and another, trying to get a hold of Rose. She hissed, twisted, scratched, spat, and sprayed urine against what she must have thought was an attack. Her claws raked the back of Dennis's hand.

I dashed to the house for a bath towel to wrap Rose in and for hydrogen peroxide for Dennis's wounds. As I reached the door, I glanced back in time to see her gyrate free. She made a limping sprint for Roger's storage facility—the box from a big-rig trailer, off its axles—and disappeared underneath.

Dennis and I got down on our hands and knees and peered

under the box. A cat-sized tunnel dropped a few inches and angled off to the left. We couldn't see Rose, and no amount of cajoling would bring her out.

When Rose didn't come home by bedtime, we set out dishes of food and water at the tunnel entrance. In the morning, they were empty. We had no way of knowing whether Rose had gotten the contents, or they'd gone to other cats, Roger's dog, or the coyotes or skunks that prowled at night. There were coatimundis, too, long-nosed raccoon relatives; and javelinas, distant relatives of (depending on which internet source you liked) hippos, rhinoceroses, and/or wild hogs.

Over the next couple of days, Dennis and I called and searched for Rose. While we worried, Peaches, Maggie, and Willie were elated to have the run of the house. They flew around and around the living room, then clung to my arms and shoulders while I prepared meals and fed them tidbits. This was more like their lives in New Mexico.

On the third night after her injury, Rose hobbled up to the screen door and meowed in a ragged voice. We leaped up from dinner. I called the birds to their cages before Dennis let her in.

Rose ate the food we put down and begged for more. Every rib stood out under her unkempt fur. She let us pet her but limped away when we got near her damaged leg.

* * *

The next morning, the Bisbee clinic had an opening. They also had a visiting vet; the regular one was out of town. My heart sank until the receptionist told me he was a cat specialist from Tucson.

Lame and exhausted, Rose was easy to catch and put in the carrier that Dennis—being unattached to her, of course—had bought. She whined and yowled all the way to Bisbee. I thought she would resist being touched by a stranger, but the vet's adept handling put her at ease.

"Severely pulled muscles, tendons, and ligaments," he diagnosed. "Nothing detached. Possible hairline fracture not worth anesthesia and X-rays."

"What can we do for her?"

"Keep her quiet. She needs thirty days of housebound recuperation. Then you can let her out for an hour or two a day."

"Oh, she's going to love that."

So, of course, were the parrots.

THE MOBILE HOME COMETH

Dennis and I managed to keep Rose indoors. To their chagrin, the birds had to make do with the bedroom again. They expressed their frustration with choruses of indignant squawks and screeches.

On a Friday afternoon near the end of Rose's recuperation, I was outside, dumping food scraps onto the compost pile I'd started. As I watched a pair of curve-billed thrashers grab the potato peels, I heard the thrum of a big diesel engine. This had to be the delivery from Casa Grande that Dennis and I had been waiting for.

As our potential new home passed, my shoulders sagged. The original roof had been covered with insulating foam and painted with rubberized roof sealer. The chemicals had reacted badly, forming a random topography of hills and valleys. Birds had pecked out nests in it, and grass and sticks stuck out.

By the time Dennis got home from work, the driver had backed the mobile home onto its lot and leveled it. We stacked up cinder blocks for stairs, hugged each other with a mix of dread and excitement, and climbed in the sliding glass door for our first look.

Despite the bizarre roof, the mobile home was snug and pleasant. The appliances were nearly new. A few gallons of white paint would fix the dark *faux* wood paneling that made the twelve-by-sixty-foot space seem smaller than it was.

We were surprised that the previous occupants had left a hide-a-bed sofa, until we tried to move it. Once we had spent ten minutes horsing it across the living room and could see how the rest of our furniture would fit, we made a handshake deal with Roger to buy the mobile on payments.

* * *

We designated the bathroom as the bird room because it could be warmed with a small electric space heater, and the counter was the right size for the two cages.

The parrots sorted out the territorial imperatives their own way. The first time they were loose, Peaches and Willie chased Maggie out, claiming the bird room for their own. That was no surprise. What puzzled me was why Maggie chose as his favorite spot the top shelf just outside the bird room door.

Later in the day, I found out what the attraction was. When I tried to get him on my finger to put him in his cage, he retreated to the back of the shelf, where he was untouchable.

Dennis had found a sawed-off broom handle in one of the closets. He slid it onto the shelf and slowly herded Maggie off. After that, we only had to hold up the stick. Maggie would shuffle out like a kid with his hands stuffed in his pockets and an *Aw, Mom* expression.

* * *

A couple of weeks after we moved in, Willie laid five eggs on the floor of her cage. Peaches fed her. Maggie stood guard every day on his shelf.

Then I took Willie to Dr. Bone for a Depo-Provera shot and removed her eggs. As soon as she stopped sitting, Maggie's protective instincts evaporated. He disputed Peaches and Willie's claim to the bird room from his shelf. The pair would fly to the top of the open bird room door, and the three would screech and squabble. The whole thing had an amusing if ritualistic quality.

To neighbors who came by for the two-bit tour, Dennis explained, "The birds live in the bird room. If we give them pine nuts, they let us use the toilet, sink, and bathtub."

We got a lot of bemused but good-natured reactions. When one man remarked that they got pretty posh treatment—they were *only birds*, after all—Dennis winked at me and said, "Cappy adores these parrots. She just tolerates me."

I laughed but wondered how long Dennis would tolerate me if I didn't start doing the one thing I was still putting off. It was time to face the daunting task of finding a job.

BACK TO WORK

I pursued work in an uncharacteristically random way, partly because my immediate survival didn't depend on having a job. I was contributing my share of the rent and grocery money from a savings account I had closed before moving and was receiving monthly payments from the sale of the Los Alamos mobile home. Dennis was substitute teaching. We knew how to live modestly.

As my savings dwindled, I checked the scant want ads and visited the state employment office. Cochise County was economically depressed, and there weren't many openings. A lot of positions required a fluency in Spanish that I didn't possess.

Then in April, a potential job at a women's and children's shelter in Bisbee fell into my lap, courtesy of our next-door neighbor, Joyce. They needed someone half time to answer phones and do the kinds of bookkeeping and secretarial tasks I had done for years. I arranged an interview.

Stacked in the director's office were boxes of materials no one had found time to file. The pile had gotten so intimidating that the director refused to look at it.

I pushed my glasses down, scanned the stack, and said, "Doesn't scare me."

The next thing I knew, the director's assistant was handing me the employment paperwork and a pen.

ROADRUNNERS AND ROSE

One evening after work, I pulled up in front of our mobile home to a chorus of parrot alarm screeches. What had Peaches, Maggie, and Willie spotted out there in the dusk? Bats? The long-eared owls that liked to perch on our neighbors' roof? A coyote?

I paused with my hand on the car door handle. What if it was a javelina? I'd come home once to find a male nose to nose with Roger and Bev's big Red Dog, so I knew they were aggressive.

I inched the door open. A few yards away sat the source of psittacine consternation: Ms. Rose Ellen Stripy Kitty Cat.

Rose dashed over and leaped into my lap, kneaded my chest, and purred. I threw my arms around her, glad that the car was out of the birds' line of sight.

What made Rose seek us out three months after we moved? For one thing, the man who was supposed to rent the house had changed his mind. It was still empty. Maybe Rose was looking for a warm place to live again, maybe for some human warmth.

Whatever the reasons, she had found us, and she wasn't leaving, no matter how much the parrots protested. When Dennis and I refused to let her in, she prowled back and forth across the deck, yowling.

When Rose realized she wasn't going to be an indoor cat again, she found hiding places in our mobile home's underpinnings and among the pots and gardening tools I'd stacked up around an old picnic table in back. She wriggled into the cab of Dennis's truck through the broken wind wing. She took the morning sun on the deck, ignoring the screeching parrots.

Rose also discovered the insulated water heater closet. The outside door was latched, so she must have wormed her way in from underneath. We found her there after a late spring freeze, curled up on top of the appliance. When Dennis tried to lift her down, she crouched behind the vent pipe, flattened her ears, and hissed. On the other side of the wall, the parrots set up a chorus of alarms.

Dennis latched the water heater door. "I don't think we can outlast her."

"Do you want to?"

With relief in his voice, he said, "Well, no, not really."

* * *

The food we put out for Rose attracted a variety of birds typical of our part of Arizona. The parrots didn't mind when cactus wrens, curve-billed thrashers, brown towhees, mockingbirds, pyrrhuloxias, cardinals, starlings, and house sparrows brought their fledglings to eat from the rim of Rose's dish.

Neither did Rose. She sat back and watched, seeming to know that there was enough for everyone. An entire generation of birds was growing up on food provided by an accommodating cat.

Roadrunners discovered the free kitty crunchies—and the birds that ate it. One morning, I found a pile of gray and red pyrrhuloxia feathers at the bottom of the stairs. Neighbors told me that roadrunners held birds down and plucked them. The smaller bird might still be alive when the roadrunner began dining.

I saw roadrunners stalk birds as large as white-winged doves—and as small as conures. Ours were in the living room one afternoon when a roadrunner peered in the sliding door. It cocked its head at each of them, tail and head crest rising with interest.

Then it pressed its beak against the door and tapped. When the glass didn't yield, it tapped harder. The parrots screamed and tore down the hall to the bird room where, for once, they didn't argue about whose territory it was.

VERMILION FLYCATCHERS

The following spring, my friend and former husband Thor phoned to ask if he could stop by on his way from California to Wisconsin.

"Of course," I said. "It'll be great to see you."

"Don't you need to ask Dennis?"

"Dennis will be fine with it." I could count on his feeling secure in our relationship.

It was a bittersweet visit. Thor had undergone treatment for rectal cancer. A scan had confirmed that the tumor was gone—and had revealed more tumors on his liver.

Thor's oncologist had urged him to try a great new chemotherapy. It would make him nauseated and exhausted, and his hair would fall out—for a fifteen-percent chance of living an extra six months. He had declined treatment—not politely, I suspected—and had decided to spend his remaining days on Deerskin Lake in Wisconsin, where he'd grown up. I supported his choice.

Thor endured enthusiastic grooming from the parrots, whom he'd met in New Mexico. It was wild birds he hoped to see, though, and quite a few obliged. His first morning with us, he looked out the sliding glass door and saw a Mexican giant cowbird. The black male, with its neck ruff and red eyes, dwarfed the brown-headed cowbirds it was feeding with.

Thor and I spent the day watching the big hummingbirds in the Huachuca Mountains, but elegant trogons eluded us in a cold spring rain. I had a consolation prize for him, though. After dinner, I said I could guarantee him vermilion flycatchers. He had wanted to see them for years.

We strolled across the park, binoculars at the ready. Sure enough, a male and female vermilion were catching insects near the stock trough. We watched until they flew off to roost in a mesquite.

Thor's cancer stirred up a lot of emotions for me. After he went to bed, I spent extra time talking to the parrots between their cage bars and giving them treats.

Before Dennis and I drifted off to sleep, I whispered, "I'm trying to remember that Thor isn't just dying of cancer. He's *living* with cancer. If I can't give him good health, at least I can add some pleasure to his remaining time."

Dennis hugged me close and said, "That's all any of us can do for each other."

IN SICKNESS AND IN HEALTH

Dennis and I called our life together "living the dream." It included running a hauling business on weekends and during the summer. The exercise kept us fit, and the income more than repaid us for the flatbed trailer we had bought in New Mexico.

The dream turned to a nightmare at the end of July, when I came down with what I thought was the flu—aches, fatigue, dizziness, a low-grade fever, and nausea. When the cottonwoods turned yellow, I was still sick. I had to give up my job at the shelter. I spent most of my days in bed, watching the digital clock blink through the hours and listening to the parrots squawk to be let out.

When I wasn't too dizzy to drive, I was seeing a doctor. The diagnostic gears ground at a snail's pace. All the tests came back within normal limits.

On afternoon, a couple of brain cells rubbed together. In recent exams, my blood pressure had been at the low end of normal. Maybe I no longer needed the blood-pressure medication I had started taking when I was dealing with a stressful job and Joe.

I staggered out of bed. Leaning on walls, I hiked to the dining table, opened the plastic containers where I kept my daily vitamins and meds, and picked out the blood-pressure tablets.

While I was at it, I plucked out the pills for the persistent acid reflux left over from the auto accident. The medication had been taken off the market in the United States because it caused cardiac arrhythmia in some people. Stubborn and ignorant, I had been buying it at a *farmacía* across the border.

Within days, the persistent dizziness and brain fog began to lift. In two weeks, I could drive, and the first place I went was the clinic. Tests revealed that on top of drug-induced low blood pressure and arrhythmia, I had an allergy to my thyroid medication.

The new medication tipped the scale. By Thanksgiving, I was getting up at six to fix Dennis's breakfast, working out with the snowbirds in the rec trailer, and letting the parrots fly while I caught up on my writing and housecleaning.

Dennis had earned his teaching certificate and was living his full-time-teacher dream. One evening, he lifted the job ads out from in front of me. "Don't go back to work. I'm making enough money to support us, if we're frugal."

My chest swelled, and tears of gratitude rimmed my eyes. This was the item I had deleted from my ideal-partner list before showing it to Dennis. At that time, it had been an unrealistic wish. Now, I could trade the little money I could make for the chance to fulfill my long-time dream.

I stammered my gratitude.

"Whether or not you ever get rich at it," he said, "you can pay me back by writing. That's thanks enough."

FAMILY

More out-of-cage time pleased Peaches, Maggie, and Willie no end. It also increased the number of minor skirmishes.

Dennis was learning that parrots were not exactly like his fifth-grade students. When squabbles broke out, he wanted to give the combatants a lecture while he hustled them to their cages for a time out. It took him a while to understand that the tiff of the moment seemed more significant to him than it did to the birds. He learned to administer immediate discipline—a sharp word, or separating the birds with a magazine or towel—and allow them to go about their psittacine business. That was how wild birds related.

Besides, their cages were supposed to represent safety. *Cage equals punishment* was the wrong message, and it would have confused the parrots. From their perspective, they'd done nothing wrong. They were just being birds.

* * *

The parrots' misbehavior, if you could call it that, set up some fun for us. When I asked, "Who do you suppose chewed the cap off my good pen?" Dennis nodded in Maggie's direction and said, "That would be *your son*. And *your daughter* just took a dump down the back of my clean shirt." Willie.

I got the idea right away. "And *your other son*"—Peaches—"just chewed a hole in the bread bag."

"Hmf! No one who would commit such a heinous crime could have sprung from my loins."

"I can't argue with that."

"They were the best of parrots, they were the worst of parrots."

I groaned at the literary pun, but I was excited, too. Our parental joking stemmed not only from Dennis's sense of humor. We were in a family frame of mind. We were talking about getting another parrot.

"She'll be our baby together," Dennis beamed one morning over breakfast. "She'll be mine the way Peaches, Maggie, and Willie are yours."

I passed him another piece of buttered toast and said, "You never know who's going to bond with whom. Add another parrot, and you toss the flock dynamics up in the air. How they land doesn't have anything to do with our egos or expectations."

"Like a lot of things," Dennis acknowledged. "But *our* bird will . . ."

I tried to roll my eyes, but my skepticism broke down into good-natured laughter.

"If Maggie and the new bird pair," Dennis reminded me, "that'll even the odds."

Dr. Ramsay's long-ago warning that I could wind up with a pair—Peaches and Willie, Maggie and Willie, Peaches and the newcomer—and two singles who didn't like either the pair or each other—wasn't lost on me. Back then, I wasn't ready to take the risk. Now, I could schedule my time around the parrots.

Dennis had never had birds before, and his ignorance allowed him to be optimistic. "However things work out, we'll deal with them—the important word being *we*."

* * *

The following weekend, we bought newspapers from as far away as Tucson. There were no breeder ads in the classifieds. We phoned the private parties offering conures, thinking they might be the equivalent back-yard dog breeders.

Instead, they were people—mostly women—with heart-wrenching tales.

"My boyfriend died and left me his parrot, and I don't know what to do with it. I don't *like* birds."

"I bought this beautiful conure from a guy my cousin works with. I'm afraid to touch it because it bites, and he won't take it back."

"My seven-year-old son wanted a parrot. Now, he won't take care of it. It hangs on the cage bars and screams. I'm a single, working mom. It's too much."

Dennis dumped the newspapers in the wastebasket.

I pulled them out. "Don't get discouraged. Let's make some more calls."

"My daughter left this bird with me when she took a job overseas," the next woman said. "I hate the mess."

"I rescued this conure from a grimy pet store," another woman told me, "and I can't stand its feather picking."

A man answered my next call. "I bought this cute little parrot. Then my girlfriend moved in with her cats, and, well, you know how it goes."

Dennis categorized these people as folks in unfortunate situations, trying to cut their losses.

"Except for the last one," I said. "He's a jerk."

Dennis shrugged. "Pussy trumps parrots. It's a no-brainer."

I threw a newspaper at him, though I appreciated his wit. Flippant though he was, he felt as compelled as I did to drive around Arizona, picking up distressed birds that people offered for free with cages, food, and toys, just to get rid of them.

But would three well-socialized parrots help a rescued bird to adjust? Or would bringing home a hard-luck case cause unforeseen problems?

"Our birds shouldn't be at risk," I said, "from our well-intended but poorly thought-out compassion."

"You and Peaches and Maggie took Willie in, and that worked out fine."

"Yes, but I knew Willie. I knew her people and her history."

"I guess we have to wait for the right parrot to fall out of the sky and hit us in the head." This was Dennis's metaphor for the way things showed up when we needed them.

Mobile homes? Okay. But a parrot, a living creature? I was skeptical.

BIRDS FOR SALE

Dennis was right about a parrot falling out of the sky. We were driving home after Saturday breakfast and shopping in Bisbee, when a sign made us double take: *Birds for Sale.* It hung on a fence surrounding a compound with a mobile home, an art gallery, and several outbuildings.

We bounced in our seats and grabbed each other's hands. Dennis pulled into the left-turn lane, then remembered that we had frozen vegetables and orange juice in La Cucaracha Azúl's trunk. I jotted down the phone number on the sign. We drove home, unpacked our groceries, and called.

The woman who answered introduced herself as Barb. "I just sold the last of my baby blue-crowned conures, but I have a pair of sun conures going to nest. They have the sweetest dispositions. Why don't you come over and meet them?"

In ten minutes, we were standing by the big cage in the corner of Barb's bird building. We *wow*ed at Sunny's and Sammy's beauty as they clambered out of their nest box to get apple slices. They were mostly orange with yellow and green wings, their primaries and tail feathers edged with purplish-blue.

"Sunny is still laying," Barb told us. "The babies are due to hatch around mid-May."

"How old would ours have to be to go home with us?" Dennis asked.

"Eight weeks, if you want to finish weaning her."

"Yes!" I said. It was a great chance to bond with our baby.

"The timing is perfect," Dennis said. "We're planning a month-long vacation trip to visit family and friends, starting the middle of June."

Barb gave us the current information on genetic sexing. The least expensive option was to test the residue inside the egg after the chick hatched. They usually hatched one or two days apart, so it was easy to determine which shell belonged to which baby. As soon as a female hatched, Barb would band her leg.

We drove home, too giddy to talk about anything else, and went straight to the bird room, where we told our parrots they would be getting a little sister.

Peaches and Willie clung to the door of their cage, begging to be let out. Maggie, whose comprehension of English had always been the best, hopped to his front perch and cocked his head as if to say, *Really?*

"It's odd," I said, as I let them all loose. "Choosing a pet has always been such an intuitive process for me. Here we are, committing to a parrot we haven't met, who may not have been conceived yet."

Dennis put his arm around my shoulders. "Given the mom and dad, we can't go wrong. And remember, you're not a single parent anymore."

WAITING GAME

Dennis and I hardly talked about anything but the end of school, our vacation plans, and our new baby. The bird's gender quickly lost its importance. Boy or girl, we would love this parrot.

That turned out to be a good thing. In mid-May, Barb called to tell us, "Two babies hatched at once. It's impossible to tell which shell belongs to which bird. Chances are one's a male and one's a female, but there's no way short of a blood test to tell which is which."

"We don't care," I said. "We'll pick up our baby as soon as we get back and take our chances."

"All right. One more thing: Do you want your baby banded? This is the time to do it, when their feet are still small enough to fit through a band."

I hadn't heard anything about vets refusing to treat unbanded birds or confiscating them as illegal. "Leave it off. Let her be as free as possible."

* * *

When Dennis got home from work, I hugged him and told him

the news.

He pulled his car keys back out of his pocket. "Let's go over and look."

"You're like a new daddy, aren't you?"

"Don't you want to see our little girl?"

"I can hardly wait, but there's nothing to see. The chicks are down in the bottom of that wooden nest box. Sunny's keeping them warm, and Sammy's bringing them food."

Dennis mumbled his disappointment. I went to the bookcase, grabbed a couple of conure books, and found pictures of chicks at different ages. Our just-hatched baby would be pink and nearly naked, her eyes sealed shut. The only things she would be able to do were open her beak and cry to be fed.

"Aw," we chorused. Or maybe it was, "Awe."

ON THE ROAD AGAIN

Around mid-June, Dennis and I crammed our camping gear into La Cucaracha Azúl, along with the parrots in their full-sized cages, for a border-to-border, ten-state loop. The birds slept in the Honda's back seat when we camped. Dennis's niece in Oregon found room for them in her bathtub. It was the coolest and most uncluttered place in her small house. At Elida and Rod's, they spent hours squawking at the turkeys and other birds from the coffee table in the cabin.

From the avian point of view, Helena, Montana, was the high point. Dennis's cousin arranged for us to stay in the vacant basement apartment of a friend's house. It was the one chance the birds got to fly. It was hard to cage them again.

* * *

High on our list of people to visit was our dear friend, Dianne, through whom Dennis and I had met. Because of her health needs, she was living in an Oregon nursing facility. Dennis's sister had happened on Dianne at a mall the year before, wheelchair bound but still riding the bus, so we assumed she was in assisted living.

Our first tip-off that things had changed was that Dianne was puffed up like a water balloon from the steroids she was taking for inflammation. The next was that she got all the pain meds she asked for. This wasn't assisted living; it was hospice care. The rheumatoid arthritis she had suffered from most of her life was destroying the veins and arteries in her feet. She was done, she told us, with the torture of medical procedures and had refused to have her necrotic toes amputated.

Dennis and I glanced at each other, understanding that gangrene would spread through her body and kill her. We could hardly breathe. Dianne was ready, though. Because we loved her, we had to support her choice.

When we said our farewells, Dianne told us, "I'm relieved you two are together. Now I don't have to worry about you. Take care of each other."

We promised to and hugged her for a long time. Then we went out to the car and cried.

SUNNY

We were still processing our shock and grief the night we arrived home, but life didn't stop for it. The following morning, as we picked our way amid vacation paraphernalia, the phone rang. It was Barb.

"Let's not bother putting this stuff away," Dennis said.

"Right. Breakfast first?" I couldn't wait, but I wanted to consider Dennis's needs.

"Let's just get dressed and go."

I pulled the last clean clothes out of my duffel bag, went into the bird room, and told Peaches, Maggie, and Willie, "We're going to pick up your baby sister."

The birds didn't complain about being left at home. We'd been gone so long they might have thought they would never see it again.

* * *

On Barb's sun porch stood a cage containing two baby sun conures in their predominantly green juvenile plumage. Their heads and necks were mottled yellow and green, and there was orange around their white eye rings and above their beaks. Their white lids were translucent. When they closed them, their dark brown eyes showed through.

The suns were as different in behavior as they were similar in appearance. The one we nicknamed Shy cringed against the cage as far from us as possible. The other, whom we called Fearless, cocked its head and nibbled our fingers between the bars. Barb let them out, and we held and stroked them and let them clamber around on us.

It was a tough choice. If we were going to have only one bird, Shy would suit us fine. But we were bringing a new bird into an established flock. Fearless might fare better in the territorial squabbles we anticipated.

Dennis named her Sunny. Probably half the sun conures in the country were named Sunny; her mother was. I shrugged and told Barb, "This is his baby. He gets to name her."

"If *she* turns out to be a *he*, the name will still work. Or your could change it to Sonny with an 'o.'"

In the wild or in Barb's breeding cage, a baby Sunny's age would still be fed by her parents, who would regurgitate food. Dennis and I would become surrogate mom and dad, courtesy of a four-inch-long soft-plastic pipette.

Barb showed us how it worked, mixing powdered food with warm water and testing it on her wrist like baby formula. Sunny stood on the counter and vibrated her wings, begging. Barb squeezed the bulb slowly, so Sunny wouldn't choke or aspirate the food. She gulped it down with enthusiastic head jerks.

* * *

When we toted the cage into the bird room, Peaches and Willie flashed their eyes, screeched, and bit at their cage bars. Sunny blinked and took a step backwards, but only one.

"This isn't going well, is it?" Dennis asked.

"Predictable, remember? To them, she's an intruder. It took months for Peaches to fully accept Maggie and that long for the two of them to admit Willie to the flock, despite her being a girl. It just takes time."

Maggie, on the other hand, leaned forward on his perch, examining the newcomer. He trembled his wings, and his eyes widened. His reaction was so encouraging that I let him out of his cage, brought him into the bedroom on my finger, and set him on Dennis's dresser. We took Sunny out of her cage and let her clamber around on the bedspread.

As he flew to the bed, Maggie squealed in an excited, high-pitched tone I'd never heard from any of the birds before. He marched up to Sunny as though it were the most natural thing in the world and gave her a head-to-tail grooming. His whole beak disappeared into her fluffy plumage. She squatted and closed her eyes. They nibbled each other's beaks, and Maggie groomed her again.

"Uh, huh," Dennis said. "Months."

I couldn't stop grinning. "Full of surprises, aren't they?"

BREAKING BREAD

We were still so heady with success the following morning that we decided to let all the birds out at once. Peaches and Willie flew to their cabinet, scrambled inside, and watched us through the holes they had chewed in the front.

Dennis and I took Maggie and Sunny down the hall on our shoulders and started making breakfast. As soon as Peaches and Willie heard the rattle of pans, they winged to the kitchen. I was engulfed in a feathered whirlwind. I'd always been able to track three of them in flight, but four were impossible.

The birds settled down enough for me to cook but kept clambering around on me, jockeying for position. Finally, Peaches and Willie flew to the curtain rod. Neither made a move toward Sunny. Her acceptance had been accomplished in twenty-four hours.

I was just serving breakfast when Barb called to see how our baby was doing. I gave her a glowing report and asked about Sunny's sibling.

"Shy dropped her act and became curious and bold as could be. She's been adopted by a woman who has no other birds."

Behind me, there was a squawk and a flap of wings. Nails parted my hair, and a four-ounce someone settled on my head.

"Incoming," Barb said. "Who is it?"

"Can't tell. My chances of guessing right are only one in four." Though Sunny's wing and tail feathers were still growing out, she could take short flights.

After we hung up, I felt a wobble of anxiety as I second guessed our decision. Despite the ease of Sunny's introduction, maybe we were overdoing a good thing. Were four parrots too many?

Questioning my choices after the fact was an old habit. I'd done it with each bird, as I'd gone from a solo to a pair to a flock to . . . I guessed I'd have to call it a gang.

We'll do whatever we have to, I thought, echoing Dennis's sentiment. *The important word being* we.

UPSTART

Once the initial hubbub of Sunny's arrival passed, having four parrots turned out to be easier than I thought. The birds themselves made it simple. Peaches and Willie—solidly paired and in possession of the bird room when they were loose—were pretty self-sufficient. Maggie spent a lot of time in the front of the house with Sunny. With the gang divvied up, I usually didn't have to deal with more than two at a time.

Mealtimes were the big exceptions. Sunny adored Maggie and mimicked everything he did. Early on, she watched him chase Peaches away from Dennis's breakfast plate. Dennis ducked as Peaches wheeled back toward the meal—and again as Sunny charged Peaches with the full force of her nine-week-old wings, slamming into him in mid-air.

"Are you watching this?" Dennis asked. "She sure has big brass—"

"Uh huh."

Peaches flew to the kitchen curtain rod and looked from the brazen upstart to me: *What in the world?*

From then on, at mealtimes, Sunny flew at Peaches, sometimes knocking him off my shoulder or a curtain rod. Peaches never retaliated. Perhaps he knew that adults had to be patient and tolerant with youngsters. Or maybe he felt secure in his position as flock elder and mate to the only laying hen.

The hen, however, wasn't having it. When Sunny attacked Peaches, Willie would fly into her as hard as she could, beak open, often coming away with a mouthful of feathers. Maggie defended Sunny and drove Willie off.

Once they got this ritualized battle out of the way—twenty seconds, max—the birds settled down to eat. Sunny nibbled from my plate. Maggie stood on my shoulder and took bits from my lips while I fed Peaches and Willie from a spoon.

Dennis learned not to come to breakfast until the ritual was over. When he did, he was likely to ask, "Are they going to leave you any?"

* * *

Sunny, like each bird before her, believed she owned unique rights to Mom. Her possessiveness peaked one morning when I sat down at the computer. Peaches, as usual, flew back to the bird room, but Willie surprised me by staying in front and claiming my right shoulder. Sunny had to content herself with perching on the computer monitor.

But Sunny wasn't content. As I pulled up my previous day's work, she launched straight at Willie. I figured Sunny would knock Willie off my shoulder and braced for a screaming, feather-pulling fight.

Instead, Willie clamped her big feet onto my shirt and leaned into the collision. Sunny bounced off, landing on the desk. She shook herself and flew back to the monitor, where she spent the following hour reassessing her flock mate's strength and determination.

Maggie had been preening on the dining room window sill and glanced around with a *What'd I miss?* expression. He squatted to launch but couldn't decide what, if anything, he was supposed to do. To cover his confusion, he ran a red tail feather through his beak as though he'd planned to all along. Then he shrilled one of those high-pitched whistles to let Sunny know he was on her side.

I took that for a good sign, certain that they would soon be snuggling in a single cage at night, fast friends forever. For now, I was covering their cages with one large towel. I was encouraged when Maggie gave up his favorite upper perch to snuggle on the floor, as close as he could to the little upstart.

CHILD'S PLAY

Upstart Sunny may have been, but she was all trust in green and yellow feathers, and she rejuvenated her big brother. She loved to flop over on her back and have her tummy tickled. When Maggie saw how much attention she got, he reverted like a human child. He rolled over on his back in my lap, begging to play Tickle Maggie's Tummy for the first time in years.

Sunny discovered the molding that ran the width of our mobile home between the lower kitchen ceiling and the higher one in the living room. She would fly to it, thrust out her feet as she landed, and hang upside down. *Squawk, chirp! Mom, Dad, look at me, I'm upside down. Look at me, Mom! Dad!*

Then she would let go with one foot and dangle until someone offered her a hand or she let go and flew. Or she would edge from one side of the molding to the other, using her beak and claws. Maggie had played this game as a baby and now rediscovered it.

Maggie often nudged Sunny with his beak, urging her to fly. She had a neophyte's optimism—and skills. Her flight was wobbly at first but slow enough that she bounced off of a lamp, the entertainment center, or a curtained window without harm.

Her flying improved more rapidly than her landings. She would hover, dodge this way and that, and circle like a jet waved off from an aircraft carrier. When she touched down, she stutter-stepped, her momentum carrying her top half forward so that she skidded to a stop on her chest and beak. She would shake her feathers and her dignity into place and be up and flying again in seconds.

Dennis watched Maggie and Sunny wing around the living room one day and commented with a satisfied smile, "The Twin Buttes Air Force has a full B Squadron."

THE PICTURE CLOUDS

Our attempt to find Maggie a friend had succeeded. He and Sunny seemed a perfect pair, almost as attentive and compatible as Peaches and Willie or Dennis and me.

As winter set in, however, Maggie stopped making that shrill whistle. He groomed Sunny less and less. When she perched next to him and lowered her head, he pecked and drove her away. She would look to me for an explanation I didn't have. All I could do was pick her up and cuddle her.

The cause of Maggie's disaffection became clear in January, when breeding season began. Maggie pursued Sunny as a male would a female, stalking behind her as she toddled across the floor.

"Does that mean Sunny's a girl?" Dennis asked.

"It's not conclusive evidence. Maggie wants a mate. He might pursue a male."

Irrespective of gender, Sunny was too young to mate. When Maggie didn't get the response he wanted, he pecked her. He spent most of his time on the top shelf in the hall, near the bird room door, harassing Peaches and Willie in their cabinet.

As mating season waned, Maggie sought Sunny's attentions again. When he approached to groom her, she scurried away. He pressed. She flew to my shoulder and hid under my hair. He had created a tough-guy reputation, and now he couldn't shake it.

MISBEHAVIOR

Despite the changes in their relationship, Maggie continued to feel Sunny's influence. He hadn't walked beyond the rim of anybody's dinnerware since the first time we had eaten together and I had asked him to get out of my eggs.

Then Dennis left a bit of toast in the center of a large plate. Maggie hesitated at the rim, leaned in, and couldn't reach it. Sunny, with a baby's brashness, brazened her way to the middle of the plate and tore off a bite.

This was too much for Maggie. His good manners collapsed, and he dashed in. I pushed the toast to the edge of the plate, and without being told to, he retreated and ate like the gentleman he wanted to be.

I explained the rules of etiquette to Sunny. She just cocked head while she chewed. Did she not understand, or was she clever enough to pretend she didn't? Food was one thing about which Sunny didn't take her cue from her big brother or anyone else.

* * *

If Maggie was in my shirt when someone came to the door, he scrambled out to see what was going on. Sunny couldn't be bothered to give up her warm cuddling spot.

One afternoon, I answered a knock from a UPS driver delivering a carton of bird kibble. "Just set it on the table," I called through the glass. "I can't open the door."

The UPS driver didn't respond, just stared at my chest. I was as accustomed to this kind of unwanted attention as any woman built the way I was, but it didn't happen much anymore, age and gravity having worked on my figure. Besides, this guy was half my age. Motioning him to raise his stare did no good. I considered phoning his supervisor to report his unprofessional conduct.

I didn't snap to what was happening until Sunny clambered out of my shirt. The poor man's eyes were practically popping at what must have looked like a third, mobile breast.

When Dennis arrived home from work an hour later, I couldn't resist telling him, "*Your daughter* almost gave the UPS driver a heart attack."

* * *

Maggie and Sunny both liked to fly around the house with food and other objects in their beaks. These often ended up in inaccessible locations—behind heavy furniture, for example. Dennis learned not to give the birds anything he wanted back when we had to move half our computer equipment and some bookshelves to retrieve his ring.

Every Sunday night during the school year, Dennis and I made up vocabulary flash cards for his class. We printed the final version on good paper from the upper paper feed. The printer sat below Elida's bluebird painting. Because the parrots liked to perch on the frame, I kept the printer cover closed.

Apparently, I wasn't vigilant enough. One night, the machine canted a sheet of paper, sucked it in, and crumpled it. I checked the next sheet, clicked *print,* and the same thing happened.

I pulled the printer off its stand, peered inside, and checked the paper jam port on the back. Nothing. I tried again. The printer chewed the next sheet with a sound like a grinding truck transmission.

My last option was to turn the printer upside down and shake it. Out fell one of Sunny's yellow body feathers, several bits of bird kibble, and a mangled red pen cap. Pieces of red plastic, ground off by the printer's gears, rained onto the desk.

Dennis and I turned toward each other and accused in unison, *"Your children!"* Then we burst out laughing.

* * *

It wasn't only the printer that Sunny sabotaged. She liked to do the Charleston on the keyboard. One day, the monitor went black. When the desktop came up, it was at a ninety-degree angle.

I couldn't fix it, so I called my ace in the hole. Lawanna and her son Charles ran a computer repair and instruction business in Douglas. We fiddled with the display until she, too, was out of options.

Fortunately, a customer who happened to be in Lawanna's office told us how to change the graphic options. It was hard to move the mouse the correct way to compensate for the desktop's orientation, but at last, the screen went black, and the desktop came up in its normal position.

"Whatever you fat-footed," I said to Sunny, "never do it again."

She looked up with a baby's adoration for her mother. What could I do but sigh and scritch her head?

SMARTER THAN THE HUMANS

Dennis always smiled indulgently when I said that the trick was to be smarter than the parrots. As it turned out, I had a surprise coming, too.

We were enjoying the kind of companionable Sunday afternoon I'd longed for during my struggles through one romantic misadventure after another. Dennis was sitting in his easy chair, reading a murder mystery. I had my unread e-mails down to a hundred and three.

Maggie was standing on one of the living room curtain rods, looking down the hall at Peaches and Willie as they flew out of the bird room, herding Sunny ahead of them. Just as they landed, Maggie cocked his head skyward and screamed with such terror that they tore back down the hall.

"What the heck is that about?" Dennis asked.

"Probably turkey vultures over by the stock trough." The broad-winged scavengers had been congregating for their migration south.

I returned to my e-mail, but something nagged at me. Peaches and Willie chased Sunny out of the back of the house again, and she landed on my shoulder. Maggie watched the action from the curtain rod.

That was just it. He was *watching.* "You petite brat."

Dennis looked around. "Who, me?"

"*Your* little green-cheeked son."

Dennis glanced at Maggie, who said, *Chip, chip,* his version of *Hi, there.*

"He isn't doing anything." Dennis's sense of fairness for the underbird was offended.

"That's just it. If there were a real danger, he would have taken off with the others. He created that panic for his own amusement. I wonder how many times he's done it, and we haven't noticed."

Dennis grinned. "Isn't that why you were attracted to Maggie in the first place, because he figured things out?"

"He's developed his own entertainment. He may be the smartest bird in the flock."

"Including us," Dennis acknowledged.

TOOL MAKERS

Dennis's and my discussion about who was the smartest bird in the flock was interrupted when Sunny hopped to the open desk drawer and gnawed the overhanging end of a paint-stirring stick held down with a pile of books.

"You break the point off that stick every day," Dennis noted, "but Sunny always sharpens it again."

We watched our baby hew the stick to a point. She scratched her head against it, eyes closed with the kind of relief I felt when Dennis scratched my back.

In the nature-nurture debate, Dennis came down firmly on the side of learned behavior. He thought Sunny had picked up sharpening the stick by watching the other birds. Peaches, I pointed out, was the only other parrot who did it, and he'd quit when he paired with Willie.

Dennis cocked his head skeptically.

"All right, how about this? She figured out how to chew a point by trial and error and found out what a good head-scratcher it made."

"Are you saying she created and used a tool? Only humans can do that."

People had once thought so. By this time, creatures as diverse as chimps and crows were known to make and use tools.

I told Dennis about Peaches dragging a piece of balsa wood and pushing it against my fingers until I got the message: *Here, hold this.*

He worked his beak around the free end, put his head down, and rubbed it against the point. Not only had he made and used a head-scratching tool; he had gotten a creature of a different species to cooperate by holding it for him.

Sunny finished scratching her head and darted to the keyboard, where she pried off the speaker mute button. I grabbed at it. She ducked but let me pull it out of her beak.

"Smart but with a short attention span," Dennis observed.

We smiled. I felt a deep gratitude and contentment for our tranquility.

A SINGLE YELLOW FEATHER

After Peaches' January molt, a single yellow feather grew in among the green ones on his right wing. I was surprised but not alarmed.

The yellow feather became more worrisome after I jerked awake at three in the morning, hearing a bird banging around in a cage.

"Whumf a mattrr?" Dennis muttered into his pillow.

Peaches was standing on the cage floor, looking dazed. Willie hopped to the lower perch and cocked her head at him. I crooned and kissed. He shook and climbed back to their food dish.

I went back to bed but didn't close my eyes. Something was subtly wrong with Peaches' face. This was the first time he'd gone sleep-flying since we'd moved into our mobile home two years before.

In the morning, all four birds flew to the kitchen for their chasing ritual and a few bites of my breakfast. Peaches ate and drank with his usual appetite.

That didn't stop me from worrying when he went sleep-flying a few nights later and a few nights after that. The interval shortened. Was he having nightmares? After each episode, I watched him, waiting for a wee-hours epiphany that never came.

Maggie sensed something wrong, too. For the first time, he picked his feathers, baring a stripe of grayish-pink skin down the center of his belly.

* * *

On a morning in late February, I uncovered the birds' cages to find Peaches standing in his kibble dish, head drooping, eyes dull. He was fluffed up and panting. He'd always been fastidious about his beak; now, it was crusted with food.

An hour and a half later, I hefted Peaches' travel cage onto the clinic's front counter and answered the inevitable questions. Lead poisoning? I was a fanatic about keeping lead out of the house. Even those curtain weights? My curtains fluttered. There was nothing chromed; zinc poisoning was out. The cleaning solutions were shut in cupboards.

"Teflon poisoning?" the veterinary assistant asked.

"I haven't used coated cookware since I was twenty-five."

"That was last year," the receptionist said with a wink that eased the tension a fraction. "Are any of the other birds sick?"

"Fine so far."

Dr. Bone listened to Peaches' recent history, looked him over, and shook his head. "He's in poor condition. I just can't tell why."

We agreed on a full battery of tests. Carrying Peaches in his cage, I followed the doctor to the operating room. Sick though he was, Peaches thrashed and screamed when I reached in to catch him with a towel. He tried to bite the assistant as she fitted a mask over his head and turned on the gas.

Unconscious, Peaches looked terribly vulnerable. His breathing was so shallow that I asked the assistant if he was all right. She removed the mask, and right away, he tried to stand.

"Parrots have small lungs that don't move much air," she said. "It takes a while to gas them down." The term sounded grisly.

Peaches didn't rouse at the mask's removal, and the assistant whisked him away for X-rays. When she brought him back, Dr. Bone took a small blood sample and invited me to the microscope. The cell walls and nuclei were purple. This was reptilian blood from birds' evolutionary past.

I asked to have Peaches' nails trimmed before he woke. Dr. Bone glanced at me as if to say something, then decided not to.

"It's an affirmation," I said, "that Peaches will recover."

Afterwards, I wrapped Peaches in a towel and carried him over my heart to the exam room, where I rocked and crooned to him until he could stand on his cage perch. Then I took a slow, deep breath and went to look at the X-rays.

No masses showed up. It was a relief not to have to make a decision about surgery.

"Parasitology shows a few nematodes," Dr. Bone said. "They can cause intestinal problems."

I looked at the roundworms in the microscope. "They must've come in on some fresh produce. Did I fail to wash something well enough?"

"Not necessarily. Remember, nematodes live in the ground. They could've come in on your shoes."

"Peaches loves to explore on the floor."

Dr. Bone handed me two syringes, each containing a small amount of white fluid. "They're easy to treat. Give him one now and the other in two weeks, when all the eggs have hatched."

I caught Peaches in the towel and squirted the contents of the first syringe down his throat. "This'll fix you right up."

Dr. Bone must have heard the relief in my voice. "There aren't enough nematodes to make Peaches this sick. Something else is going on. I'll call you when the blood work comes back. Meanwhile, keep him quiet and warm. That's all we can do for now."

CHIRICAHUA DEATH MARCH

Before Peaches got sick, Dennis had committed to leading his school's fourth- and fifth-grade classes on a field trip to Chiricahua National Monument, an hour and a half away. I had volunteered to chaperone, along with another teacher and several parents.

When the day came, there was nothing I could do for Peaches, so I kissed his beak and left him in the company of his flock.

Some hyperbolic thinker later named the hike the Chiricahua Death March. Nobody else got more than a blister or two, but I came down with severe altitude sickness. It manifested as a pounding headache, nausea, and such profound fatigue that I could barely lift my feet. My heart hammered. Within a couple of miles, I was sitting down every hundred yards, then every fifty. Sucking on my emergency asthma inhaler didn't help.

A mile and a half from the end of the trail, I couldn't get up. We agreed that Dennis would get everyone on the buses, headed home. Then he would see if the rangers could bring a hospital horse.

I lay down on my back across the narrow trail, head up the slope and feet down. The breeze cooled my sweat-soaked face and filled my nose with the scents of pine and warm earth. The combination of relief and oxygen deprivation made me euphoric. Where the intense sky met the intense volcanic ash formations, the colors vibrated as if electrified. Leaves whispered as though for my ears alone, while rufous-sided towhees called overhead, each note a bell-like quaver I could almost see.

I pictured each of my parrots, imagined their soft, shiny feathers against my cheeks, their beaks grooming my hair and nibbling my ears. Even over the forest waft, I smelled the clean, dry scent of their feathers. I believed I was going to recover, get off the mountain under my own power, and go home to them. Yet, perhaps because of Peaches' illness, I was struck by the thought, *What a beautiful place to die.*

I tipped my hat to shield my eyes from the sunlight flickering through the trees and either fell asleep or passed out.

* * *

Perhaps half an hour later, I woke, energized. I got up and brushed off the leaves and dirt. I was thirsty. I'd started the hike with my day pack full of water bottles but had given most of them to kids who hadn't brought enough. I drank the last few ounces in the remaining bottle and set off up the trail at a brisker pace than I'd managed all day.

In half a mile or so, I encountered the ranger who had led the hike. While I guzzled from her canteen, she said, "I'm glad you can walk. The hospital horse is at the farrier's."

We hiked on until we came upon another ranger, carrying four canteens. No one had to urge me to drink some more.

A quarter of a mile from the ranger station, we encountered Dennis. The strength of his embrace told me how worried he'd been. He'd taken a brief rest and had called Roger, the owner of Twin Buttes, who was on his way to pick us up.

Back at the visitor center, with my own wellbeing assured, I dropped a quarter into the pay phone.

"Not all the results are in," Dr. Bone said, "but a few important chemical profiles came back negative. His potassium is low. That's consistent with malnutrition. We still don't know the cause."

COLLAPSE AND REBOUND

As more test results came back, my hope for something definitive and treatable sank. We received a single clue: a low enzyme level typical of nerve trauma and viruses, including cancer.

Peaches was now struggling to appear normal. He would come out of the cage with Willie in the morning and fly through the house, raising my hopes. Then he would slump on his perch, in a food dish, or on the bottom of their cage, where I'd folded a thick towel to break his falls.

He shivered occasionally at first, then all the time. With a small electric heater, I kept the bird room at eighty degrees. Peaches felt warm to the touch. Dr. Bone believed the shaking was caused by cancer working on Peaches' brain and nervous system at the cellular level. There might never be a detectable mass.

At Dr. Bone's suggestion, I gave Peaches the medication I'd dosed him with for feather-picking. It contained thyroid that would stimulate his appetite, plus an anti-inflammatory to reduce the effect on his nerves.

Peaches became too weak to crunch up bird kibble. I mashed

fruits, vegetables, and grains for him. He refused to eat Sunny's baby food from the pipette. When he was particularly weak, I would pry his beak open and dribble the liquid down his throat. He spent so much of his meager energy resisting, and seemed so humiliated, that I stopped.

To increase the protein content of Peaches' diet, I bought live mealworms. I kept the beetle larvae in a plastic bag in the refrigerator, where the cold made them torpid. When they warmed in the birds' food dishes, they wriggled. While the other birds gulped them down, Sunny pulled her head back and flashed her eyes. She picked out other food and backed away from her dish to eat.

Giving the parrots mealworms triggered my vegetarian resistance to feeding anybody to anybody else, but I didn't care. In an over-the-top moment of anxiety, I told Dennis I would slaughter a cow with my bare hands, chew it up, and feed it to Peaches from my teeth for a chance to restore him to health.

Because he was weak and slow, Peaches had to spend a lot of time eating. I watched him for long periods to see whether he ate or just pushed his food around—and because I suspected these were our last few days together.

I couldn't shut the recurring questions out of my mind: Was I prolonging his agony by medicating him? Should I—*gulp*—have him put down?

It looked as though euthanasia wouldn't be an issue. Peaches paused one day after a shaky feeding session and laid his head sideways on the edge of his food dish. His body went into a slow collapse. I dissolved into sobs.

All at once, he stirred, straightened, and took a deep breath, blinking his way back from whatever boundary he'd approached. He dug into his food again as if nothing had happened.

* * *

Peaches collapsed and rallied so many times that I stopped counting. As long as he fought for his life, I would think no more about euthanasia. I prayed to the Green Parrot Goddess to either restore Peaches to health or take him quickly and relieve his suffering.

Neither happened. I sat with Peaches numerous times each day, making the kissing and whistling sounds he knew. I pictured moments that had left strong impressions on me—white light beaming from his eyes in the pet shop, his fascination with yellow earthmovers, his free flight among the trees—and hoped that these images and my love would reach and heal him.

When I thought I couldn't bear the pain, I made myself sit still, breathe, and be present and mindful. It became a spiritual practice, the most difficult I'd ever undertaken.

Maggie would linger in his cage when I let everyone out, as close to Peaches as he could get without sending Willie into a territorial tizzy. With his usual head-cocking curiosity, he tried to figure out these disturbing changes.

One morning, I explained the situation, withholding nothing. Maggie listened, then sidled closer to the bars that separated him from Peaches' and Willie's cage. He didn't leave until he heard me assembling breakfast, then flew out to nibble from my lips before going back to his honored duty.

THE LIGHT GOES OUT

On a Thursday night in April, it was clear that Peaches was nearing the end. He lay on the towel on the bottom of the cage and couldn't get up, even when Willie groomed and nudged him.

Willie knew. She lay down and snuggled up to him. There they stayed, wing to wing, cheek to cheek, through dusk and into the night, as Peaches slipped into unconsciousness.

With trembling hands, I covered Maggie's and Sunny's cages, switched on a small lamp, and sat in its glow. Peaches' breathing slowed and became shallower.

I longed to hold him and comfort him but would mostly have been comforting myself. Hadn't Willie earned the right to stay beside him? It seemed right for Peaches to end his life in the caring company of his own kind.

A little after ten, Peaches' breathing became barely visible. Without fanfare, it stopped.

Willie stayed beside him, eyes closed, no longer trying to rouse him. When she did get up, I lifted Peaches' cooling body. She didn't protest.

I closed the cage door, covered Willie's cage, and turned off the light.

GRIEF STYLES

After Dennis left for work the next morning, I lifted Peaches' body out of its plastic bag in the refrigerator and carried it into the bird room. I showed his remains to Willie first. She looked, turned away, and hung her head.

Maggie pushed his beak between the cage bars and preened Peaches' feathers, then poked, trying to rouse him. That smart little parrot stood back, looked over his big brother's body, then lifted his head and stared straight into my eyes. His gaze seemed to say, *Oh, now I understand.*

Sunny backed away, eyes wide, head averted. She was still a baby, fully grown but less than a year old. Death confused and frightened her.

I slipped Peaches' body back into the bag and returned it to the refrigerator before going out for our exercise group's traditional Friday desert walk. I didn't want my absence to become an object of curiosity. I mentioned Peaches' death only to Donna, before everyone else showed up.

"Have a busy day," she urged.

I knew what she meant. I had made a list of domestic chores that wouldn't involve too many of my barely firing synapses and would sop up some of my grief.

* * *

Willie found her own way to cope. During Saturday breakfast, she flew to the back of a dining chair and perched less than a foot from Maggie. He blinked with surprise but allowed her to stay.

She edged toward him. He didn't lunge at her, as I expected, but fluttered to the floor. She pursued him at a distance. She repeated this behavior several times during the day.

"What's going on?" Dennis asked at dinner.

The implication was as clear as it was startling: "Willie is courting Maggie."

Dennis feigned moral outrage. "Without a decent mourning period? Has she no shame?"

"Probably not. This might be her first stage of grief: denial. Her self-image is *I'm a parrot who has a mate*, so she has to have one."

As I put Maggie in his cage that night, Willie hurtled into the room and dove in after him. Maggie leaped back, then sprang at her with his beak open. Willie scrambled out and flew to Dennis's bath towel. It took some urging to get her to step onto my finger and enter the cage where her mate had died.

I felt the need for meaning I could cling to. The best I could come up with was a weak cliché. "If there's a lesson in this," I told Dennis, "it's that life goes on." That didn't do justice to Willie's impulses. "And life is more than bare survival."

Peaches had known that. In the face of capture, sickness, and a life with humans, he had chosen to live as fully as he could.

I hoped that in his absence, I would be able to follow his example.

RESTING PLACE

Three days after Peaches' death, Dennis and I loaded tools and a bag of birdseed into GW. During the forty-five minute drive, I held Peaches' body, sometimes over my heart, sometimes on the leg of my jeans, where I spread his wonderful wings.

His eyes were dull now, his feathers losing their sheen, but I couldn't stop looking. I wanted to lock into memory everything about him, from where the orange feathers on his head gave way to turquoise and then to green, to the particular shade of blue in his wing feathers, to the curves of his beak and nails.

I fingered the quarantine band on his right leg. Should I have taken it off? I pictured myself wearing it on a chain around my neck or on my MedicAlert bracelet. I could still remove it but couldn't face the possibility of breaking his fragile leg bone. Peaches was beyond pain, but the violence would have traumatized me.

Maybe it was all right to leave the band on. Peaches had worn it for a long time. It was a symbol, not just of his brutal capture, but of our years of affection.

We drove past mesquite that were just greening up and creosote studded with bright yellow blooms. That Peaches would become part of this natural beauty failed to comfort me. The prospect of leaving him in the ground was almost unbearable. I reached for Dennis's arm, ready to tell him to turn back. What made me willing to go on was the certainty that I would have to face this eventually—and the doubt that it would get easier.

The wind whipped our jackets as we climbed Taylor Butte, below the ridge where a golden eagle pair had fledged both their young the previous year. A hundred yards up, a small, pale gray boulder lay embedded in the soil. Dennis started digging a hole on the uphill side.

Motion caught my eye as a diamondback rattlesnake unwound from a jackrabbit scrape and glided away. Dennis lunged, shovel raised. I stepped between them, reminding him that we were there to grieve one death, not cause another. The snake, after all, just wanted to be left alone.

"Sorry," he said, "I have this knee-jerk fear of snakes."

"Maybe the snake is Peaches' grave guardian," I said as I sprinkled bird seed into the finished hole, an offering for Peaches' journey in the afterlife.

Because of the angle of the slope and my weak knee, I couldn't get down and put Peaches in the earth. Dennis held the shovel, and I laid his body on the blade, spreading his wings as in flight. As Dennis lowered him into his final resting place, my chest constricted around a huge *NO!* that couldn't get out past the tightness in my throat.

We alternated layers of soil and flat rocks and stacked a cairn against the boulder to discourage scavengers. I sprinkled more seeds on top. Southeastern Arizona was in its eleventh year of drought, so I held out little hope that millet or sunflowers would take root. Perhaps our offering would help Peaches' wild cousins survive.

Dennis and I stayed there for a while as the wind whipped our hair. I wept quietly, hands clasped in a wordless prayer for Peaches' soul.

COMFORT

Most people were consoling. When I worried that I hadn't done enough for Peaches, Beverly assured me that I had given him a better and longer life than he would otherwise have lived. She reminded me that we didn't know how old he was. He might have been captured well into adulthood and died of old age.

Naomi phoned from Phoenix to suggest that everything and everyone in our lives was on loan, and to urge a gentle process of letting go.

Elida e-mailed a sentiment I greatly appreciated: *Fly free, little Peaches!*

Most salving was Dennis's daily sympathy. This was one thing I'd wanted out of a partnership: the small but vital comfort of a touch, a hug, a hand squeeze. He had never expected to live with a house full of parrots, but he loved Peaches and grieved with me.

Some people were unable to offer consolation. Perhaps they couldn't imagine how deeply bonded a person could become with a bird. I sloughed off, "Don't be sad, you have three others," and, "You can always get another parrot." But when a woman I had considered a friend chastised, "You haven't accepted that death is a natural part of life," I became more careful who I revealed my feelings to.

LOVE OF MY LIFE

I was reminded every day of what grief could make me want to believe. I longed to wrap the whole experience in a blanket of meaning against the indifference of natural forces. A variety of images captured my mind by turns: Peaches flying free with his home flock in Brazil, winging across the highway ahead of GW, and spreading great green and blue wings above our home to bless and protect his flock.

My greatest longing—to see Peaches again in this life or the next, if there was one—intensified when I received a sympathy card from Dr. Bone and his staff. It spoke of the lost pet looking up from his endless play in the afterlife, thrilled to see his person coming to join him.

I had to be mindful not to follow my longing to go wherever Peaches was, especially behind GW's wheel. Edgar Allan Poe wrote about the Imp of the Perverse, that urge to do something contrary to a person's good. One afternoon, the Imp wanted me to spin the steering wheel toward an oncoming eighteen-wheeler—a fine irony in view of Peaches' aversion to big rigs.

Like anyone who had lived a few decades, I'd faced some painful losses, yet I'd never felt so unmoored, so adrift, so unable to come to terms with death.

It took someone else's self-awareness to guide me. I was sitting at my desk one summer afternoon, reading Susan Richards' *Chosen Forever*. She wrote about Georgia, the Morgan mare she had lost years before, as the love of her life.

The words snapped my head up, and my heart thrilled with recognition. Peaches was the love of my life. I knew it in every cell.

In a secret cranny of my heart, I'd held the wish that Peaches had been left to live a natural life with his own kind. Saying so had seemed like a jinx. I acknowledged it now as a small tribute to my wonderful companion.

GRIEF GOES ON

It came as no surprise that, of all the birds, Willie suffered the most overtly. I was dismayed, however, when she developed a ritualistic behavior. Standing on the catch dish under her water dispenser, she craned her head in a circle, spun around, and hopped to her lower perch before climbing onto the dish and repeating the choreographed moves. She did it over and over. A dozen times a day, she called for Peaches in a forlorn and sometimes desperate-sounding voice.

Then one weekend morning, instead of sequestering herself in her cabinet, she flew to the dining table and landed on Dennis's shoulder. She nibbled his lips, begging for food. When he lay down on the couch to read, she snuggled against his cheek.

I was lounging in bed the next morning when I heard Dennis in the bird room, crooning. Willie squawked and chirped and, Dennis told me later, let him scratch her head and chest between the cage bars for the first time. Later, she perched on top of the refrigerator while he serenaded her with "Getting to Know You" from *The King and I*.

Maggie also sought Dennis out. They became so close that when Dennis took a weekend nap, Maggie chewed off a corner of the bedroom door, trying to get to him.

Willie couldn't stand that. When Dennis came out, she flew out of the bird room, thudded onto his shoulder, and held on with an iron grip, screeching and biting at Maggie when he flew close.

Maggie could have chased her away, but he chose not to. Any time Willie and Dennis communed, Maggie stood nearby or stationed himself on my shoulder, awaiting his turn.

These apparently good intentions didn't always earn Maggie the rewards he deserved. Sunny continued to claim the inside of my shirt and liked to poke her head out and nip his feet. That would set off a screaming, pecking fight.

Willie started doing with Dennis what she had done with me before pairing with Peaches. As he reclined with his head propped up on a pillow, she would land on his chest and rub her vent against his chin, flirting with him over her shoulder. Her desire for a mate was unmistakable.

And sometimes humorous. The first time she dove down the front of Dennis's shirt, his eyes widened. "Ouch! I just learned what you've probably known for years."

"What's that?"

"Protect your nipples."

* * *

Willie wanted to crawl down the front of my shirt, too, even if Sunny was already there. A noisy, biting squabble would ensue. My only option was to pull my shirt up and shake it, a flapping dance accompanied by the chant, "Out, out, out!" that never failed to crack Dennis up.

Sunny had mental powers on her side. One evening while I was cooking dinner, Willie claimed the inside of my shirt. Sunny flew to my shoulder and baited her, squawking and threatening. When Willie charged out, Sunny darted across my shoulders and plunged down my shirt front from the other side.

After Dennis and I stopped laughing, he asked whether Sunny had thought up the ruse beforehand. She was smart enough. Or she might have taken spur-of-the-moment advantage of Willie's reaction.

Either way, she was an opportunist, but with a soft side. She showed no lasting signs of distress from Peaches' death, but my sorrow and the shifts in flock dynamics must have made her anxious. She begged for the pipette every day, seeking that baby comfort. After drinking until her crop bulged, she would doze on my shoulder. I would lean my cheek into the rise and fall of her chest, the soft rub of her feathers.

I was an opportunist, too, taking comfort where I could find it.

* * *

Elida, in one of her consoling e-mails, asked if we planned to get another parrot to bring the numbers up from odd to even.

No plans at the moment, I wrote back, *but you never know. It's too early to tell.* At that point, I didn't want another parrot. I wanted only Peaches.

Age was a consideration, too. Three weeks after losing Peaches, I had turned sixty. I'd never intended to have a flock that would outlive me, though it was possible that some or all of the surviving parrots would. If I died first, Dennis might not want or be able to keep the birds. Hard as it was, I'd started to assemble a list of parrot sanctuaries, rescuers and re-homing organizations.

HEALING TOUCH

On a summer afternoon almost four months after Peaches' passing, I went into the bathroom to apply some hand lotion—a staple in the arid Southwest—and didn't see Willie.

My heart didn't skip when she failed to answer my calls. She might have been napping in her nest box. I didn't want to disturb her by opening the cabinet doors. Besides, I'd have had to sweep up the shredded toilet paper that would rain down.

When I checked the bird room a few minutes later, Willie popped up in the hole in the side of the cabinet, calling for her mate in a now-familiar cry, insistent and forlorn.

I patted my shoulder, an invitation to fly to me. "You've been up there all day. How about using the wings the Green Parrot Goddess gave you?"

Willie ducked back into the cabinet.

I went to the kitchen and brought back some fresh food, including half an almond. She didn't come out to perch on her dish and eat, so I rattled the sunflower seed jar, a sure-fire lure. Maggie and Sunny flew in to get their share. Willie didn't even look out a peep hole, much less chase them out of her territory.

The next day, Willie spent all her cage time huddled underneath her wash cloth. Afraid that she wasn't eating, I scooped her out and set her on the postage scale. Her weight was normal, but I still made an appointment with Dr. Bone.

* * *

"Has she laid any eggs this year?" Dr. Bone asked, as he felt Willie's breastbone for fat reserves.

"No. She's almost seven years old. Could she be past breeding age?"

"Maybe. Was Peaches too ill to mate with her?"

"I think so. Could the distress of his illness and death prevent her from ovulating?"

"It wouldn't surprise me." He palpated her pelvis. "She's not egg-bound." This was a potentially fatal condition in which the bird produced eggs but couldn't pass them.

He felt her crop. "There's food in there, so we know she's eating. I'm concerned about her hiding, though."

As he released her into her travel cage, he said one of those things that endeared him to me. "Many people believe that animals don't have complex and profound emotional lives. It's clear to me that Willie is suffering from grief. She's depressed by the impulse to lay eggs and the absence of her mate."

He suggested a vitamin and mineral supplement to increase her energy. More important, Dennis and I were to involve her more with the rest of the family.

Apparently, Willie also needed some rock 'n' roll therapy. I found an oldies station on our way home and sang along with The Beach Boys' "Good Vibrations." Willie clambered around in her cage and squawked in rhythm.

The next day, after we all ate Saturday breakfast together, Dennis and I lay on the bed, giving everyone bird-like talk and grooming. We held the birds above us, pulling our hands down to make them flap their wings. Willie was as lively as ever.

I called Dr. Bone's office on Monday to report Willie's improvement, suggesting that she just needed a ride to Sierra Vista with Mom and some animated music. I sang, "Give me that old-time rock and roll," from the Bob Seger song.

The receptionist laughed. "And a little touchy-feely with Dr. Bone."

When I related the conversation to Dennis, he said, "Maybe she has a thing for him."

After seeing Willie pursue Maggie and bond with Dennis, anything seemed possible.

FEATHERED COP

Maggie took on a different role after Peaches died, using his position as alpha parrot to become the flock peacekeeper. He was an equal-opportunity cop who flew at the aggressor, whether it was Willie or Sunny. Just a squawk—*Don't make me fly over there*—could break up a squabble.

He also became an active protector, usually of Sunny. He would see that silly little girl yelling at Ms. Rose Ellen Stripy Kitty Cat through the sliding glass door and would fly over, knock his little sister off the wicker bookcase, and chase her to safety.

One day, I asked Dennis to grab a pen because Sunny was about to pry out the ball point. Maggie was quicker. When he flew at her, Sunny dropped the pen and winged to a living room curtain rod.

Dennis stared. "Did he understand what you said?"

"Maybe he picked up on our attention to her. On the other hand . . ."

REMEMBRANCE

The air was cool one autumn morning when I woke, not to parrot squawks, but to an unfamiliar bird call. I clambered to my knees and pushed the bedroom curtain aside. Two male red-cockaded woodpeckers stood in the desert willow. I had never seen any before and didn't expect to, this far from their southeastern pine and oak woodland.

I jumped out of bed and hurried for the phone to call Thor. Half-way down the hall, I stopped, realizing, *My phone won't reach that area code.*

Thor had been living in a Wisconsin hospice facility since having a severe heart attack the previous December. Liver cancer had spread to his kidneys and stomach. My former husband—my friend of forty years—had died in his sleep a few days earlier.

I shuffled back and plopped down on the end of the bed. It was another chance to see how much I wanted to believe something that comforted me: that Thor had sent the woodpeckers as a sign, a remembrance, a greeting from the other side.

Or maybe Dianne had sent them. Or a Southern California friend who had died of a botched gall bladder surgery.

Or maybe Peaches.

It had been a tough year.

ANNIVERSARIES

I believed that remembering the exact date Peaches had died would be a setup for future sadness and had allowed myself to forget it, or so I thought. As March ended, I was overtaken by a persistent, shapeless longing that made it hard to concentrate.

On April 20, I couldn't stop crying and couldn't figure out why. Even playing with the parrots didn't ease my pain. To distract myself, I was deleting old e-mails when I ran across several dated April 21 of the previous year, telling friends we had lost Peaches the night before. The date had been engraved in my subconscious.

* * *

In June, my grief began to change. Dennis and I visited friends in New Mexico, staying in Beverly and Bob's pop-up travel trailer in Chimayó. The parrots were excited at the sounds of wind rustling the tall trees, wild bird calls, and the burble of water running in the irrigation ditches.

That natural music lulled me into profound sleep. In the healing dream it produced, Dennis and I took a private plane to Central America with Peaches, Maggie, Willie, and some people we didn't know. I thrilled at the sight of our parrots flying free in the jungle. When it was time to leave, however, I became frantic because I couldn't find them.

Maggie finally flew to the airstrip. I lifted him from a branch, put him in his cage, and took him to our pile of luggage. Willie was there, standing with one foot on each of two suitcases. Even in my sleep, that seemed symbolic. Perhaps she was straddling life with Peaches and life without him. I caged her, too.

The pilot urged Dennis and me toward the plane, where others were boarding. I saw no alternative but to surrender to my loss. I sobbed and said, "I'm giving Peaches back to the jungle."

Everyone thought that was commendable. If only they had known what an emotional defense it was against the agony of losing my friend.

And then Peaches zoomed into the clearing and landed on my hand. I could have gotten him into a cage. Instead, I looked into his eyes, saw how they flashed with the excitement of free flight, and tossed him back into the air.

In the days following the dream, Peaches felt less present in the ether around me. My sadness, though constant in the background, became less intense. The natural and necessary healing process kept rubbing at the rough edges off my grief.

FLOCK DYNAMICS

At the start of mating season in January, a year after Peaches' yellow feather came in, Maggie stopped harassing Willie from the hall shelf and invaded her territory. He would cling to the cabinet doors, screeching and pecking at her through the peepholes.

I kept waiting for Willie to run Maggie off. She did him one better, reaching through a hole and biting his foot. Maggie leaped off, landed on the counter between his cage and Willie's, and hopped around on his uninjured foot, shrieking the parrot equivalent of *Ow, ow, ow!*

By the time I quit rummaging through the medicine cabinet and a box of bird supplies for the styptic I knew I had but couldn't find, the bleeding had stopped. I put on my glasses, got a hold of Maggie, and examined his injured toe. It appeared no bones were broken.

Did this trauma discourage Maggie from harassing Willie? If

anything, it intensified his efforts to get her attention. Clear into March, the bird room was their daily battleground.

One afternoon, I turned my head from the computer screen with a start. No noise was coming from the back of the house. I walked down the hall with Sunny on my shoulder to find out what Maggie and Willie were up to.

Willie wasn't in sight; I assumed she was in the cabinet. Maggie didn't seem to be around, though, and that worried me. I looked under the counter where we kept the travel cages, behind the shower curtain and the toilet. I expanded the search to the rest of the house, my breath quickening with anxiety.

As I passed the bird room, I heard scuffling and glanced in. Willie appeared in the cabinet's entrance hole—then Maggie.

Sunny squawked her surprise: *Mom, do you see that? I can't believe it!*

I couldn't, either. So *that* was what all the furor had been about. Maggie hadn't been trying to evict Willie, as I'd suspected. He was like a grade-school boy trying to get the attention of a girl he liked by harassing her. His persistence, along with the spring hormone surge, had won out.

I was so thrilled that I thanked the Green Parrot Goddess over and over. At last, Maggie had a mate. I re-interpreted the previous summer's dream: Willie had been between one *mate* and another.

That night, Maggie flew into Willie's cage as though it were the most natural thing in the world. They were little Velcro parrots, snuggling together in one of their food dishes. I covered them, then Sunny, and told Peaches about the latest developments. I thanked him for any part he might have played.

* * *

Only Sunny was displeased by the new union. It was the first time she had been in her cage without being able to see Maggie, and it made her anxious. The following day, she nipped me, not hard but often. She hunkered in my shirt for hours and begged for the pipette every time she came out.

I spent extra time with her over the couple of weeks it took her to adjust, scratching her head and playing Tickle Sunny's Tummy. And remembering Dr. Bone's comment about the complex emotional lives of animals.

Parrots had been seeing me through heartbreak for nearly two decades. The least I could do was return the favor.

EPILOG

Even in the face of Peaches' absence, our home is full of life. As I finish our story, we're having a companionable Sunday morning. Dennis is typing up a lesson plan for his eighth-grade English class. I'm at the kitchen table, writing by hand on scratch paper.

Maggie is nestling in my left hand, playing with my replacement MedicAlert bracelet. He doesn't do it often anymore, but he can still take it off in five seconds flat.

Maggie spends most of his time guarding Willie while she sits on a clutch of three pale coral-colored eggs. He feeds and grooms her and sleeps shoulder-to-shoulder with her. They pipe to imprint their sounds on the chicks.

Maggie's visit doesn't owe to a husbandly hiatus. Earlier, I heard him playing with the plastic bird kibble container on top of the toilet tank, heard it *bang* as it hit the toilet lid, then the rapid rhythm of Maggie's wings. He was standing nonchalantly on the dining table before the jar stopped rolling across the floor.

Being nowhere near the scene of the crime is one of Maggie's blossoming talents. Dennis calls him "Mile-Away Maggie."

Sunny, the perpetual baby, is standing on the neck of my blouse, leaning her back against my chest, grooming her yellow and orange breast feathers. Her large, dark eyes give her an appearance of childhood innocence. Though still snuggly most of the time, she's having episodes of bity irritability. She's a teenager now, with the attendant hormonal changes. We hope she (?) will answer the gender question within the year.

Peaches is resting in his grave by the boulder on our land, his departed soul a drop in the vast ocean of spirit. I often gaze across the valley and speak his name. He's the bright thread that continues to weave through my days—the wild green founder of our flock, who grabbed my heart and never let go.

###

ABOUT THE AUTHOR

Cappy Love Hanson has lived three distinct lives: on the California beaches, in the New Mexico mountains, and in the Arizona high-desert grasslands, where she currently resides with her husband and their parrots, dogs, and cat. She loves to read, write, play music, take long walks, and watch birds.

Her third-grade teacher labeled her a poet for a piece about spring. Probably the most significant aspect of her education at UC Santa Barbara and USC was the time she spent ditching classes and sitting in the library, writing everything from Gilbert and Sullivan knockoffs to futuristic fiction. Fortunately, none of it survives.

Cappy's work has appeared in *Writer's Digest, The Santa Fe New Mexican, Blue Mesa Review, New Millennium Writings, CutThroat,* and other publications. She was on the editorial staff of Cochise College's literary and arts magazine *Mirage* for nine years and is cofounder of the Cochise Writers Group and member of the High Desert Writers Association.

CONNECT WITH CAPPY

Friend me on Facebook at:
http://www.facebook.com/cappy.hansongordon

Email me at::
cappylove1211@gmail.com

38536812R00142